HI CIATION

COUNTRY HOUSE GUIDE

By GEORGE PLUMPTRE

Please note that because of their special status as charities the Leeds Castle Foundation (page 94) and the Trustees of Arundel Castle (page 100) are unable to offer free admission to Friends of the Historic Houses Association.

The Duke of Devonshire and the Chatsworth House Trust (page 27) support the work of the HHA and are contributors to the Association but, not being formal Members of the Association, do not participate in the scheme for free admission to Friends of the HHA.

April, 1994

SPONSORED BY SOTHEBY'S

First published in Great Britain by Sotheby's
34 - 35 New Bond Street, London W1A 2AA.

In association with

Historic Houses Association
2 Chester Street, London SW1X 7BB.

ISBN: 0-85667-434-6

Printed and bound by Quadsect Ltd., London.

This book is distributed by:

H.H.A. Publishing Department, PO Box 21,
The Business Park, Letchworth, Herts SG6 2JF.

Sotheby's, 34 - 35 New Bond Street, London W1A 2AA.

Introduction

It gives us great pleasure to introduce this book, written by George Plumptre. The Historic Houses Association has long felt the need for a guidebook covering virtually all of its Member houses that are open regularly to the public, a need that has now been met thanks to the generous sponsorship of Sotheby's.

The entries for all the individual houses have been written in close collaboration with the owners concerned. They include the practical information the visitor needs - where to go and when to go there - with a summary of the particular interest of each of the properties and, in many cases, anecdotal material about the history of the buildings, or the families involved with them over the years. We believe that this will make the Guidebook more interesting than many similar publications.

We hope that all of its readers will find it useful in planning their visits to historic houses and that it will add to their understanding and pleasure when they get there.

William Proby
President, H.H.A.

Preface

The houses included in the book are all member houses of the Historic Houses Association, open to the public on an advertised basis. As well as the general public opening details given with each entry, the houses are also open by appointment or for groups and special parties - during the public opening periods and often at other times. The details of these openings can be obtained by telephoning individual houses.

As the book is not an annual gazetteer, the opening details given are not date-specific as the actual days of opening change from year to year, although the periods usually remain constant. Therefore, if necessary, visitors can telephone individual houses to check any uncertainty, or alternatively consult one of the annual historic house gazetteers or directories. Prices and other details given were correct at the time of going to press.

Most important, the houses are, with the exception of only a couple of ancient fortified towers, all occupied family homes. Their architectural and artistic qualities are hugely enhanced by the warmth of family inhabitance which in most cases has been continuous for generations, in some for hundreds of years.

The evolution of the country house from squalid mediaeval castles and towers was a vigorous, complex process. The web of links between land and estates, architecture, art and gardening, social advancement and vanity, developed through successive generations. In the evolutionary process old houses were replaced as architectural fashions changed, their surroundings were similarly landscaped or terraced. At the same time many succumbed to disasters - fire or bankruptcy.

Today the situation is rather different. The evolution of new country houses, dependant, as in the past, upon a landed estate for much of their economic support, has slowed almost to a halt. This has sharpened the focus on historic house owners who preserve and maintain, against increasing economic odds, such a considerable part of our national heritage. Public support by visitors can often make the difference between a house surviving as a viable entity, and being broken up in sale. It is this support that THE COUNTRY HOUSE GUIDE hopes to encourage.

In the year of their own 250th anniversary, and having enjoyed a close relationship with country houses and collectors through those two and a half centuries, Sotheby's are proud to play a part in celebrating and supporting the country house. Any contribution made to future health and survival, and to the appreciation of owners' unstinting work, will be of lasting value.

George Plumptre
Sotheby's. January 1994

Contents

CVMBRIA
Hutton-in-the-Forest

DALEMAIN, *Penrith*

Robert Hasell-McCosh Esq.
Tel: 07684 86450.

3 m south of Penrith on A592.
Open: April to Oct daily except Fri and Sat 11.15-5.
£4, children £3.
Home-made teas.

The passing road leading from Penrith to the Lakes heartland presents an irrestible view of Dalemain, a balustraded house of the utmost restraint, built of wonderfully pink sandstone quarried a mile away and facing down to where Dacre Beck joins the River Eamont before running into Ullswater. Behind the well-mannered early 18th-century facade of Dalemain exists a fascinating mixture of the domestic and the unusual. The elegant staircase hall hung largely with family portraits leads through to one of the best 18th-century Chinese rooms in England. The dining room, which has a mellow, clubable quality, abutts the mediaeval stone vaulted hall now used as a restaurant. An ancient stone spiral staircase leads to the charming small panelled rooms characterising early-18th century domesticity.

The estate was purchased in 1679 by Mr Hasell, agent to Lady Anne Clifford, and has remained in the family ever since. They established themselves as the largest landowners on the northern shores of Ullswater. Hasell's house was built around the existing Pele tower and stone staircase dating from Dalemain's fortified past to repel Border raiders. Hugh de Morville took refuge in the tower with his brother after he had taken part in Becket's murder in Canterbury. Hasell added his house around a courtyard and during the 1730s another Edward added the two Georgian fronts to the block's grander apartments for entertaining. The cantilevered staircase is of the same period.

The main rooms contain the family portraits extending from Lely, Beale and Richardson, to Devis and Zoffany and continuously to the present day. Here too is furniture by Gillows of Lancaster, porcelain and other works of art. Elsewhere are a good collection of glass and silver. The rooms have a nicely judged mixture of the expected and unexpected: of the latter the hall contains a massive view of Venice, one of the small upstairs rooms a splendid pair of globes. There is a nursery exhibition, a Yeomanry Museum and a recently established museum devoted to local agriculture and crafts.

The present owner's mother created the garden which is full of quality and greatly enhances the setting; her work brought the family history full circle as the walled garden and buttressed terrace that she has made such features were originally built by Sir Edward Hasell.

HOLKER HALL, *Cark-in-Cartmel.*

The Lord and Lady Cavendish.
Tel: 05395 58328.

1 m north of Cark-in-Cartmel,
4 m west of Grange-over Sands, exit 36 M6.
Open: April to end-Oct daily except Sat 10.30-4.30.
Prices/concessions available from Administrator.
Restaurant.

Where the foothills of the Lake District drop away into Morecambe Bay a large Tudor-revival Victorian house is a surprising discovery. Holker's inaccessibility tells much about its history: it enjoyed a lengthy period as a subsiduary home of the Cavendish dukes of Devonshire, until the 19th century when William Cavendish, who had been brought up at Holker, married one cousin, inherited the dukedom from another, but retained his love of his childhood home in preference to his other main seats, Chatsworth and Hardwick Hall.

Parts of the house are much older and date from 1604. But its immediate impression is Victorian, vividly portraying the home of a patrician, politically active family. Both the 7th duke's sons became cabinet ministers and the younger, Lord Frederick, was the target of a political assassination that stunned Victorian society. His wife Lucy was a niece of Gladstone who, in 1882, appointed Lord Frederick Secretary of State for Ireland. On the day he arrived in Dublin to take up the appointment he was murdered in Phoenix Park.

The 7th duke made substantial alterations to the house between 1838 and 1842 and later built the stable block. But most of his work met a tragic end; in 1871 fire swept through the west wing - the largest block - and gutted it. Undeterred the duke set about rebuilding and enlarging the house. It is his second effort which visitors to Holker admire today.

The detail of craftsmanship, in linenfold panelling, plaster ceilings and marble fireplaces, is unfailingly excellent. Even when electricity was installed in 1911 great care was taken so that modern comfort did not intrude; in the library the light-switches are concealed behind dummy books. As befits a ducal home the four monumental twisted oak columns that flank the dining room fireplace were carved from trees felled on the estate; the cantilever oak staircase was built with similarly local timber, and the limestone for the monolithic archway which divides the hall from the staircase was quarried at nearby Allerston.

Among the typically Victorian ensemble are the three and a half thousand books with which the 7th duke filled his library, the mixture of French and English furniture and Old Master paintings in the drawing room. The family played carpet bowls with heavy granite balls along the broad upstairs gallery.

HUTTON-IN-THE-FOREST, *Penrith.*

Lord and Lady Inglewood.
Tel: 07684 84449.

6 m north-west of Penrith on B5305, M6 exit 41.
Open: Easter Sun-Fri, Tues, Fri, Sun May to Oct,
Wed in Aug and Bank Hols 1-4.
£3, children £1.

Both house and garden are well worth discovering, folded into the understated country north of Penrith. Distinguished for the successive waves of architectural improvement wrought in every century since 1600 when Hutton was developed around a defensive Pele tower, the house continued to throw out shoots. The 1620 long gallery is an unusual survivor in the county; having fallen into disrepair in the 18th century it was restored by Webster c.1830. It is now hung with family portraits and contains good early-17th century furniture.

In the late-17th century Edward Addison, William Talman's master-mason at nearby Lowther Castle, added the exuberant Baroque facade. This encloses an enfilade of rooms, confirming the pattern of the first-floor overlooking the gardens. The staircase, richly carved with putti and foliage, leads to the library, ante room and drawing room. The Fletchers, as can be seen in the fine sequence of portraits, were a cosmopolitan family; the inlaid 17th-century furniture supports blue and white oriental porcelain, the height of fashion at the time. Mainly Chinese, there is also a rare Japanese piece as well as Dutch and English Delft. The period decoration continues with fine Mortlake tapestries on the stairs, and the elaborate gardens also date from this period, laid out in the formal Dutch style.

The 18th century saw the house pass to the Vane family and the series of elegant 1740s rooms - recently superbly restored - are their work. The Cupid room has a delicate plaster ceiling and set against the panelling is good period furniture. One of the house's highlights, the early Hogarth of Walter Vane and his family hangs in this room.

The house was the subject of almost constant work during the19th century, first by Webster, subsequently by Salvin in a surprisingly sympathetic mood. The collections were also enriched by Sir Henry Vane and his wife Margaret Gladstone, cousin of the Liberal prime minister. She introduced the William Morris decorative schemes and the William de Morgan studio pottery. With its successive changes, Hutton is an excellent example of how 'contemporary fashionable improvements' were introduced harmoniously to the advantage of the old house.

LEVENS HALL, *Kendal.*

C.H. Bagot Esq.
Tel: 05395 60321.

5 m south of Kendal on A6.
Open: April to end-Sept daily except Fri and Sat, 11-5.
£3.90, children £2.30, concessions.
Tea room.

House, interiors and garden at Levens present an unusually integrated whole, together celebrating the Elizabethan and late-17th century periods when the major developments took place. Even the uncomfortable proximity of passing main roads cannot disturb the place's air of establishment which dates back to the 13th century and the construction of the pele tower which forms part of the present house.

In 1562 Levens was bought by Alan Bellingham and at the hands of his son James defensive tower became comfortable home. James Bellingham, later knighted by James I, rebuilt Levens and the irregular but well-assembled exterior has changed little since. His interior work was more spectacular; panelling with local oak, plaster wall decoration and moulded plaster ceilings. Most vigorous of all are the carved oak overmantels, especially that in the drawing room which has ascending pilasters in the three classical orders dividing and flanking heraldic panels with the arms of Bellingham and Elizabeth I. Bellingham was obviously a loyal subject; the Queen's arms in brilliantly painted plaster also surmount the great hall fireplace.

James Bellingham's great-grandson Alan gambled Levens away and in 1688 it was bought by his kinsman, Colonel James Grahme, Keeper of the Privy Purse to James II. Lely's fine portraits of the colonel and his wife hang in the drawing room along with his daughter by Hudson and he was responsible for much of the important late-Stuart and William and Mary furniture which is so well suited to the panelled rooms. Carved oak and walnut chairs abound, with pride of place going to the Charles II walnut set in the dining room.

Grahme also commissioned Levens best-known feature, the now wonderfully mature topiary garden laid out by the Frenchman Guillaume Beaumont who lived in a small house at Levens. The assembly of clipped yew trees that fill the garden to the east of the house are a feature of national importance and Beaumont's work extended to the very early ha-ha and avenue in the parkland beyond.

MIREHOUSE, *Keswick.*

Mr and Mrs Spedding.
Tel: 07687 72287.

4 m north of Keswick, on A591.
Open: April to Oct Sun and Wed, and Fri in Aug 2-4.30.
£3, children £1.50, concessions.
Tea room.

Of Cumbrian houses open to the public Mirehouse most closely reflects the Lake District. Set on the shore of Bassenthwaite with the ground rising dramatically behind, it has long been the home of the Spedding family, whose friends including Wordsworth, Tennyson and Carlyle, have left an indelible mark on the place. The contents accurately tell of the family's activities: a portrait of the Mayor of Newcastle; rare Whaling paintings; portraits by the local George Romney; and a clock by Jonas Barber of Winster; and confirm their involvement in literature, history and philosophy through the 19th century.

The library is impressively full of books and documents relating to Thomas Carlyle and Tennyson while the parlour contains manuscripts by Sir Francis Bacon whose works were edited by James Spedding during this period. The walls are hung with important portraits by Samuel Laurence and photography by Julia Margaret Cameron. Not only the library but most of the house presents history in a most digestible and enjoyable fashion. Each room from the dining room to the school room contains interesting artefacts clearly shown and waiting to be explored. There are coins 'hidden' for children to find, a Queen Anne cabinet with sweets hidden in secret drawers for the enquiring to discover and a gong for the outgoing to bang.

Outside the walks by the lake incorporate the spot where Tennyson composed 'Le Morte d'Arthur', and the adventure playground in the woods provides further enjoyment for children.

MUNCASTER CASTLE, *Ravenglass.*

Mrs P. Gordon-Duff-Pennington.
Tel: 0229 717203/717614.

1 m south-east of Ravenglass on A595.
Open end-March to end-Oct Tues to Sun and Bank Hols 1-4,
Gardens and Owl centre daily all year 11-5.
£4.90, children £2.50, concessions.
Restaurant.

Ruskin called the view from Muncaster over Eskdale to the peaks of the Lake District 'the gateway to paradise' and the castle's position is among the most spectacular in the country, enhanced by its remoteness. Defensive potential accounted for the 14th-century Pele tower built by the Penningtons, but today Muncaster is as transformed by Anthony Salvin from 1862.

Externally his design in warm pink granite is in the style of noble restraint that he employed at Peckforton, rather than one of his more fantastical efforts such as Harlaxton. Inside the variety of the hall, dining room, octagonal library and drawing room pay tribute to his skilful versatility. In the library a high brass-railed gallery surmounts the bookcases that are broken by doorcases, panels and niches and the ceiling is imaginatively ribbed and vaulted. Equally enjoyable is the barrel ceiling of the drawing room with plasterwork by Italian craftsmen.

Salvin was commissioned by the 4th Lord Muncaster (the title acquired by the Penningtons in 1783). On the death of his brother in 1917 the castle passed to his mother's family the Ramsdens. It is their first incumbant, Sir John Ramsden, whose hand is most evident inside and out. He brought Ramsden portraits of quality, including four Reynolds, which hang together in the drawing room; the Penningtons decorate the walls of the dining room. Sir John was a discerning collector and among the items that he acquired are the alabaster nude by John of Bologna and Italian bronzes. They add variety to fine 17th-century furniture, silver by Paul Storr and important porcelain. For family history, however, the most prized possession is the 'Luck of Muncaster': a drinking bowl presented by Henry VI to Sir John Pennington who took in the king at Muncaster after his defeat at the battle of Hexham. So long as the cup remains intact it will ensure that the family continue to thrive at Muncaster.

Sir John Ramsden's other major contribution was the gardens. He financed a number of plant-collecting expeditions to the Himalayas during the 1920s and from the seeds brought back by Ludlow, Sheriff and Kingdon Ward, established the superb collection of rhodendrons and azaleas ideally suited to their woodland setting. Muncaster's other garden feature is the 18th-century terrace which provides unforgettable views over the landscape beyond.

RYDAL MOUNT, *Ambleside.*

The Trustees of Rydal Mount.
Tel: 05394 33002.

Between Ambleside and Grasmere off A591.
Open: daily March to end-Oct 9.30-5; Nov to end-Feb 10-4 (closed Tues), £2, children 80p.

Rydal Mount is a shrine to William Wordsworth who lived here from 1813 until his death in 1850, brought by his great great grandaughter, Mary Henderson and now preserved by her family. The typically Lakeland house, extended from a 16th-century cottage during the 18th century, with views out to Windermere in one direction, Rydal Water in another and fells all around, encapsulates the area's appeal to the poet. He designed the garden to consist of, in his own words, 'lawn and trees carefully planted so as not to obscure the view.'

The warm, homely rooms recreate the life of the group who lived harmoniously together: William, his wife Mary and their three surviving children John, Dora and William, his sister Dorothy and his sister-in-law Sara Hutchinson. Work and relaxation were obviously carefully separated, a visitor was apparently told by a member of the staff, 'this is my master's library where he keeps his books: his study is out of doors.' Sadly the library does not survive intact but the happy domesticity is brought to life in the various pictures: a number of Wordsworth himself, including the drawing by B.R. Haydon whose original hangs in the National Portrait Gallery and a softer likeness by the American Henry Inman. Originally he was painting a portrait to mark Wordsworth's appointment as Poet Laureate; Mary Wordsworth was so taken with the result that she commissioned another for herself.

Contrastingly unsettled is the portrait of Dorothy by S. Crosthwaite, painted three years before her mental collapse. It is her only known portrait. Although Wordsworth and Coleridge had fallen out before he came to Rydal Mount the friendship is perpetuated in Coleridge's portrait by Northcote in the library.

East Anglia
St Osyth

HEDINGHAM CASTLE, *Castle Hedingham.*

The Hon Thomas and Mrs Lindsay.
Tel: 0787 460261.

1 m off A604 between Cambridge and Colchester.
Open: Easter week to end-Oct daily 10-5.
£2.50, children £1.50, concessions.
Teas by arrangement.

The strategic importance of Hedingham's position is clear as you enjoy the commanding views in all directions from the upper floors of the Norman tower. It was built around 1140 - one of the few Norman keeps to survive from that period - by Aubrey de Vere whose family were among the most powerful in Norman England. In 1142 Aubrey was made Earl of Oxford, a title which the family held for 20 generations until 1703. Macaulay called them 'the longest and most illustrous line of nobles that England has seen.' After the soldiers of the Middle Ages came scholars and aesthetes; Edward the 7th earl is widely believed to have been the author of Shakespeare's plays.

The keep remains an imposing edifice, its pale ashlar stone quarried at Barnack near Stamford - an expense testifying to the de Veres importance. One hundred and twenty two spiral steps lead from the basement where food was stored past the ground floor guard room and on up to the first floor banqueting hall spanned by a fine Norman arch - reputedly the broadest in Europe. A gallery still runs around the banqueting hall and above is the dormitory floor. The rooms on each level are kept plain encouraging the visitor to slip back in time; school children imagining arrow-slits and pots of boiling oil account for a large percentage of the castle's visitors. Today the sloping lawns and lakeside walks that surround the castle present an altogether more peaceful atmosphere, conducive to picnics rather that warfare.

INGATESTONE HALL, Chelmsford.

The Lord Petre.
Tel: 0277 353010.

Off A12 at Ingatestone.
Open: April to end-Sept Fri, Sat and Sun (also Wed, Thur mid-July to 1 Sept).
£3, children £2, concessions.
Tea room.

After the royal palace of Hampton Court Ingatestone boasted the first example of a long gallery, completed around 1543 and setting the house in the vanguard of Tudor fashion. William Petre was Thomas Cromwell's proctor for the Dissolution. His post demanded that he visit abbeys up and down the land and so, in 1539, he was able to purchase the Manor of Ingatestone from the lands of Barking Abbey which had been surrendered to the crown. He replaced the existing modest dwelling at Ingatestone with one, 'very fair, large and stately, made of brick and embattled' - substantially the house that survives today.

Petre carried on to be Secretary of State to Henry VIII and to enjoy the rare distinction of surviving in office through the reigns of both Edward VI and Mary Tudor; perhaps because he was in the view of one contemporary, 'the man who said nothing.' The 7th Lord Petre flirtatiously snipped a lock of hair from his cousin Arabella Fermor and caused the family feud that inspired Alexander Pope's 'The Rape of the the Lock'.

From Ingatestone the Petres spread to Thorndon Hall nearby on their Essex estates, which James Paine transformed into sumptuous Palladian. In 1876 fire virtually gutted the great house and in 1919, following the death of the 16th Lord Petre as a young soldier in 1915, his widow returned to Ingatestone and set about a painstaking restoration which reaffirmed the house's Tudor character. Visitors go through the arch of the clock tower range and approach the long U-shaped house of warm brick, with crow-stepped gables, tall patterned chimneys and a delightful octagonal turret staircase in one corner.

The succession of panelled rooms evoke the Tudor mood. Some panelling is original while other, such as the oak linenfold in the dining room, is period but put in during the restoration. Portraits represent almost all generations of the family; many of the earlier 16th and 17th-century figures, such as the 2nd Lord Petre and his wife by Cornelius Johnson are very arresting, while the troublesome Arabella Fermor hangs in the one main room left with its 18th-century decoration. Furniture combines much from the 17th century such as the fine Charles II 'Harlequin' chairs with later 18th-century and Regency pieces from Thorndon. The dining room contains three important tapestries, two from the Mortlake factory, the third 17th-century Flemish depicting the Siege of Troy.

LAYER MARNEY TOWER, *Colchester.*

Mr Nicholas Charrington.
Tel: 0206 330784.

6 m south of Colchester, off B1022.
Open: April, May, June, Sept, Sun and Thur 2-6
July and Aug daily except Sat 2-6, Bank Hols.
Price on application.

Layer Marney is a building of sparkling originality and could not disappoint the most expectant of visitors. Not only is it the tallest of the select group of Tudor gatehouses, it is the most flamboyant, architecturally assured and decoratively avant-garde. The arrangement of the eight storeys of windows in the towers, the expansive three storeys of the central block and the diapered brickwork together exemplify Tudor vigour. But most important is the terracotta decoration, for window mullions and the crestings on the towers where the initials J and C (for John and Christian Marney) flank crestings, which puts Layer Marney amongst a tiny select group of buildings that enjoyed this fleeting brush with the Renaissance. Terracotta was only introduced to England by Italian craftsmen working for Wolsey and Henry VIII; the dissolution terminated the conducive relationship with Italy. It is most likely that the work at Layer Marney was carried out by English craftsmen who had learnt from the Italians, which explains a little haziness over the classical vocabulary.

It was the last - and by all accounts - only, flourish of the Marneys who had occupied the manor since the 12th century. Henry Marney rose to prominence during the reigns of Henry VII and VIII; around 1520 he determined to build himself a suitably fashionable and grand house. He died as building was beginning and six weeks after being made a peer; two years later in 1525 his son died also and the family line was extinct. Henry Marney's house was left largely as it is today, the gatehouse with its wings which would have formed the first range of an expansive courtyard of buildings, and the separated building to the south called the long gallery.

After the Marneys Layer Marney was owned by another prominent Tudor family, the Tukes, thereafter changing hands sucessively and falling into considerable disrepair. After some restoration during the 19th century it was bought in 1904 by Walter de Zoete who carried out far more extensive restoration and gave the interiors their present appearance. He also restored the church to the south-west of the house and contains the tombs of Henry and John Marney, each with canopies that are the most striking of all the terracotta work. In 1958 Mr Charrington's father bought Layer Marney and the family have continued Walter de Zoete's work and opened the house to the public.

SAINT OSYTH'S PRIORY, *Clacton-on-Sea.*

Somerset de Chair.
Tel: 0255 820492.

Off B1027, 10 m south-east of Colchester, 3 m west of Clacton.
Open: Easter and May to end-Sept, daily except Sat.
£3, children 75p, concessions.

St Osyth's can justly claim to contain the finest monastic remains in England and is a surprising discovery hidden away on the edge of the Essex marshes. The earliest parts of the monastery are 13th-century while additions from successive centuries through to the 19th link together around an expansive quadrangle. Most impressive is the 15th-century gatehouse. Mr de Chair bought St Osyth's in 1954 and first restored the gatehouse for occupation. The 18th-century range in particular now contains his art collection and outstanding paintings inherited by his wife from her father, 8th Earl Fitzwilliam, including celebrated Stubbs's.

EUSTON HALL, *Thetford.*

The Duke and Duchess of Grafton.
Tel: 0842 766366.

3 m south of Thetford, off A1088.
Open: Thur June to end-Sept and last Sun in June and 1st Sun in Sept, 2.30-5.
£2.50, children 50p, concessions.

Euston was rebuilt for Henry Bennet, 1st Earl of Arlington. His only daughter Isabella married Charles II's son by Barbara Villiers, Henry, 1st Duke of Grafton. Arlington left nothing to chance, she was betrothed at five and married at twelve. The house was considerably altered for the 2rd duke by Matthew Brettingham who removed the domes from the corner pavilions and replaced then with the more demure Palladian pyramid roofs evident today.

The collection of royal Stuart portraits is only rivalled at Windsor Castle. Arlington's daughter is shown with her son in one of Kneller's most sophisticated portraits and the 18th-century Graftons added further quality to the collection, such as Reynolds portraits and Stubbs's famous Mares and Foals at Euston. William Kent designed chairs for Euston and landscaped the park (on which John Evelyn had advised Arlington), and built the octagonal temple. Capability Brown completed the park in 1769.

HOLKHAM HALL, *Wells.*

The Viscount Coke.
Tel: 0328 710227.

2 m west of Wells, off A149.
Open: Daily except Fri and Sat, end-May to end-Sept, 1.30-5 and Bank Hols.
£2.70, children £1.20.
Tea room.

Holkham's austerity disguises the fact that it is as Robin Feddon confirmed, 'the ultimate achievement of the English Palladian movement.' The riches of the interior are more easily appreciated and present an unparalleled ensemble. One can hardly imagine anyone daring to make alterations to Holkham and it remains as built surrounded by William Kent's park to soften the coastal site which a contemporary of Holkham's builder called, 'a most unpleasant place.'

Young Thomas Coke spent six years between 1712-18 on the grand tour in Italy. In 1744 he was created Earl of Leicester. The house, begun in 1735 but not completed until after his death in 1759, is the fruit of his education and collecting during those years, and his association with the high priest of English Palladianism, the Earl of Burlington and his protege William Kent. Much of the work was carried out by Leicester's surveyor, Matthew Brettingham.

Externally no decorative flourishes were allowed to distract from the precise Palladianism - emphasised by the blandly pale brick baked nearby and used throughout - of the central block with state rooms filling a piano nobile and four identical wings each joined to a pyramid-roofed corner tower. On the garden side the spatial arrangement of the broad facade, the subtle minor differences in window style, and the central portico, is breathtakingly assured.

The marble hall is memorable. 18 enormous pink fluted columns supporting the coved and coffered ceiling, broad stone steps leading up from the basement level between walls faced in pink Derbyshire marble. Roubiliac's bust of Leicester surveys the scene from above the door leading to the saloon, the central state room on the garden front. The rich coved ceiling and doorcases, wall hangings of Genoese velvet and chimneypieces of Sicilian marble, suggest the hand of Kent who designed the gilded furniture covered in velvet. The paintings compliment the decoration, especially Rubens' The Return of the Holy Family. In the south dining room hang two full lengths of Leicester's great-nephew 'Coke of Norfolk' the farming entrepreneur, one as a young connoisseur on the grand tour by Batoni, the other as an English squire by Gainsborough.

For most visitors the quality of paintings reaches a zenith in the smallest state room, the landscape room, hung only with landscapes by Claud, Poussin and Gaspard. Such undiluted quality typifies Holkham.

HOUGHTON HALL, *Kings Lynn.*

The Marquess of Cholmondeley.
Tel: 0485 528569.

13 m east of Kings Lynn, 10 m west of Fakenham, off A148.
Open: Easter Sun to end-Sept Sun, Thur and Bank Hols.
£4, children £2, concessions.
Tea room.

Blenheim and Stratfield Say were gifts of a grateful nation to military heroes, Marlborough and Wellington. Houghton, however, a house of equal stature to both, was created out of the fruits of political office - the successes of England's first Prime Minister, Sir Robert Walpole. It was built in just thirteen years (1722-1735) to a design by Colin Campbell, adapted by James Gibbs, Thomas Ripley and William Kent. Externally its massive square plan is remarkably lightened by the satisfying Palladian proportions and the cupolas that surmount the four corner towers, giving Houghton one of the most distinctive skyines of any English house. Inside the decoration is William Kent as his most brilliantly unrestrained, assisted by the plasterwork of Artari. The series of state rooms on the piano nobile, encircling the central hall aptly convey the authority and wealth of the most powerful man in the land.

Kent's interiors demonstrate the clever reinterpretation of classical and Renaissance models, enhanced by Roman Baroque, which gave such early-Georgian houses their combination of elegance and vigour. Walpole's great picture collection - at the time without rival in England - was sold to Catherine the Great by his ungrateful grandson; but Kent's interiors and furnishings remain as ample testament to its splendours. Particularly noteworthy are his sets of gilded chairs, the French and Italian 16th and 17th century bronzes, the tapestries including the famous Mortlake of the Stuart kings, and the state beds.

The survival of Kent's rooms was both an accident of history (the house was largely unoccupied for over a century) and the result of the energy and taste of George, 5th Marquess of Cholmondeley and his wife Sybil Sassoon - whose considerable fortune enabled Houghton to be revitalized and who brought to it new collections such as the exquisite French furniture, porcelain and Old Masters. Between the wars they restored both house and gardens and their work has been continued by the present marquess.

In recent years the enormous collection of model soldiers assembled by the present marquess's father has been brilliantly displayed; it is an absorbing addition, not just for schoolboys. On the walls around are more family portraits and - suitably - good 18th and 19th century military paintings, notably a splendid Reinagle of the local militia.

KENTWELL HALL, *Long Melford.*

Mr and Mrs J. Patrick Phillips.
Tel: 0787 310207.

Off A134 on north edge of Long Melford.
Open: late-March to mid-June Sun, Bank Hols and other days/week-ends, mid-June to mid-July Sat and Sun and other selected days, usually 12-5.
£4, children £2.50, concessions.
Home made teas.

The attractive village of Long Melford has the unique distinction of two important houses of identical style and period, the National Trust property Melford Hall and Kentwell, approached from the north of the village along a majestic three-quarter mile avenue of 300-year old limes. At the far end the Tudor house with protruding wings flanking a generous courtyard is immediately welcoming, the combination of warm brick, tall gables and paired cupola-topped towers enhanced by the encircling moat crossed by a central bridge.

Patrick Phillips bought Kentwell in 1971 and has carried out admirable restoration to both house and its gardens. Sir Thomas Clopton built the house and his mother's will of 1563 refers to 'the new mansion', and the interiors saw continual alteration thereafter. The main staircase is 17th century, chimneypieces and doorcases 18th century, but the most substantial alterations came after a fire in 1827. The owner, Robert Hart Logan commissioned Thomas Hopper (who had previously been working at neighbouring Melford Hall) to carry out the work, which he did in rich Gothic and Tudor revival style. He worked on almost all the main rooms with varying treatment; the most impressive are the dining room and great hall, whose towering bay window contains rare 15th-century armorial glass (of which there is more in the billiards room). In the library he introduced dazzling sciagola columns and, as in the drawing room, a fine chimneypiece.

The daunting restoration by Patrick Phillips was carried out over a number of years and involved painstaking redecoration and the introduction of furniture. The overall effect has been to bring the venerable house to life, especially on the occasions of the 'Tudor Re-creations' for which Kentwell has acquired a reputation.

OTLEY HALL, *Ipswich.*

Mr J.G. Mosesson.
Tel: 0473 890264.

7 m north-east of Ipswich on B1078.
Open: Bank Hol week-ends and by appointment for groups.
£3.50, children £2.50, concessions.

Martha's Vineyard, the fashionable holiday island in Massachussetts, was named after the daughter of Bartholemew Gosnold, whose family lived at Otley from 1440-1674 and built the 15th and early-16th century moated house with a later Jacobean wing, all of which survives remarkably unchanged 500 years later. The combination of steep gables, herringbone brickwork, half-timber and pargeting, and vigorously tall brick chimneys makes for an immediately arresting picture while inside many mediaeval features can be discovered.

The great hall at the core of the house has an outstanding timber ceiling with carved joists and moulded beams, and retains its original screen and 8-light mullioned window. Equally important is the panelling in the linenfold room, used as dining room while upstairs the banqueting room retains panels of delicate 16th-century wall painting incorporating coats of arms.

Dorothy Sherston, who lived at Otley from 1910-1950, was largely responsible for the preservation of the mediaeval character of the house and its major features, as well as carrying out judicious restoration. Architectural work was carried out by Morley Horder while Francis Inigo Thomas (co-author with Reginald Blomfield of *The Formal Garden in England*) supplied a plan for the garden. A picture of Thomas's plan hangs in the house, and although it was not carried out to completion, in 1987 the addition of the canal and mount took up one of his ideas. Mr Mosesson bought Otley in 1976 and first opened it to the public, for whom it provides a rare example of mediaeval vernacular architecture.

THE PRIORY, *Lavenham.*

Mr and Mrs A. Casey.
Tel: 0787 247003.

In Water St, Lavenham.
Open: April to end-Oct, daily 10.30-5.30.
£2.50, children £1.
Restaurant.

It is fitting that one of the most important houses in Lavenham, renowned for its mediaeval buildings, has since 1979 been restored from an advanced state of dereliction by Mr and Mrs Casey. Pevsner wrote, 'there is nothing in Suffolk to compare with the timber-framed houses of Lavenham' and a return to the house of 1600 was the aim of the Casey's restoration. From a 13th-century hall house belonging to the Benedictine order it passed through successive owners, some connected with the cloth trade which brought Lavenham its fortune, who made various additions and alterations, accounting for the house's rambling appearance.

The timberwork, much of it exposed during the restoration is of primary interest, in particular the crown-post roofs of the solar and great chamber, and the Jacobean staircase. Decorative pargeting is preserved on the gables of the front facing onto the passing street, which also have finely embattled barge boards. The great chamber has Elizabethan strapwork over the fireplace and parts of the Elizabethan wall paintings that once decorated the whole painted chamber survive. Equally important as the surviving decorative and structural features, the arrangement of the rooms well illustrates how they would have been during the house's heyday.

SOMERLEYTON HALL, *Lowestoft.*

The Lord and Lady Somerleyton.
Tel: 0502 730224.

5 m north-west of Lowestoft, off B1074.
Open: Easter to end Sept Thur, Sun and Bank Hols,
July and Aug Tues and Wed, 2-5 (house).
£3.50, concessions.
Tea room.

Somerleyton was built by the fortune of one Victorian plutocrat and embellished by another. Such a combination brings a surfeit of riches both inside and out. The diversity is not only architectural: the gardens contain glasshouses by Paxton and a maze and parterre by Nesfield; the fabulous winter garden has, alas, gone but its loggia and the conservatory survives; inside is lavish carving, a monumental staircase hall, and an array of fine furniture, porcelain and paintings.

Morton Peto, who bought the Somerleyton estate in 1843, was a meteoric and philanthropic entrepreneur. From bricklaying in his uncle's firm he rose to be the leading building contractor and railway constructor of the day, an MP and, in 1855, a baronet. The highlight of his career was the contract for the new Houses of Parliament and when he set about modernising the existing Jacobean Somerleyton he chose as architect John Thomas, a sculptor and mason who had assisted Charles Barry at Westminster.

Peto's idea was Victorian Jacobean; the end result was ornately heterogeneous. The entrance front has a Jacobean feel with its advancing wings whose gables recall the old house. In addition there is a tall Italianate tower at one end, a French flavour in the balustraded screen, and rich stone work everywhere, balustrades, towering porch, and statues along the parapets. The stable tower clock was made by the royal maker Vulliamy for Big Ben. A row broke out over the cost, Vulliamy withdrew and Sir Morton bought it for Somerleyton.

Thomas's work continued inside. The pair of white marble chimneypieces in the ballroom reveal him in his outstanding metier, as a craftsman carver; as do the oak columns in the entrance hall and the imposing staircase. The combination of rich oak and the glittering white and gilded woodwork and crimson hangings in the ballroom perpetuate a strong sense of mid-Victorian affluence.

Sir Morton's affluence did not last. Generosity - he guaranteed £50,000 towards his friend Paxton's Crystal Palace - and extravagance plunged him into debt and in 1861, ten years after his new house had been finished, he put the whole estate on the market. It was bought in 1863 by Sir Francis Crossley (perhaps to celebrate his baronetcy of that year), whose family fortune came from their carpet-making mills in Halifax.

When Sir Morton sold Somerleyton the fittings and works of art were included and many remain at Somerleyton today, such as the two paintings from the Napoleonic Wars by Clarkson Stanfield which Sir Morton had commissioned, and the mirror from the Doge's Palace, which he bought at the sale of the Duke of Buckingham's Stowe in 1848. Sir Francis and his successors (his son Savile was made 1st Lord Somerleyton and was the grandfather of the present owner) have made outstanding additions, none more so than the wonderful Wright of Derby in the dining room. The 1st Lord Somerleyton collected the 2,200 volumes in the library which was made out of Sir Morton's grand two-storey banqueting hall. Successive generations of Crossleys hang in the staircase hall, but the most delightful family likeness is the Carrera marble figure by Thomas Durham of Savile Crossley as a boy with a spade and hatfull of seashells. The 12 acres of gardens are maintained to the highest standard.

WINGFIELD OLD COLLEGE, *Eye.*

Ian Chance.
Tel: 0379 384505.

7 m south-east of Diss, off B1118.
Open: Easter to end-Sept, Sat, Sun and Bank Hols 2-6.
£2.20, concessions.
Tea room.

Wingfield College presents a piece of architectural trickery. The demure 18th-century front is only a facade, built onto the rooms of the existing mediaeval college, many of which were retained but disguised with false walls, ceilings and plasterwork. The college, whose church stands adjacent to the house was founded in 1362 by Sir John de Wingfield a friend of the Black Prince. The imposing church was built over Sir John's tomb. His daughter married a de la Pole whose family became earls and dukes of Suffolk and were generous benefactors for the college. It was surrendered during the Dissolution and the college became a private house to which Squire Buck added the Georgian facade.

Mr Chance bought Wingfield in 1971 and has uncovered much of the mediaeval fabric. The most impressive room is the great hall with a fine oak roof, linenfold panelling and a screen incorporating three carved Tudor portraits. The church contains a series of important tomb effigies including Sir John Wingfield and John de la Pole, 2nd duke of Suffolk and his wife Elizabeth Plantagenet (sister of Edward IV). In 1981 Mr Chance founded Wingfield Arts and Music which has festivals through the year.

EAST MIDLANDS
design for West Wing by John Webb
1654
Lamport Hall

CHATSWORTH HOUSE, *Bakewell.*

Chatsworth House Trust.
Tel: 0246 582204.

4 m east of Bakewell on A263.
Open: end-March to end-Oct 11-4.30.
£5.50, children £2.75, concessions.
Restaurant.

Chatsworth presents an unrivalled image of a ducal country seat: a great house, set in noble parkland, surrounded by impressive gardens, with splendid stables, quaint farms, and inside, endless evidence that it has been for centuries the home of an illustrious family. Most of these generations have left their mark and part of the appeal as you wander the passages, mount cavernous staircases or gaze in the state rooms, is the sense that far from being a period piece preserved with subsequent titivation, Chatsworth has evolved, accumulating steadily along the way. Today a good deal of the accumulation is from other Devonshire houses (the absent-minded Victorian statesman the 8th duke could never remember how many homes he had), in particular Devonshire House in London, Chiswick villa (the home of Lord Burlington whose daughter married the 4th duke), and Compton Place in Eastbourne.

Bess of Hardwick's Tudor house was replaced at the end of the 17th century by the 1st Duke of Devonshire in a building programme of 20 years and just completed whe he died in 1707. The duke was closely involved and may himself have designed the west front that greets visitors from the park; a first view few ever forget. Prior to this William Talman designed the south front facing the long canal and the east front looking across gardens to the wooded hill beyond. The west front came next then, in 1705, after the architect Thomas Archer had already given Chatsworth the most exciting garden building in the country - the cascade house - he rebuilt the north front. Just over a hundred years later Jeffry Wyatville rebuilt the east front and added the north wing. In between the periods of activity at the house the 4th duke commissioned James Paine to build the suitably ducal stable block, and the bridge over the River Derwent whose course had been altered in 'Capability' Brown's landscaping of the park.

The 1st duke employed a team of craftsmen who together gave Chatsworth some of the finest Baroque interiors in England. Walls and ceilings were painted by Verrio and Laguerre and later Thornhill, Tijou provided ironwork, and Cibber executed designs for rich carving. Much of this was executed by Samuel Watson who was born a few miles from Chatsworth but despite his humble origins produced quantities of work of unrivalled quality, an interesting parallel to the degree to which house and estate are proudly self-sufficient today.

Much of Wyatville's work for the 6th duke was making Chatsworth convenient to live in, while his more substantial internal alterations included the series of libraries for his employer's ever-increasing quantity of books. Outside, the duke's gardener, Paxton, was ever busier constructing and planting. Even if his great conservatories have gone his Emperor fountain - planned for a visit by the emperor of Russia - glass wall-cases, cascades and rockeries, pinetum and arboretum all survive to celebrate this tireless polymath.

Both house and garden - as well as all other estate enterprises -have been energetically and lovingly attended to by the present duchess and it is her contribution that has added a vital element for visitors.

EYAM HALL, *Eyam.*

R.H.V. Wright.
Tel: 0433 631976.

In Eyam off A623, 12 m west of Chesterfield.
Open: Easter Sun to end-Oct, Wed, Thur, Sun and Bank Hols 11-4.30.
£3.25, children £2.25, concessions.
Tea room.

The spectacular countryside of the Derbyshire peak district is justifyably among the most popular in England and heading from the sprawling metropolis of Sheffield to Eyam, a mere 15 miles to the west, one is reminded why. But of the thousands of annual visitors few have yet discovered Eyam Hall, which first opened to the public in 1992. The village gained a reputation for self-sacrifice during the plague of 1665, when having suffered an outbreak via a parcel of cloth from London, it imposed its own quarantine to prevent the disease spreading.

A few years later, in 1671, Eyam Hall was rebuilt and extended by Thomas Wright for his son John who had married a local heiress, Elizabeth Kniveton. The family have occupied the house ever since. John's house was built with local millstone grit and its low, gabled entrance front with mullioned windows, looking onto a protective courtyard seems to reflect the tough but impressive peak landscape that surrounds it. Inside, the house retains a small-scale intimacy; the succession of rooms are full of interest but never imposing. An extensive collection of family portraits illustrate the characters of successive generations, while good English furniture - an unusual pair of settles and fine tester bed contemporary with the house, and George I chairs - make an enjoyable ensemble. The collection of toys and dolls in the nursery dates back to 1850 and is in keeping with this welcoming family home.

HADDON HALL, *Bakewell.*

The Duke of Rutland.
Tel: 0629 812855.

2 m south-east of Bakewell on A6.
Open: April to end-Sept, Tues-Sun and Bank Hols 11-6.
Closed Sun July and Aug except Bank Hol.
£4, children £2.50, concessions.
Restaurant.

Haddon's air of romance comes from its position on a wooded hillside above the Derbyshire Wye, its castellated stone walls and towers and hanging terraced gardens, its ancient establishment, and neglect for nearly two centuries. Its heroine Dorothy Vernon eloped from Haddon with John Manners and their subsequent marriage gave the house to the Manners family who have owned it ever since. By 1703 when their earldom became the Dukedom of Rutland they were based at Belvoir castle and Haddon was maintained empty. In 1912 the 9th duke began the restoration that became his life's work.

William the Conqueror's illegitimate son Peveril of the Peak owned Haddon but the house dates from the 12th century. It remains superbly mediaeval, a link between defensive castles which produced the west front rising from Norman walls, and later country houses. From the Norman beginnings Haddon evolved around its two courtyards, divided by the great hall and associated rooms, principally during the 200 years from 1370 when Sir Richard de Vernon IV built the great hall. Later highlights were Sir Henry Vernon's completion of the dining room and great chamber and, finally around 1603, the decoration by John Manners of the Elizabethan long gallery overlooking the gardens.

All the main rooms are of considerable importance. The hall retains much of its original timber structure; the dining room has panelling surmounted by carved heraldic emblems and portrait medallions and with bright heraldic paintings in ceiling panels. Above are the great chamber and the long gallery with renaissance-patterned panelling. Suitably in a primarily mediaeval house, tapestries are of primary decorative importance: the oldest is French, dating rom around 1460 and carries the English royal arms; it may have been a gift from Henry VIII's older brother Prince Arthur, to whom Sir Henry Vernon was Treasurer. Hanging over the gallery fireplace is a painting of Haddon by Rex Whistler, done in 1933, which captures the place's alluring atmosphere. For most visitors the series of stone-terraced gardens that descend beneath the rose-clad walls of the south front are integral to this atmosphere, their different size and levels given uniformity by balustraded walls and continuing the theme of variety so noticeable in the house itself.

MELBOURNE HALL, *Melbourne.*

Lord Ralph Kerr.
Tel: 0332 862502.

In Melbourne, 9 m south of Derby off A453.
Open: daily in Aug (not Mon) 2-5.
Price available on request.
Tea room.

Melbourne is an almost perfect small country house. Once the home of Queen Victoria's favourite prime minister, Lord Melbourne, it stands in the manner of a French petit chateau, on the edge of its eponymous village and beside a beautiful Norman church. In addition to the enduring attraction of the overall scene, Melbourne is of great importance for its formal garden in the manner of Andre le Notre, a rare survivor from the early 18th-century . From the sweep of lawn descending to a sheet of water in front of the house radial avenues and walks between clipped hedges lead off into woodland on one side. There are waterworks and superb ornaments including the delightful Birdcage Arbour made of wrought iron by Robert Bakewell whose smithy was in Melbourne village and the lead Four Seasons Urn by Jan van Nost; the two are the finest work of their kind in any English garden.

The architecture of the house is irregular, 17th-century at the back, with a fine provincial 18th-century facade by William Smith of Warwick looking over the sloping garden. The colourful interiors contain an unusual collection of 17th-century English portraits, including Jacob Huysmans' masterpiece.

ROCKINGHAM CASTLE, *Corby.*

Commander Michael Saunders-Watson.
Tel: 0536 770240.

2 m north of Corby off A6003.
Open: Easter to end-Sept Sun, Thur, Bank Hols and Tues following, Tues in Aug, 1.30-5.30.
£3.60, children £2, concessions.
Tea room.

1994 witnesses the 900th anniversary of Rockingham Castle, a span which divides with distinguished symmetry into two identical periods; 450 years as a royal fortress and 450 years as home of the Watson family. The views from the castle's pre-eminent position overlooking the broad Welland valley would have been equally commanding when William the Conqueror built one of the formidable castles which served as a network of secure bases from which he was able to subdue the native English. Successive monarchs used Rockingham for the next four centuries; KIng John was a frequent visitor and Edward I made substantial alterations to improve the secure but uncomfortable Norman castle for his queen Eleanor. But towards the end of the 15th century the castle had lasped into disrepair, Henry VIII leased it to Edward Watson and in 1619 his grandson Sir Lewis Watson bought the property from James I.

Edward I's gate with round towers was retained as was the walled enclosure of the Norman outer bailey, but Edward Watson began the transformation from castle to house which his successors continued into the 17th century (especially after extensive damage by parliamentary forces during the Civil War who captured Rockingham. Edward Watson added buildings to both ends of the 13th-century great hall and this range has steep Elizabethan gables. At one end is a long gallery wing, part Tudor but largely rebuilt after the Civil War, and altered again during the 19th century, when Anthony Salvin was commissioned to carry out internal work and external additions including the flag tower.

Sir Lewis Watson was made Lord Rockingham, his grandson became an earl but those titles died out in 1746. Marriage to the daughter of Sir George Sondes of Lees Court in Kent meant that the family used Rockingham as an occasional home during the 18th century, although some of its artistic highlights date from the this period, when the Watsons were Lords Sondes. Eventually the Sondes family remained in Kent and a Watson brother stayed at Rockingham.

The mediaeval character of Rockingham is best preserved in the cobbled 'street' of service rooms and buildings; the old great hall was divided by Edward Watson into the present hall and adjacent panel room. The hall contains Tudor portraits in keeping with its period and including an important picture of Francis I of France Joos van Cleeve. The elegant librray has an 18th century feel to it and the fine collection of books were largely assembled by the Sondes; but Rockingham's most memorable interior is the long gallery, successively remodelled until given its present form during the late-1830s when Salvin was commissioned and built the flag tower whose bay window became a major new feature of the gallery. Charles Dickens immortalised the room when he used Rockingham as the model for Chesney Wold in Bleak House.

Generations of the Sondes family are represented in a series of outstanding paintings of fascinating variety: single portraits by Lely, Reynolds and Angelica Kauffmann, a family group by Dahl, but, most memorable are two period pieces of rare quality; the children of the 1st Lord Sondes playing cricket by Zoffany, and the four sons of the 2nd Lord Sondes with their hounds by Ben Marshall. Few other rooms can boast two such pre-eminent, different sporting paintings.

STANFORD HALL, *Lutterworth.*

Lady Braye.
Tel: 0788 860250.

7 m north-east of Rugby off A5, exit 18 M6.
Open: Easter Sat to end-Sept, Sat, Sun, Bank Hols and Tues following 2.30-6 (last admission 5.30).
£2.90, children £1.30, concessions.
Home-made teas.

Robin Feddon described Stanford's south front as 'a textbook example of the William III style' and the visitor has to agree. Immaculately proportioned and faced in grey ashlar, its hipped roof with dormers over two storeys with tall sash windows and side projections, it exemplifies the elegant style of the period. From the park which extends to the River Avon the south front can be enjoyed at the same time as the similar one facing east; similar but different in period. Around 1690 Sir Roger Cave, whose famiy had been at Stanford since the 15th century, commissioned the architect Smiths of Warwick to build a new house. The estimate for £2,137.10 for demolishing the old house and building a new one is preserved in the library. William Smith executed the south front, his son Francis built the stables whose juxtaposition to the house is so integral to Stanford's charm. He probably also built the east front looking towards stables and river at the same time, forsaking the expensive ashlar for mellow red brick.

Sir Roger Cave's son Thomas married Margaret Verney, who brought the ancient barony of Braye to the family - albeit in abeyance, which it remained until revived in 1839 in favour of Sarah Otway-Cave who became the 3rd baroness. Family portraits bring together the stories of Cave and Verney and testify to the latter family's devoted royalism. The are Van Dyck's of Charles I and his wife Henrietta Maria and of the king's standard-bearer, Sir Edmund Verney, who was killed grasping the royal standard at Edgehill and whose hand had to be cut off to release the standard. Two hundred years after the battle Sarah Otway-Cave, who had become lady Braye, purchased in Rome the collection of pictures and Stuart relics that had belonged to Henry Stuart, Cardinal Duke of York.

Stanford's elegant surroundings are as enjoyable as the house's history and artistic quality, and the visitor should not leave without paying tribute to the generations of the Cave family preserved in spectacular tombs in the adjacent church of St Nicholas. An unexpected discovery is the aviation museum in the stables which honours the friend of the 6th Lord Braye, Percy Pilcher, the first man to fly in England. Pilcher was killed in 1899 when his glider crashed in the park at Stanford. A replica of his machine 'The Hawk' is the museum's main exhibit, having been presented by the Royal Aeronautical Society.

BELVOIR CASTLE, *Grantham.*

The Duke of Rutland.
Tel: 0476 870262.

7 m south-west of Grantham, between A607 and A52.
Open: April to Oct, Tues, Wed, Thur, Sat 11-5, Sun, Bank Hols 11-6, Sun in Oct 11-5.
£4, children £2.50, concessions.
Restaurant.

Belvoir should be approached from the Grantham to Melton Mowbray road. Dropping down into the village of Woolsthorpe the castle appears proudly surmounting its wooded eminence, the realisation of Victorian picturesque mediaevalism. From this distance the whole is satisfyingly harmonious and the continued approach offers a shifting picture of turrets, towers and battlements.

Inside, cavernous rooms date from the rebuilding of the castle carried out by the 5th duke and, more especially his duchess Elizabeth, who hailed from Castle Howard. In 1801 James Wyatt, was commissioned and continued work until his death in 1813, by which time two of the main fronts and many interiors were complete. Three years later fire destroyed most of his internal work and reconstruction was carried out by the duke's chaplain the Rev Sir John Thoroton with the amateur-architect duchess closely involved.

In the Elizabeth saloon the duchess commissioned Matthew Cotes Wyatt to create the sumptuous room with its white and gilded wall panels; he painted the rich ceiling panels depicting Juno and Jupiter and arranged the red damask and gilded Louis XV-style furniture made for the room. He also sculpted the duchess full length in white marble to stand at one end.

The one marvel of the fire was the survival of Wyatt's Regent's gallery - named in honour of a royal visit in 1814. Despite its overpowering size is the most splendid room in the castle. The central bow perfectly offsets the huge length, the rose-red ground of the Gobelins tapestries illustrating the adventures of Don Quixote compliments the damask shade of the original curtains and woven carpet with a pattern of arum lilies, and maplewood doors and a variety of grand regency furniture add to the overall composition. Gilded rococo pier glasses and portraits alternate with the tapestries while a succession of Nollekens busts on cool pedestals give continuity from one end to the other.

In the picture gallery the 4th duke's contribution to Belvoir is clear; although most of the Old Masters that he collected were destroyed in the 1816 fire, there remains ample evidence of his connoisseurship: five Poussins depicting the seven sacraments, works by Teniers and van Steen, and three Gainsborough landscapes being a selection of the best.

BURGHLEY HOUSE, *Stamford.*

Burghley House Preservation Trust.
Tel: 0780 52451.

1 m south-east of Stamford.
Open: April to Oct daily 11-5.
£5.10, one child per adult free, concessions.

Completed in 1587 Burghley is the place where Tudor becomes Renaissance, exuberant, sophisticted and reflecting the status of its builder, William Cecil, 1st Lord Burghley, pre-eminent statesman. Built around a central courtyard, with a series of adjoining state rooms on the first floor, the house continues to evoke the period of its construction and the personality of William Cecil - captured in his portrait by Marcus Gheeraerts. Contributions of subsequent generations over four centuries have made it a treasure-trove of collecting and patronage.

Burghley's son was made Earl of Exeter. Under the 5th earl, John, during the last two decades of the 17th century, interiors were painted in rich Baroque style by Louis Laguerre and - in particular - Antonio Verrio - whose decoration of the Heaven Room is his masterpiece. Edward Marten provided ornate plaster ceilings and Grinling Gibbons exquisite wood carving. The 5th earl travelled extensively on the continent collecting for Burghley. His acquisitions included Gobelins tapestries and furniture from France, paintings and works of art from Italy. He also built up a notable library now in the great hall.

His great-grandson Brownlow, the 9th earl, completed the decoration of the interiors. He commissioned a large quantity of the house's most important furniture, much of it from the leading firm of Loondon cabinet makets, Ince and Mayhew (who built two of Burghley's four magnificent state beds), and added the marble chimney-pieces in the set of four 'George' rooms.

Like the 5th earl, he collected extensively on the continent, including further groups of Old Masters. He commissioned Capability Brown to landscape the park. Brown also made a number of architectural alterations to the house, demonstrating to good effect this lesser known of his skills.

Highlights of later periods are the portraits of Brownlow's son Henry (who was made Marquess of Exeter) and his wife and daughter by Lawrence; the pair of portraits by Gainsborough of Sir Christopher Whichcote and his wife (ancestors of the 4th marchioness); and a selection of medals and trophies won by the 6th marquess - famous as a gold-medal winning Olympic hurdler and painted in his Cambridge 'blue' blazer by Oswald Birley.

Burghley is the focus of a thriving estate and owned by a private charitable trust for whom Lady Victoria Leatham (the youngest daughter of the 6th marquess) and her husband and family occupy and care for the house.

DODDINGTON HALL, *Doddington.*

Mr and Mrs A.G. Jarvis.
Tel: 0522 694308.

5 m west of Lincoln on B1190.
Open: Easter Mon then May to Sept, Wed, Sun, Bank Hols daily except Sat in Aug, 2-6.
£3.50, children £1.85.
Restaurant.

Doddington Hall was designed by Robert Smythson. Only its trio of cupolas lighten the confident symmetry of the stone-quoined brick exterior which is reminiscent of Burton Agnes in Yorkshire, where Smythson began work in 1601 - the year after he finished at Doddington. Like Burton Agnes, Doddington is approached via a delightful gate house and a square walled courtyard.

Unchanged Elizabethan outside, inside Doddington is Georgian thanks to restoration by Sir John Delaval, one of the more sober members of the notorious Delaval clan, who inherited from his grandmother. The hall - recently redecorated to its original Delaval colour scheme, sets the tone for the succeeding rooms with its cool Palladianism. Sir John preserved the long gallery which fills most of the top floor along the west front. He replaced the Elizabethan staircase with the present double one of restrained elegance.

Despite changes in name through marriage family successon of Doddington has been unbroken for 400 years. This is reflected in the paintings. Smythson's patron, Thomas Tailor is shown, there are Husseys by Michael Dahl, and many Delavals, including a Reynolds of Sir Francis Delaval in uniform and his important group of Sarah Delaval, her husband Lord Pollington and their son dressed for George III's coronation. There are two portraits of Sarah Gunman, who in the early-19th century left Doddington to her lover Captain George Jarvis from whom the present owner is descended. The glorious bed in the Tiger room came from Seaton Delaval where it had been slept in by the Duke of Cumberland on his way to Culloden - when he weighed 23 stone.

There is much good porcelain in the house much collected by Edwin Jarvis during the 19th century. Furniture includes a rare set of Cromwellian bobbin chairs, Venetian and Dutch marquetry chests, an impressive pair of Naples ebony cabinets with painted glass panels and an 1805 Broadwood satinwood grand piano. The enjoyable mixture was not all there in Sir John Delaval's day but he was so fond of Doddington that when his ownership was disputed by his brothers on his inheritance of Seaton Delaval he cut down all the trees on the estate in rage and, as Antony Jarvis says, when a compromise was reached, 'lived out his life in a treeless and windswept parish.'

FULBECK HALL, *Grantham.*

Mrs M. Fry.
Tel: 0400 72205.

On A607 between Lincoln and Grantham, 1 m south of A17.
Open: Daily from first to last Sun in July and Bank Hol Mon 2-5.
£3, children £1, concessions.

The Fane family have owned Fulbeck since 1622 when Francis Fane, (created Earl of Westmorland two years later) acquired the property from his cousin, Sir George Manners. The family have survived at Fulbeck despite various calamities: in 1731 a fire destroyed the house all but the service wing; the Fane owner went bankrupt in 1887 but the property was bought by a Fane cousin; and the house was nearly ruined by the military after it was requisitioned for World War Two. The present owners, Mary (nee Fane) and Michael Fry are still restoring parts of the house damaged during the war.

Elegant wrought-iron gates lead, via an avenue of ancient limes, to the handsome Georgian house. 1730s rebuilding during was carried out by a local Stamford architect and his work predominates, with additions from later in the 18th century. The most prominent of these is the bowed north extension which was added in 1784. It offered welcome extra space to the then owner, the Hon Henry Fane, his wife and their fourteen children. The last addition was completed in 1902 by William Vere Reeve Fane.

In the interior the 1730s panelling has survived in the hall, staircase and landing. Pilasters, such a distinctive feature in stone on the exterior, re-appear flanking the front door inside the hall doorway, opposite on either side of the staircase arch and, in reduced scale, in the oak panelling of the stairs. The drawing room and morning room are both of the 1840s, remodelled for General Sir Henry Fane. The dining room dates from his parents' additions of 1784 and the library was created by William Dashwood Fane in 1894.

Fulbeck has connections with the 1st Duke of Wellington. Harriet, twelth child of the Hon Henry Fane, became the Duke's closest woman friend and intimate confidante from 1820 to her death in 1834. The family stress that she was not his mistress; the relationship was based more on their mutual passion for politics. Harriet's cousin, Lady Georgina Fane daughter of the 10th Earl of Westmorland, had rather different intentions as a letter preserved in the drawing room, from the 80-year-old duke to her mother explains. He asked the Dowager Countess to use her influence on Georgina to cease molesting him with 'daily vituperative letters'. She had mercilessly pursued the the great soldier-statesman for decades, following a brief romance. She threatened to publicise his love letters to her and sue him for breaking a promise to marry her.

GRIMSTHORPE CASTLE, *Bourne.*

Grimsthorpe and Drummond Castle Trust.
Tel: 0778 32205.

4 m north-west of Bourn on A151.
Open: Easter and Sun and Bank Hols end-May to mid-Sept 2-5.
£2.50, children £1.25/free, concessions.
Tea room.

Grand and remote, Grimsthorpe sits improbably and dramatically on the edge of a Lincolnshire plateau. The approach, long and straight is almost continental in its formal grandeur and much as Sir John Vanbrugh intended when he transformed the existing Tudor castle. The scale of the park laid out later by Capability Brown, including the enormous lake increases the impressive nature of the scene.

It was a Duke of Suffolk who began the castle in the 16th century and Dukes of Ancaster who commissioned Vanbrugh and Brown in the 18th. The ancient Willoughby de Eresby title dates from 1313 and can be held by a female while the dukedom of Ancaster (created in 1715) became extinct in 1809 and the later Earldom of Ancaster (created in 1892) similary disappeared on the death of the present Lady Willoughby de Eresby's father in 1983, there being no male heir.

Lurking behind Vanbrugh's brooding facade, is a 16th-century quadrangle of great charm. Internally the house is romantic and almost exotic with ceilings painted by the Italian Francesco Sleter, grand continental furniture and tapestries. The hall is considered by some Vanbrugh's noblest interior. Despite its size the house has an air of considerable privacy which compliments the unspoilt remoteness of its position.

ALTHORP, *Northampton.*

The Earl and Countess Spencer.
Tel: 0604 770006.

6 m north-west of Northampton, off A428.
Open: selected days in April, May, July and Sept, daily in Aug, 1-5.30 (last admission 4.45).
£4.50, children £2.50, concessions.
Tea room.

Althorp remains brimming with evidence of generations of Spencer connoisseurship. Wealth from wool was the basis for political and social supremacy as Earls of Sunderland. When the 5th earl inherited the Marlborough dukedom in 1733 his younger brother John inherited Althorp. His son was created Earl Spencer in 1765 and the house has passed in male descent to the present 9th earl who inherited on the death of his father in 1992.

The present house is principally the work of Henry Holland. After part of the roof collapsed in 1772, he was commissioned by the 2nd Earl Spencer to transform the existing building, part Tudor and part as altered during the 17th century. Holland's exterior, covered in grey mathematical tiles is impressive but austere; the warm stone of Roger Morris's 1730 stables is more appealing.

The Wootton Hall was commissioned by the 5th earl of Sunderland before he departed for Blenheim and hung with his favourite horses, the canvases all ordered to fit the walls. Despite its vast proportions the staircase hall or saloon is densely covered with portraits of unfailing quality. The collection reaches its zenith in the picture gallery which survives from the old house. At the far end is one of Van Dyck's greatest pictures, the double portrait of 'War and Peace' Lords Digby and Russell. To one side are the Hampton Court beauties by Lely, all in the Sunderland frames named after the 2nd earl who commissioned them. The ensemble is a rare experience.

The Marlborough room is hung principally with consummate portraits by Reynolds, as well as works by Gainsborough and Kaufman. Old Masters, many collected by the 1st Earl Spencer, hang in other rooms, which also bear witness to successive 18th-century craftsmen including Rysbrack, Vardy, Scheemakers and James 'Athenian' Stuart. After the sale of Spencer House during the 1920s, the richness of Althorp's contents was increased. The splendid state dining room is largely furnished from the London house; including most of the dining chairs from a set of 54 made by George Seddon. Among such a quantity of artistic riches most people would be daunted by the challenge of making their own contribution, but the present earl has restored the chapel to its status and modified some of the redecoration carried out for his father and stepmother.

BOUGHTON HOUSE, *Kettering.*

The Duke of Buccleuch and Queensberry.
Tel: 0536 515731.

3 m north of Kettering on A43.
Open: Aug daily 2-5.
£4, concessions.
Tea room.

Approaching Boughton for the first time a visitor might be forgiven for dreaming they were in France; no other house in England looks so strongly - and authentically - like a chateau. The effect is exactly as intended by Ralph, 1st Duke of Montagu, who returned in 1678 from spending a decade as ambassador at the court of Louis XIV, to introduce England to French architecture and decoration. The Mansard roof, arched colonnade and style of window are all in the French classical tradition. And yet the surprise of Boughton is that the first impression conceals the Tudor building extended from a monks' hall by Sir Edward Montagu, Lord Chief Justice to Henry VIII.

Ralph Montagu's additions were married to the existing building so that many of the interiors retained their simplicity, small-scale and low ceilings to a degree completely disguised by the grandeur of his north facade. Decorative changes were most noticeably applied to the great hall which lies at the centre of the village-like group. Its ancient hammer-beam roof is concealed above a richly-painted barrel ceiling. The French flavour of the painting of the staircase hall by Louis Cheron and the 'Parquet de Versailles' floors extends to the furniture (including many exquisite gifts from Louis XIV himself), but not to the exclusion of English craftsmanship. In 1674 Ralph bought the Mortlake tapestry factory and ran it until 1691 and there is rich evidence of this patronage at Boughton.

His collection of paintings was added to by his successors and today the array is the equal of the other Buccleuch houses. Ralph's son the 2nd duke, known as 'John the Planter' as during his lifetime he added 70 miles of avenues to Boughton's estate. John's daughter Mary married the Earl of Cardigan from neighbouring Deene Park who was created Duke of Montagu. When their son the Marquis of Monthermer died aged thirty-five Boughton was inherited by their daughter, Elizabeth who had married the Duke of Buccleuch.

The Buccleuch match meant - given they were mainly in Scotland or London - that Boughton was little used by the family for long periods, absence which preserved the atmosphere of the house's formative decades. Today Boughton is very much occupied by the family, its estates run with the admirably forward-thinking custodianship that they bring to all their extensive properties, and its works of art readily available to both scholars and the more casual visitor.

COTTESBROOKE HALL, *Northampton.*

Captain and Mrs John Macdonald-Buchanan.
Tel: 060 124 808.

10 m north of Northampton, off A50 at Creaton.
Open: mid-April to end-Sept, Thur, and Bank Hol Mon 2-5.30 (last admission 5).
£3.50, children £1.75.
Tea room.

A rose-brick house is a surprise in Northamptonshire, a county blessed with one of the best English building stones. Otherwise Cottesbrooke effortlessly joins the ranks of the county's most distinguised houses. Aligned on an axis with the spire of Brixworth church, three miles away, it stands surrounded by gardens and 18th-century parkland. One can well imagine why Jane Austen was possibly inspired to use it as a model for Mansfield Park.

Attributed to Francis Smith of Warwick and completed in 1713, the plan of a central block and flanking pavilions facing a courtyard exemplifies the architecture of that period. The outstanding internal addition was the mid-18th century Rococo papier-mache decoration by John Woolston of Northampton, carried out in the hall which retained its original marble cantilevered staircase.

Captain Macdonald-Buchanan's parents bought Cottesbrooke between the wars and made it a house of rare distinction. His mother was the only daughter of James Buchanan, Lord Woolavington who used the fortune derived from his family whisky firm to built up the finest private collection of British sporting paintings in the world - rivalled only by the Mellon collection. The upper and lower curving corridors that link the west wing with the central block are both galleries giving a representative idea of the collection's quality. Outstanding in the upper - China - corridor is the Ferneley of Lord Craven's hunters at grass. Below is the comprehensive collection of Munnings, many depicting Lord Woolavington's and his daughter's winning horses.

Ben Marshalls hang in the entrance hall with the Barraud brothers' painting of the Beaufort Hunt, while the dining room contains Marshall's masterpiece, Thomas Oldaker on Pickle, and Stubbs' Gimcrack on Newmarket Heath - among the most famous English racing pictures. In the drawing room an equestrian bronze of Empress Elizabeth of Austria recalls the period during the 19th-century when she rented Cottesbrooke for hunting with the Pytchley. Among extensive collections of English, Continental and Oriental porcelain are a rare Pinxton service and sets of Kangxsi pieces. English and continental furniture includes a large Chippendale desk, Louis XV fauteuils and a Flemish cabinet-on-stand. Although mainly gathered together during the last 100 years, the ensemble is an example of English connoisseurship in the best tradition.

DEENE PARK, *Corby.*

Mr Edmund and the Hon Mrs Brudenell.
Tel: 0780 450223/450278.

8 m north-west of Oundle, 6 m north-east of Corby, on A43.
Open: Sun June, July, Aug and Bank Hols 2-5.
£3.50, children £1, concessions.
Tea room.

The intimate, mainly Elizabethan courtyard through which the visitor enters Deene would seem to set a tone; further progress reveals that it is only one flavour of the intriguing whole which Brudenells have added to and embellished since 1514. A tour of the outside moves from Elizabethan to Jacobean and then, along the south garden front, Tudor is extended by matching Georgian gothic to give great length repeated in the gardens beyond, and canal and lake.

17th-century Brudenells were fiercely Royalist and Catholic. Their loyalty was rewarded in 1661 when Thomas Brudenell was made Earl of Cardigan. More settle times came in the 18th century, reflected in the set of three gracious rooms added along the south front sometime between 1750 and 1800, the bow room, drawing room and dining room.

The bow room's library reflects the scholarly leanings of generations of the family - the 1st earl was especially upset when his books were removed from Deene by Cromwell's troops when the house was sacked in 1643. Over the fireplace hangs Reynolds' sensitive portrait of Lady Mary Montagu, daughter and heiress of the 2nd Duke of Montagu. In the drawing room family portraits mix with members of the Stuart royal family on account of the marriage of Anne Brudenell to Charles II's illegitimate son the Duke of Richmond.

An unexpected change comes in the dining room, which introduces the most flamboyany member of the family, the 7th Earl of Cardigan who led the Charge of the Light Brigade. Over the fireplace is his dashing portrait by de Prades leading the charge. The artist's equestrian portrait of his second wife, Adeline de Horsey, hangs among Victorian Brudenells on the main staircase which is part of the 5th earl's additions. In the hall below is James Sant's group of the earl describing the Battle of Balaklava to Prince Albert and the royal children. The earl did not marry Adeline until 1858 and their subsequent behavious scandalised their relations and society; not least the Queen who had originally been in the group but insisted on being removed when she heard of their goings-on.

Mr and Mrs Brudenell have carried out spirited restoration since the war and a note of their gratitute to many helpers is to be found in the group of small portraits of members of the Deene staff by Richard Foster which hang in the Octagon.

ELTON HALL, *Peterborough.*

Mr and Mrs William Proby,
Tel: 0832 280468.

On A605, 5 m west of Peterborough.
Open: Bank Hols, Wed and Sun in July, Wed, Thur and Sun in Aug.
£3.80, children £1.90 (under-fives free), concessions.

The Proby family's occupation spans over three centuries, dating from Sir Peter Proby, whose grandson greatly extended the existing 15th-century tower and chapel, completing his work in 1666. During the late-18th and early-19th century further extensions gave the house a theatrically Gothic appearance, but during the mid-19th century some of these were removed so that now the Gothic style is largely limited to the south-facing garden front.

The outstanding attractions, however, are the library, furniture and paintings. Reynolds's friendship with the family is confirmed by his likenesses of them, as well as his self-portrait and another portrait of Kitty Fisher - banished to the housekeeper's room during the 19th century on account of her loose reputation.

During the 18th century the family acquired the title Earl of Carysfort. In 1828 the 1st earl's collection - excepting the Reynolds and other portraits - was sold. This dispersal partly inspired the 5th earl to collect himself which he did with assured and varied taste. In addition to Old Masters, which are arranged with early portraits in the main dining room upstairs, he collected the works of his Victorian contemporaries. In the lower octagon room are Henry Nelson O'Neil's Eastward Ho! and Sir Lawrence Alma-Tadema's A Dedication to Bacchus. The Minuet by Millais, showing the artist's daughter, hangs over the fireplace in the yellow drawing room. Upstairs in the ante dining room a Constable of Dedham Vale and a Gainsborough landscape whet the appetite for the array in the main dining room which includes works by Girolamo Genga, Hobbema, Poussin and Luini.

The 5th earl purchased the magnificent pair of cabinets in the yellow drawing room which were made to order for William Beckford and many other of the finest items of furniture at Elton. He was also able to make good much of the damage done to the library by fire in 1894, so that its 12,000 or so volumes (especialy strong in liturgical books and bibles, such as Henry VIII's Prayer Book), remain one of the finest private collections. Built up steadily from the time of Sir Thomas Proby, the library contains contributions from almost all generations of the family.

LAMPORT HALL, *Northampton.*

Lamport Hall Trust.
Tel: 060 128272.

8 m north of Northampton on A508.
Open: Easter to end-Sept, Sun and Bank Hols, Thur in July and Aug, 2.15-5.15.
£2.80, children £1.20, concessions.
Home-made teas.

Lamport's long, low facade looking out over parkland is easily enjoyed; it is also important for the central block is a rare example of the architecture of John Webb, Inigo Jones's son-in-law. Webb was commissioned by Sir Justinian Isham, whose father had been given a baronetcy and whose family could boast settlement in the area from at least the Conquest.

Webb was commissioned to add to the existing house in 1654, but the troubles of the time often intruded; on occasion his patron sent instructions from prison. Sir Justinian's royalist sentiments were confirmed by his purchase of Van Dyck's huge paintings of Charles I on horseback which he hung in the High Room built by Webb. This caused Parliamentary displeasure and his subsequent arrest was hardly surprising. The family's royal enthusiasm also accounted for the full length portrait of Anne of Denmark by Van Somer's and another similarly sized Van Dyck of Charles I with his horse, the original of which hangs in the Louvre. Sir Justinian's connoisseurship was continued by his son as evidenced by the two magnificent Venetian cabinets that he collected on the grand tour, and his portrait by Maratti, but he died on the eve of his wedding aged twenty-four.

The 5th baronet commissioned Francis Smith of Warwick to continue Lamport's changes, adding the wings that now flank Webb's central five-bay block. The library is the scholarly 5th baronet's and the 18th century witnessed Lamport's elevation to a house of rounded quality with distinguished family portraits adding to Old Masters and more unusual earlier work such as the scene of Stag Hunting in Richmond Park by Joan Carlile, and the accumulation of good funiture, porcelain and other works of art.

The nineteenth century saw regular rebuilding at Lamport and the entrance front was changed twice. It is sad that the 10th baronet's collection of gnomes was almost entirely destroyed; now only one original survives in the library and the quaint figures thad adorn the rockery are replicas. Visitors should cross the road to the adjacent church to see good taste restored in the superb monument to the 5th baronet by Scheemakers. They should also acknowledge Gyles, the 12th baronet, who bequeathed Lamport and its estate into an endowed trust to preserve it for public enjoyment.

SOUTHWICK HALL, *Oundle.*

Christopher Capron.
Tel: 0832 274064.

3 m north of Oundle.
Open: Wed in May to end-Aug and Bank Hol Sun and Mon, 2-5.
£2.50, children £1.50, concessions.
Tea room.

Surrounded by some of the most palatial houses in the country, Southwick is refreshingly modest, its gables typifying the lesser manor houses of this area. Modesty does not mean lack of distinction and interest, nor of long establishment; of the original Knyvett family Sir John Knyvett was Edward III's Lord Chancellor and the house passed from them to the Lynns after the financial constraints of raising a ransom in the Hundred Years War.

Much of the mediaeval house remains, notably the 14th-century turreted tower overlooking a small courtyard, a vaulted room with distinctive doorways with shouldered heads and a circular stair turret, but the Lynns made considerable extensions during Tudor times and again during the 18th century. The oak panelling in one bedroom survives from the former, while the hall, study and parlour - with a fine Gothic bay window, date from the latter. In 1841 the house was bought by the Caprons and they rebuilt the east wing into two storeys.In 1909 they made an new entrance through the original undercroft.

The three families are best commemorated in the hall, originally the Knyvett's great hall, remodelled by the Lynns during the 18th century and now hung with portraits of three generations of Caprons. There are enjoyable exhibitions of Victorian dress and Victorian and Edwardian children's clothes and nursery paraphenalia while the stables contain a more eclectic museum of rural life. One of the most distinguished occupants of Southwick was the 18th-century George Lynn, who observed the eclipses of Jupiter from a 13-foot telescope erected on the main tower and his moving monument in the church next to the garden, depicting his wife mourning beneath a classical urn, is attributed to Roubiliac.

HOLME PIERREPONT HALL, *Nottingham.*

Mr and Mrs Robin Brackenbury.
Tel: 0602 332371.

3 m east of Nottingham, off A52.
Open: June, July and Aug, Tues, Thur, Fri 2-6.
£2.75, £1.
Home-made teas.

Holme Pierrepont Hall is a surprising discovery beyond the outskirts of modern Nottingham. Despite the city's proximity the ancient house has an undiscovered feel encouraged by the knowledge that is was for centuries a subsidiary home for the Pierreponts of Thoresby Hall. The house evolved from a mediaeval one built around an internal courtyard which survives as a charming enclosed garden, surrounded on three sides with the churchyard wall along the fourth. The entrance front retains much of its original early-Tudor character and brickwork dates from 1510. Inside the survival of the mediaeval lower and upper lodgings intact is a rare distinction; the superb roof timbers in the upper one contain the only cusped wind braces in east England and run the whole length of the building. Later alterations saw a 17th-century north wing go up only to be pulled down in 1730; the florid Charles II oak staircase with carved panels was almost certainly moved from the demolished wing.

During the 17th and early-18th centuries the Pierreponts were earls and dukes of Kingston. These titles became extinct after the 2nd duke and his bigamous wife Duchess Elizabeth Chudleigh failed to produce a son, and in 1806 the nephew who had inherited was created Earl Manvers. Kingston and Manvers portraits are one of the house's chief attractions. The most impressive is the full length of Robert 3rd Earl of Kingston, attributed to Wissing, in an elaborate French carved frame. Manvers's hang on the staircase, including the French third countess who lived here with her husband while Thoresby was being rebuilt by Salvin, and who added the colonnade around the courtyard. A fine portrait of her ancestor, Count de Coigny hangs in the long gallery.

Holme Pierrepont suffered badly from requisition during both World Wars, but brave restoration was begun by Lady Sibell Argles, daughter of the 4th Earl Manvers. Mr and Mrs Brackenbury bought the house in 1969 because she is descended from the 3rd earl and they have continued the work. The wide-ranging furniture includes many peculiarities such as the pairs of unusual Yorkshire and Derbyshire chairs and the Victorian bed made of Ceylonese rosewood. Brackenbury additions such as the self-portrait of the talented artist Georgina Brackenbury, a fervent suffragette whose portrait of Mrs Pankhurst hangs in the National Portrait Gallery, blend in happily.

HEART of ENGLAND
Stanway House

BERKELEY CASTLE, *Bristol.*

Mr and Mrs R.J. Berkeley.
Tel: 0453 810332.

Mid-way between Bristol and Gloucester off A38.
Open: daily except Mon April (2-5) to end-Sept, 11-5 (Sun 2-5), Sun in Oct 2-4.30, Bank Hol Mon 11-5.
£3.80, children £1.90, concessions.
Tea room.

If ever there was a home that should be better known it is Berkeley. It offers the visitor all the excitement of a mediaeval castle together with works of art from one of the most cosmopolitan, discerning of families. Just a few miles off the M5 between Bristol and Gloucester it stands proudly in its gardens and landscape still looking out over the Severn estuary which it was originally built to protect.

Berkeley was originally built in the mid-12th century and a great deal of its mediaeval grandeur remains in a series of towers, castellated walls and courtyards. A great hall, chapel, twisting stairs and narrow corridors all add to the excitement.

The potent mediaeval qualities which make the murder of Edward II at Berkeley seem quite in keeping were enhanced during the second quarter of this century when 19th-century additions were done away with to return both the fabric and atmosphere of a mediaeval castle. At this time the pictures and other works of art were swelled with additions from other family houses. Sometimes the result was an embarrassment of riches, why else Old Masters in the kitchen other than shortage of space? Overall Berkeley affords a charming and intimate sequences of rooms for looking at paintings by Stubbs, van de Velde, Gainsborough and Reynolds, Batoni as well as many others. These are accompanied by similarly distinguished works of art including bronzes and sumptuous tapestries.

STANWAY HOUSE, *Broadway.*

Lord Neidpath.
Tel: 038 673 469.

Off B4632 and on B4077 between Toddington and Stow-on-the-Wold.
Open: June to Sept inclusive, Tues and Thur, 2-5.
£2.50, children £1, concessions.
Tea room.

Tucked beneath the steep wooded edge of the Cotswolds, where the road runs down towards Tewkesbury, Stanway and its village that clusters around has an undisturbed romanticism that few visitors forget. In addition to its long continuity, only one change of ownership in over 1200 years, and that by marriage not sale, its atmosphere is enhanced by the halcyon period at the end of the nineteenth century when, under its chatelaine Lady Elcho, Stanway was a favourite haunt of the 'Souls' group. Elcho is a subsidiary title of the Wemyss earldom, the family name being Charteris.

The Wemyss ownership of Stanway dates from the 18th century with marriage to the heiress of the Tracy family. They had been established at Stanway since its mediaeval ownership by Tewkesbury abbey and during the 17th century built the present Jacobean house and the superb gatehouse, decorated with the shells of their coat-of-arms, that adds so much to the collection of buildings. Another highlight is the meiaeval tithe barn that dates from the abbey ownership.

The Wemyss connexion brought many outstanding works of art to Stanway during the 18th century, notably the portrait of Lord Elcho by Raeburn, the two Charteris children by Romney, and two 'Chinese' Chippendale day beds with pagoda tops. During the late 19th and early 20th century the Souls connexion brought to the house wallpapers by William Morris, and paintings and drawings by Burne-Jones, Poynter and Sargent.

SUDELEY CASTLE, *Winchcombe.*

Lord and Lady Ashcombe.
Tel: 0242 602308.

7 m north-east of Cheltenham on B4632.
Open: April to end-Oct daily, 12-5.
£4.75, children £2.50, concessions.
Restaurant.

The riches of Sudeley's history, in particular its royal ownership from Edward IV through to Tudor times when it was granted to successive royal favourites, are very evident in its atmosphere. Jane Seymour's brother was created Lord Sudeley and lived here; he married another of Henry VIII's wives Katherine Parr but his ambitions led him to the scaffold. She died at Sudeley a year after their marriage and is buried in the chapel. Thereafter Queen Mary granted Sudeley to Thomas Brydges, 1st Lord Chandos, whose family remained until the 19th century. In 1837 it was purchased by two brothers, John and William Dent.

Much of the castle is 15th century, the work of Ralph Botelar, including St Mary's chapel where Katherine Parr is buried and Portmare Tower by the gatehouse, named after a French admiral whose was imprisoned by Botelar and whose ransom was part of the fortune he acquired during the wars against France. Extensive destruction was wrought by Parliamentary forces during the Civil War followed by nearly two centuries of neglect.

The Dents commissioned Sir Gilbert Scott to carry out restoration which was added to by other architects and by the 1850s much of the castle was again habitable, a fine restoration of its original mediaeval and Tudor period character. After its inheritance by John Coucher Dent his wife, Emma Brocklehurst, made the most telling contribution to the castle by collecting many of its most important contents. One notable source was the sale in 1842 of Horace Walpole's home Strawberry Hill, including the most important picture, Hans Eworth's The Tudor Succession, and Turner's delightful view of Pope's villa at Twickenham.

The Victorian Dents re-established Sudeley to a high degree. Their restoration was matched by new gardens and the works of art they carefully gathered together. Other outstanding paintings include Van Dyck's portrait of Charles I, The Four Evangelists by Rubens, distinguished Dutch Old Masters, and works by Lely, Poussin and Claude. Nedlework and tapestries are another highlight, in particular the 16th-century Sheldon Tapestry.

Lady Ashcombe was previously married to Mark Dent-Brocklehurst who died in 1972 aged only forty. Today, distinguished history, and the combination of the venerable castle walls, encircling gardens which have been considerably redeveloped, and the treasures inside, provide a range of enjoyment.

WHITTINGTON COURT, *Andoversford.*

Mrs Robert Charleston.
Tel: 0242 820218.

4 m east of Cheltenham on A40.
Open: 1st half of April and 2nd half of Aug daily 2-5.
£2.00, children £1, concessions.

Whittington's history is that of manor houses up and down the country; ancient origins followed by construction, continuous occupations and alteration durin the 16th and 17th centuries; subsidiary status to another house and irregular occupation during the 18th and 19th centuries; welcome return and restoration during the 20th. Now the gabled house that so typifies Cotswold manors contains accumulated evidence of its often-changing history.

It must have been a substantial house when built by John Cotton during the 16th century, for Elizabeth I lunched there on her progress through Gloucestershire in 1592. His son Ralph extended the house around 1600 and internal alterations were made later in the century, notably the replacement of the existing staircase with the present Jacobean one. With the demise of the Cottons during the 1660s Whittington became a secondary house. It passed through successive hands - and via an acrimonious court case in 1823 - to the Lawrence family, a member of whom finally took up residence as owner in 1910 after decades of tenancy.

LIttle visual evidence of the Cottons survives, but there is ample testimony to the quality of their house, not least the early-classical stone chimneypiece in the library. Most of the portraits are Lawrences and the furniture came from their main homes at Sevenhampton and Sandywell - especially the latter, which provided Whittington's finest posession, the set of three bookcases in the library which were almost certainly made by Gillows of Lancaster.

BURTON COURT, *Leominster.*

Lieut-Commander and Mrs R.M. Simpson.
Tel: 0544 388231.

5 m west of Leominster off A44.
Open: end-May to end-Sept Tues, Wed, Sat, Sun, Bank Hols 2.30-6.
£2.00, children £1.50, concessions.
Home-made teas.

Burton Court's hilltop position is adjacent to an ancient British camp and in 1402 the dashing Henry Prince of Wales camped here before moving on to deal with Owen Glendower. Such historical mists are today concealed by the house's Victorian and Edwardian appearance; carried out in two periods for the Clowes family who bought Burton in 1865 from the Brewster family who had occupied since the 17th-century. The Hereford architect Frederick Kempson carried out the earlier work which replaced the old half-timbered house. Boosted by the fortune of a shipping heiress from Liverpool, in 1912 Colonel Peter Clowes commissioned the then young and rising Clough Williams-Ellis to remodel the entrance front to its present appearance.

Williams-Ellis was responsible for the billiards room that every fashionable Edwardian house required. Kempson's period is retained in the dining room with its ornate set of High-Victorian furniture. The style of the cantilevered stone staircase with an open lantern would suggest that it was inserted into the old house, but all this disguises the main feature and surprise of Burton Court, the survival of a substantial 14th-century hall which retains its original five-bay sweet chestnut roof. The elaborately carved oak overmantel is later, dated 1654, but exactly suits the hall's scale. Here - and in other rooms of the house - is the extensive costume collection which is Burton's main attraction. The oldest item is a pair of Charles II gauntlets; possibly even rarer is the 19th-century uniform of an officer of the Chinese Imperial Guard. Mrs Simpson, whose husband bought Burton Court in 1960 is engagingly knowledgeable and enthusiastic about the collection.

EASTNOR CASTLE, *Ledbury.*

Mr and Mrs James Harvey-Bathurst.
Tel: 0531 632302/633160.

2 m east of Ledbury on A438, exit 2 M50.
Open: Sun and Bank Hol Mon Easter to end-Sept, Sun to Fri in Aug 12-5.
£3.50, children £1.75, concessions.
Home-made teas.

Few buildings in England are as uncompromisingly massive as Eastnor Castle, which the visitor discovers brooding in the gentle foothills of the Malverns. A member of the family, Lady Henry Somerset, wrote blithely in 1889 that; 'It is castellated in the style of a Norman baronial castle at the time of Edward I combining the comfort and convenience of a modern home with the stately grandeur of a feudal fortress.' Visitors entering the enormous great hall which towers through four floors to a height of 60 feet would question its qualification as a typically convenient modern home.

Lady Henry was the granddaughter of Eastnor's builder, the aggressive 1st Earl Somers, who commissioned Robert Smirke to replace his existing family home with something more substantial. Inside the baronial character continues - most obviously in the great hall - in the staircase hall and dining room which retains Smirke's original furniture. The fan-vaulted plaster ceiling of the drawing room is theatrically Gothic but the decoration was changed for the 2nd earl by Pugin and at the same time the set of Brussels tapestries (a wedding present to his wife) were introduced.

The 3rd earl built up an outstanding collection of armour - notably half of the famous Meyrick collection - confessing to a weakness for what he called 'armouritis'. He also commissioned George Fox to redecorate the great hall in Venetian Romanesque style and his Italian enthusiasms account for the library which contains tapestries collected in Mantua and originally woven for Catherine de Medici and two Verona marble chimneypieces.

Impressive Italian furniture and paintings - among which Bassano's Last Supper is a highlight - add to good family portraits mostly hung in the dining room. The 3rd earl fell in love with his wife when he saw her full-length portrait by G.F. Watts which he purchased; her friendship with Watts accounts for the quantity of pictures by the artist. Recently many items of the 3rd earl's collection of Italian furniture and works of art have been retrieved from store and their display in various rooms has coincided with enlivening redecoration.

The 3rd earl built up one of the best arboretums in the country. The rare conifers are fascinating to the enthusiast and their towering forms compliment the architecture in a manner flower gardens would struggle to achieve.

HELLEN'S, *Much Marcle.*

The Pennington-Mellor-Munthe Trust.
Tel: 0531 84440

In Much Marcle on A449.
Open: Good Fri to Oct, Wed, Sat, Sun and Bank Hols 2-6.
£2.50, children £1.

Hellen's, part mediaeval, part Tudor and part Stuart, internally re-arranged at different times with somewhat haphazard results, has an atmosphere of long slumber that one feels disguises much of interest, which indeed it does. The house's story is dotted with names familiar to schoolboys; wicked Roger Mortimer, who arranged the murder of Edward II in Berkeley Castle and whose sister Yseult lived at Hellens, the more popular Black Prince, friend of James Audley of Hellens who supposed built the chimneypiece in the hall or court room and decorated it with the prince's feathers in honour of a visit; and Mary Tudor who is reputed to have stayed and slept in the room whose overmantel bears her initials and the Tudor portcullis. The house's descent was made tortuous by constant inheritance by females and actually takes its name from the son of a steward, Sir John Helyon who went on pilgrimage to the Holy Land and was so revered by the local people that they named the house Hellyon's Home.

The complicated descent eventually simplifies with the inheritance of Hellens by Hilda Pennington-Mellor who married the Swedish doctor and philanthropist, Axel Munthe. They were the parents of Major Malcolm Munthe, who established the trust that now owns the house. For visitors, in addition to the charmingly undisturbed atmosphere the major interest is the distinguished collection of pictures, in particular fine portraits of many generations of inhabitants of Hellens, their relations and other connected personages, and demonstrating that patronage was a strong suit at many times.

The collection includes works attributed to Mytens, Cornelius Johnson, Van Dyck, Lely and Raeburn and there are many surprises: one of three editions of Reynolds' delightful work The Laughing Girl; the 18th-century courtesan Kitty Markham by Hogarth; and a splendid full length of another of Hellen's blackguards, Philip, Duke of Wharton (whose aunt lived at Helen's), a Jacobite plotter who dabbled in black magic with the Hell Fire Club and died an outlaw aged thirty-two. His presence at Hellen's well illustrates the surprises that the ramshackle house disguises.

MOCCAS COURT, *Hay-on-Wye.*

R.T.G. Chester-Master.
Tel: 0981 500381.

1 m off B4352 on River Wye, between Hereford and Hay-on-Wye.
Open: April to Sept Sun, 2-6.
£1.80.

In 1771 Sir George Amyand Bt., a successful banker, married Catherine Cornewell the heiress of Moccas. As well as assuming her name he wished to impress his bride by rebuilding the home where her family had lived for a hundred years. No doubt they were planning the change when painted together in front of the scar on the far side of the Wye valley looking back to the old house, a delighful watercolour preserved at Moccas. The result was the present house, austerely elegant outside, full of surprises within, set in parkland laid out by 'Capability' Brown and later altered by Humphry Repton. The architect was Anthony Keck, but the most important contribution was made by Robert Adam who supplied the plans from which Keck worked and himself designed and decorated the series of outstanding rooms.

The music room celebrates the Cornewell's musical interests (his father was a friend and trustee of Handel) and Adam's decoration carries a theme of instruments in the frieze and marble chimney-piece. In the library the frieze, doorcases and mahogany doors, and rich scagliola chimney-piece are of similar quality, but the decorative climax comes in Adam's glorious circular drawing room with an elaborate plaster ceiling and curved doors and chimney-piece. Adam's 'Pompeian' decoration of the walls was carried out, but not in paint as he suggested, instead with an intricate pattern of paper panels from Paris. One moves from decorative to architectural quality in the oval inner hall rising through three storeys, where a curving cantilevered stone staircase ascends to the first floor landing.

The notable contents of Moccas - including the 3,000 books from the library - were sold in 1946 and the house has been refurnished by the Chester-Master family who inherited on the death of Sir Wlliam Cornewell in 1962. Their contributions are entirely fitting with the house; fine Japanese and Chinese porcelain, English and French furniture and paintings including an accomplished 18th-century portrait of Mrs Richard Master and Mmme Saladin by their sister Ariana Egerton, and van Meulen's painting of Louis XIV travelling with his entourage.

SUFTON COURT, *Mordiford.*

Major and Mrs J.N. Hereford.
Tel: 0432 870268.

In Mordiford on B4224.
Open: last two weeks of May and last two weeks of Aug.
£1.50, children 50p.

John Martin Robinson, the authority on the Wyatt family of architects, wrote of Sufton, 'I have no doubt at all that the house is by James Wyatt.' Many details suggest a fastidiously skilful hand such as Wyatt, working here in his early years of neo-Greek enthusiasm before the castles and Gothic houses that later clients demanded. At Sufton he was working for a squire not an extravangant grandee; he made the best of a limited budget and gave his client a gentleman's residence with select features of quality.

The exterior is typically late-Georgian, a neat formal box built of traditional Hereford brick faced in stone - an economic but distinctive combination in an area where the brick predominates. It rises through four storeys, but Wyatt appreciated that to make all four show would look cumbersome so he disguised the top floor within the roof and lit it from a central well.

Inside features of Wyatt's decoration are typical of his high standards, but again with a clear order of priority. The most important room was the music room, now the drawing room and its decoration is more extensive and elegant than in the others. The mahogany doors with inlaid panels are set in doorcases with fine plasterwork which continues in the freize and chimneypiece; all bearing delightful arranagements of musical instruments set in floral cartouches. In the dining room across the central hall the level of decoration is sightly reduced; the doors have no inlaid panels or plasterwork on their cases; here the freize contains a pattern of goblets with grapes flowing out of them. The staircase at the end of the hall continues the theme of unostentatious quality.

No doubt it greatly appealed to Humphry Repton who was called in in 1795 to advise on the grounds. His contribution is the second of Sufton's strings of distinction. His Red Book with suggested designs is preserved in the house and has the mix of salesmanship and light artistry which made the technique such a success. He made the most of the house's enviable position on an eminence overlooking the Wye valley and his planting survives today.

The Hereford family have lived in Mordiford since 1140 and have occupied Sufton since it was built. Sadly much was sold during the 1950s to pay death duties, and it is an enjoyable feature of the house that its most charming pictures - a series of watercolours - were painted by a member of the family, Edward Hereford who died in 1921, a naval officer and a talented, prolific artist.

SHIPTON HALL, *Much Wenlock.*

J.N.R.N. Bishop Esq.
Tel: 074 636 225.

6 m south of Ludlow and 10 m north-west of Craven Arms off A49.
Open: Easter to end Sept Thur, Bank Hol Sun and Mon 2.30-5.30.
£2.50, children £1.50.

Set in the Corve Dale, positioned enticingly above a walled garden with stone steps ascending, with Saxon church on one side, Georgian stables on the other and its mediaeval dovecot perched above and encircled by lawn and flower garden, Elizabethan Shipton Hall idealises an English manor house in its community a feeling perpetuated by the present owners. The dovecot was probably built by monks from Wenlock Abbey who owned Shipton then. The first - timber-framed - house was destroyed by fire and replaced in 1587 by Richard Lutwyche. His family owned Shipton until 1759 when Elizabeth Lutwyche married Thomas Mytton and took the house as her dowry.

The stable block hints at what the gabled Elizabethan facade conceals, a series of distinguished 18th-century interiors executed by Thomas Pritchard, best known for building the Iron Bridge that symbolised the start of the Industrial Revolution. Pritchard extended the garden front but the most impressive addition was interior plasterwork. The Italian craftsman Francesco Vassalli executed the ceiling in the hall; Pritchard himself was responsible for the staircase hall with its tall Gothic window and plaster ceiling, and the upstairs library's outstanding plaster overmantel.

Part of Shipton's charm derives from the fact that these additions blended with rather than replaced the old Tudor features. Thus from Georgian plasterwork and pedimented doors one goes to oak panelling and diamond panes in the windows. One window records the sorry imprisonment of 18-year-old Harriet Mytton to prevent her romancing with a local squire. She scratched in the glass; 'By dint of time this argument Ann learned, who'd be happy must be unconcerned, must all her secrets in her bosom wear, and seek for peace and comfort only these; hope travels thro' nor quits now.' Her fortitude was rewarded; in 1795 she married the squire, Thomas More of Larden.

A hundred years since they bought Shipton Hall the Bishop family successfully perpetuate its appealing informality and the sense of evolution from generation to generation.

UPTON CRESSETT HALL, *Bridgnorth.*

William Cash Esq.
Tel: 074 631 307.

4 m west of Bridgnorth off A458.
Open: May to Sept, Thur 2.30-5.
£2, children £1.

Few houses can rival Upton Cressett for blissful seclusion, the approaching lane winds for miles between high banks and hedges before climbing the wooded hill that once hid a Saxon village and now conceals only the manor and its small adjacent Norman church. Throughout most of its long history - from the Conquest until the early 20th century - Upton Cressett belonged to just two families and their intermarriage in the 14th century made the ownership continuous. The de Uptons, who held a series of evocative sounding mediaeval positions including Verderers of the Royal Forest of Morfe, were succeeded by the Cressetts who were responsible for the houses's present appearance. One of their number is reputed to have entertained the boy King Edward V on his last tragic journey from Ludlow to his death in the Tower. The family let the house from the 18th century and in 1919 it was sold. When Mr Cash bought it in 1970 it was derelict and he has carried out spirited and sensitive restoration.

The house is most intriguing for the relationship of mediaeval manor and the Elizabethan gate house which faces it across a courtyard garden. Drastic reduction in the manor's size during the 18th-century - possibly by half - has made the gate house assume far greater prominence in the relationship than would originally have been the case. The manor was probably encased in red brick when the gate house was built, but retaining inside the 14th-century great hall and 15th-century cross wing. The great hall is divided, the lower half now a dining room with oak panelling, but impressive timbers disappearing through the ceiling suggest continuity which is confirmed when one climbs the oak newel staircase to the bedroom above where the old timber roof survives.

Although the manor's reduction has increased the impact of the gate house, it was always a building of consequence. Facing the house the central block with the entrance arch is flanked by delightful octagonal turrrets, behind are steep gables and tall chimneystacks, the whole constructed of diapered brickwork. Inside the two rooms on the first floor have plaster ceilings and an overmantel whose quality confirm the gate house's status. Above are two further rooms. With bathrooms skilfully fitted in the turrets the gatehouse can be rented for holidays; a more romantic prospect would be hard to imagine.

WESTON PARK, *Shifnal.*

Weston Park Foundation.
Tel: 095276 207.

On A5 at Weston-under-Lizard, junc 12 M6.
Open: Aug daily 1-5.
£4, children £2, concessions.

Weston Park was designed in 1671 by its owner, Lady Wilbraham, a formidable character and the Mytton heiress through whom Weston passed. The house was in the vanguard of Palladio-inspired classicism in England as Lady Wilbraham's copy of his architectural work in the archives confirms. The symmetrical broad facades, the unusual semi-circular pediments on the park front and the warm brick with stone quoins and window dressing are immensely satisfying.

The park is one of a series by 'Capability' Brown's in the West Midlands including Chillington, Coombe Abbey and Tong Castle which together represent some of his most distinguished work. Brown was commissioned by Sir Henry Bridgeman who built the farms and was a renowned improver. James Paine designed the Roman bridge at one end of the lake and the Temple of Diana, a garden building of rare distinction.

Lady Wilbraham's house was altered internally during the 18th century, again in the late-19th century and finally during the 1960s when the present Earl of Bradford's mother carried out redecoration - demonstrated in the ravishing dining room - and reversed a number of the Victorian alterations. The tapestry room is hung with one of the six sets of Boucher-Neilson tapestries woven at the Gobelins factory for English customers.

Weston's descent has often been plagued by a lack of male heirs. Lady Wilbraham and her husband had no sons, their daughter married Richard Newport, 2nd Earl of Bradford; that title died out with the next generation (despite there being six sons!) and Weston passed on to the Bridgemans; Sir Henry Bridgeman married Lady Ann Newport who inherited Weston in 1762. He was made Lord Bridgeman and his son Earl of Bradford in a new creation.

The changes and different characters make for a house full of interest; paintings, furniture and porcelain in particular are outstanding. Van Dycks, Lelys and Reynolds set the standard among the family portraits, but the rarest likeness is the Holbein of Sir George Carew; Jacopo Bassano's 'The Way to Golgotha' excels among distinguished Old Masters. As well as the Gobelins there are Aubusson and Soho tapestries, 18th-century French furniture, and Bow, Derby and Chelsea porcelain. Most intriguing is the extensive correspondence between Disraeli and his confidante, Selina, Countess of Bradford.

CHILLINGTON HALL, *Wolverhampton.*

Mr and Mrs Peter Giffard.
Tel: 0902 850236.

4 m south-west of A5 at Gailey; via A449 through Coven following signs to Codsall.
Open: Easter Sun and Sun before May Bank Hols, May to mid-Sept, Thur, Sun in Aug, 2.30-5.30.
£2, children £1.

The arrival at Chillington is a surprise. Sprawling Wolverhampton leads to winding country lanes to the north, at different points along which you glimpse an estate - park walls, plantations, and gates. At the Brewood lodge the visitor suddenly comes upon the vista down a great avenue looking like a 17th-century bird's eye view by Kip. In the far distance the red brick house, standing four-square on an eminence, presents an arresting eye-catcher.

Long establishment adds to the sense of the estate's dominance of this rural enclave; the Giffards have lived at Chillington since 1178 and inasmuch can claim to be one of the oldest resident family in Britain. The house and estate represent the ebbs and flows of the family's fortunes. The mediaeval structure still lies beneath the present building redesigned in the 18th century by Smith of Warwick then John Soane. Inside are wonderful early 18th-century Baroque rooms with plaster work thought to be by Altieri, or maybe Vassalli, alongside the more monumental Soane interiors. His magnificent central saloon was made on th site of the Tudor hall. The outstanding works of art date from the Soane period, notably a bust by Hewetson and - unusually - portraits of two generations of Giffards by Batoni. Other treats are the early-19th century paintings and the charming depictions of the Pool, with the Giffard yacht.

The Pool is the major feature of the 18th-century landscape which lies beyond the park surrounding the house; the two together are one of 'Capability' Brown's most skilful works. The park provides the imposing house with a setting of suitable scale, while the landscape beyond contains an ideal mix of trees and architecture around the enormous lake or pool which he created with a dam. Outstanding among the various buildings is Soane's classical temple, most delightful is James Paine's arched bridge at one end of the pool - matched by false bridge by Brown over his dam at the far end. Peter Giffard has carried out superb maintenance of this landscape, in spite of the horror of a motorway carving through and separating park and pool from the lodge gates.

It was to nearby Boscobel, then a Giffard property, that Charles II escaped after the Battle of Worcester and hid in his oak tree. Chillington's hidden qualities - its antiquity and beauty - are somewhat more accessible today.

WHITMORE HALL, *Newcastle-under-Lyme.*

Rafe Cavenagh-Mainwaring Esq.
Tel: 0782 680478.

4 m from Newcastle on A53.
Open: May to end-Aug, Tues and Wed 2-5.30.
£2.

Whitmore is an unexpected rural haven within a few miles of the connurbation of Newcastle-under-Lyme and the Potteries and the property has survived undisturbed through eight centuries, changing hands only by descent or marriage, never sale. The setting is enviable, the warm brick Carolean entrance front looks down an avenue of limes to the parish church, to one side the 18th-century park (so Brown-like that, given his quantity of commissions in the area, it is hard to believe he did not have a hand in it although there is no evidence), stretching along a gentle valley and up the slope beyond, and on the far side of the house gardens stretching down to an expansive lake.

Edward Mainwaring (the fourth of eight successive Edwards) added the Carolean front to join the wings of the existing Tudor house and closed in the small courtyard to form an entrance hall. The striking stonework around the door is contemporary but the porch was added by Admiral Rowland Mainwaring who lived at Whitmore from 1837 until his death in 1862. His arrival is recorded in his diary; he and his family were met at the station by 'about 120 tenantry and friends on horseback, the children of the national schools and the band playing "See the Conquering Hero Comes"' and his presence is very evident. He was painted in uniform by John Phillip and collected the fine marine pictures by Luny, including a superb view of The Battle of the Nile where he served as a midshipman.

After his death the furniture and other contents of Whitmore were sold - against his wishes - but fortunately not the fine collection of portraits. These include works attributed to Mark Gheeraerts and Cornelius Johnson and a fine double portrait by Michael Dahl of Edward Mainwaring VII and his wife. Throughout the 17th century the Mainwarings were staunch parliamentarians in a royalist area and he continued the tradition by leading his tenantry against the advancing Jacobite army during the 1745. He made important alterations the house, including the elegant screen of Corinthian columns in the hall and curving staircase behind, as well as creating the park.

Whitmore's main distinction is, however, neither house nor park, but one of the most important stables in the country. The modest sandstone building dates from the turn of the 17th century and inside are nine bays with turned columns, carved arches and hay racks. The family also built a later and more elaborate set at their other home, Peover Hall in Cheshire, which also survive.

ARBURY HALL, *Nuneaton*

The Viscount Daventry.
Tel: 0203 382804.

2 m south-west of Nuneaton off B4102.
Open: Sun from Easter to end-Sept and Bank Hols, 2-5.30.
£3, children £1.60
Tea Room.

Sir Roger Newdigate was among the foremost scholar-connoisseurs of the 18th century; he left twin legacies of the prize named after him at for verse at Oxford University and his home Arbury Hall, England's finest 18th century Gothic house. Newdigate was a pioneer of the Gothic revival, work at Arbury (contemporary with Horace Walpole's Strawberry Hill) began in 1750 and went on for half a century until the year before Sir Roger died in 1806.

The long gallery survives as evidence of the Elizabethan house that Sir Roger transformed. Externally Arbury's Gothic character is announced on all sides but especially on the south looking out over park and lake. The interiors were executed room by room with Sir Roger employing a succession of architects, the gifted amateur Sanderson Miller, then Henry Keene and finally Henry Couchman of Warwick. Although copied from noble mediaeval originals in stone (in particular Henry VII's chapel at Westminster Abbey), Arbury - like most 18th-century Gothic schemes - was decorative not structural and executed in plaster. The three elaborate rooms are the dining room, drawing room and saloon with different but equally striking detail. The dining room was made out of the old great hall and its height allowed for fan vaulting that recalls church interiors; the drawing room has a vaulted ceiling with groining; while the saloon ceiling reaches a decorative climax.

Sir Roger's changes extended throughout most of the house and the sense of continuity is emphasised by the vaulted corridor or cloisters which extends around two sides of the Elizabethan courtyard. He was painted by Arthur Devis in his Gothicised library, the gallery was given a delicate ribbed ceiling and lesser rooms were given fan vaulting and Gothic chimney-pieces. The chapel was untouched, preserving its fine plaster ceiling executed for Sir Roger's grandfather, Sir Richard, who also commissioned from Sir Christopher Wren the design of the classical doorway to his new stable block.

Sir Roger's portrait shows him as the gentle scholar described in Scenes of Clerical Life by George Eliot who was brought up on the Arbury estate. There are many other Newdigates and other fine paintings include Elizabeth I by John Bettes and Old Masters, happy among the exuberant plasterwork. The most important piece of furniture is Archbishop Laud's cabinet.

RAGLEY HALL, *Alcester.*

The Earl and Countess of Yarmouth.
Tel: 0789 762090.

2 m south-west of Alcester on A435.
Open: Easter to end-Sept daily except Mon and Fri (open Bank Hols), 12-5.
£5, children £3.50, concessions.

Wyatt's monumental portico disguises Ragley's age, and not many country houses can have been so long in the making. In 1677 Sir Edward Seymour wrote, 'Here you will find me playing the fool in laying out money upon building...' He commissioned Robert Hooke (the little-known contemporary of Wren) to carry out his most important commission. Over half a century later internal decoration was still going on.

The delay was fortuitous, for it enabled Ragley to acquire what Robin Feddon calls, 'the finest late Baroque interior in England' - James Gibbs' great hall, a memorable assembly of plasterwork, pilasters and pink-painted walls. Gibbs executed the room in 1750 and the furniture was specially made in 1756. The Prince Regent was a friend of the 2nd marquess and, more particularly, of his wife. There are portraits of the Prince by Lawrence and Hoppner and the bed specially built for his first visit, surmounted with gilded Prince of Wales's ostrich feathers. His bust by Nollekens in the hall was a gift to Lady Hertford.

The urge to compete with the Prince Regent led their son, the 3rd marquess to assemble the art collection which his son further increased to form what is now the Wallace Collection in London. Both collectors neglected Ragley - living in London and Paris respectively. Only when the 5th marquess, a cousin, inherited, were house and estate's fortunes rosier.

Today the healthy condition of the house is thanks to the spirited efforts of the present Lord and Lady Hertford. Against all advice they moved into Ragley after their marriage in 1956, opened it to the public and carried out extensive redecoration over a period of many years. Successful continuity has been established and they have now been succeeded in the house by their son Lord Yarmouth and his family. Lord and Lady Hertford's most significant addition was to commission Graham Rust to decorate one of the two matching staircases with a sparkling ascending series of murals.

In all the main rooms the fruits of generations of connoisseurship are evident. Important furniture and mirrors by Chippendale and later Regency pieces are complimented by Louis XV commodes, a suite of Louis XVI chairs and Sevrès porcelain. One drawing room contains Seymour portraits by Reynolds, other highlights include Vernet's Salt Mines near Rome, The Raising of Lazarus by Cornelius van Haarlem and the Holy Family by Cornelius Schut.

WARWICK CASTLE, *Warwick.*

Madame Tussauds Group.
Tel: 0926 495421.

In Warwick.
Open: daily all year (except Christmas). April to late-Oct, 10-6; late-Oct to end-March 10-5.
£7.75, children £4.75, concessions.
Two restaurants, tea room.

Since 1978 when the Earl of Warwick sold Warwick Castle to the Tussauds group, it has become a tourist attraction on an impressive scale; it is the most visited member of the HHA. Its high exposure and a strongly theatrical note notwithstanding, it remains an indelibly impressive mediaeval castle, its position on the banks of the Avon greatly enhanced by 'Capability' Brown's park. Inside are magnificent 17th and 18th-century state rooms and quantities of evidence of its illustrous occupants, earls of Warwick from 1068, mediaeval lords and leading figures in the Hundred Years War and Wars of the Roses, and from 1604 the Greville family, who became barons Brooke and, in 1759, earls of Warwick.

The series of state rooms are all lavishly decorated and furnished. One drawing rooms has red lacquer panelling, another the same in carved cedarwood and throughout are sets of rich English, French and Italian furniture - gilded tables and gilded tapestry chairs. One room contains Queen Anne's imposing state bed and its attendant gilded furniture from Windsor Castle, given to the Earl of Warwick by George III, but probably the most monumental piece of furniture is in the great hall, the Kenilworth cabinet made by Cookes and Sons of Warwick for the 1851 Great Exhibition. Its carving depicts Elizabeth I's visit to Kenilworth and it was given to Lord Brooke (later the 4th earl) as a wedding present.

Portraits from the studios of Van Dyck and Lely abound, other paintings include a powerful likeness of Henry VIII after Holbein and a pair of lions by Frans Snyders which could have been a study for the lions in Rubens' The Chariot of Victory in the Louvre. As one might expect, there is a formidable collection of armour - up to 1,000 pieces, much of it rare and important, including the suit worn by the daredevil Scottish royalist general, James Graham, Marquess of Montrose, whose portrait by Dobson hangs in the red drawing room. A miscellany of such distinguished but unrelated figures greatly adds to Warwick's rich historical tapestry.

HAGLEY HALL, *Stourbridge.*

The Viscount and Viscountess Cobham.
Tel: 0562 882408.

Between Birmingham and Kidderminster, off A456.
Open: Jan to March daily except Sat, and major Bank Hols, 2-5.
Price available by telephone.

Hagley Hall and its Lyttelton occupants are often overlooked in discussions of 18th century taste to which both made important contributions. Sir Thomas Lyttelton married the sister of Lord Cobham of Stowe (whose title the family later inherited); their son George, 1st Lord Lyttelton was acquainted with most of the leading artistic figures of the day, many of whom made contributions to his new house at Hagley. The house itself, designed by Lyttelton's friend Sanderson Miller and built during the 1750s is the last of England's great 18th-century Palladian houses and much of the decoration, notably the plasterwork is reminiscent of the earlier part of the century in its light, rococo character.

Before beginning his new house Lyttelton set about transforming the park. When complete with a variety of buildings of which many survive including Miller's ruined castle and James 'Athenian' Stuart's Grecian temple, it was among the most influential picturesque landscapes in the country.

Miller's fastidious house of pink-tinted stone, with four corner towers reminiscent of Holkham or closer Croome Court makes an imposing picture with the park rising behind. As befitted a Palladian plan the arrangement of rooms is symmetrical around central hall and saloon with staircases on both sides. In 1925 a disastrous fire destroyed the rooms on one side, including the important library, with quantities of paintings and furniture being lost. Meticulously faithful restoration was carried out by the 9th Viscount Cobham and his wife and in recent years the present Lord and Lady Cobham have redecorated most of the main rooms.

Although restrained in colour the hall gives an introduction to the plasterwork that follows, notably in the medallions and the overmantel of Pan by Vassalli. Rysbrack's marble busts of Rubens and Van Dyck compliment the 18th-century one of a young Roman soldier which Lyttelton collected in Italy. Beyond, the saloon contains Vassalli's most exuberant plasterwork with winged putti, festoons and trophies hanging from ribbon bows. The tapestry drawing room was designed for its set of Arabesque Soho tapestries. Their decorative lightness is perfectly suited to the house's mood and the Rococo theme is continued in the outstanding pair of pier glasses with legendary Ho-ho birds, above matching console tables and in the picture frames.

Although the library was one of the main losses of the 1925 fire the present collection extends to some 3,500 volumes, most of them in the classical bookcases of the present library. This room is dominated by the portrait of Alexander Pope by Richardson over the fireplace. In the broken pediments of the bookcases stand four busts by Scheemakers of Shakespeare, Milton, Dryden and Milton given by Pope to Frederick Prince of Wales, who bequeathed them to his secretary, Lyttelton.

The gallery running the length of the east front has a plaster ceiling of now familiar quality and is given classical character by the bold fluted Corinthian columns. It contains a second fine pair of pier glasses, attributed to Thomas Johnson and was originally planned by Lord Lyttelton to display sculpture and paintings, in particular the collection of 17th-century portraits that were bequeathed to Sir Charles Lyttelton (his grandfather) by Lord Brouckner which are still in situ, having survived occasional direct hits during the 19th century when the precocious eight sons of the 4th Baron Lyttelton used the room for cricket practise.

Other good portraits, include a rare venture away from landscape work by Richard Wilson who painted the full length of Admiral Thomas Smith, which hangs in the saloon with - among others - Batoni's portrait of Sir Richard Lyttelton. For most visitors, however, it is the vibrant combination of decoration and furnishings which leaves the most lasting impression, along with Hagley's memorable setting - only miles from the centre of Birmingham.

North of England
MEOLS HALL

ADLINGTON HALL, *Macclesfield.*

Mr and Mrs A. Barnett Legh.
Tel: 0625 829206.

5 m north of Macclesfield on A523.
Open: Good Fri to end-Sept, Sun and Bank Hols 2-5.30.
£2.70, children £1.25.
Tea room.

Cheshire is famous for its black-and-white timbered houses but Adlington presents a startling contrast of the old house in this style fronted with a 18th-century red-brick wing with a central portico of bizarre size. The stables to one side are the same date and style and equally imposing. These Georgian additions were carried out by Charles Legh who considerably altered and extended the old courtyard house where his ancestors had lived since the 13th century, although his work was reduced to a more practical scale in 1928. His staircase, drawing room and dining room survive, the last two with warm classical panelling and there is an overmantel of carved fruit and foliage in the drawing room. Both rooms and the staircase hall contain good Legh portraits by Cornelius Johnson, Hudson, Van Reyschoot and Opie among others.

But none of Charles Legh's work compares with Adlington's oldest and - with later additions - most important room, the great hall; indeed it is one of the most astonishing interiors to be found in an English country house. It was built by Thomas Legh between 1480 and 1505, with a lofty hammerbeam roof and towering spere trusses hewn - so it is said - out of live oak trees. Between the oaks is the house's chief glory, the great Baroque organ built during the 17th century by "Father" Bernard Smith, the master of his trade. It rises with increasing bravado through the delicately balustraded gallery to clusters of pipes and up to the family arms with their unicorn crest between trumpeting angels. Handel played on it when visiting Adlington in 1741 and wrote a Hunting song with words by Charles Legh. It was silent for over a century until restored in 1959 by Noel Mander.

At the opposite end of the hall is a coved canopy that dates from the original building, with sixty later heraldic panels, continuing the heraldry of the angels on the roof hammers who carry shields. The windows are only on the south side and the other three walls bear enormous murals depicting scenes from the Trojan legends, whose date is uncertain but which were plastered for a long period until accidentally uncovered in 1859 during a game of shuttlecock.

Mr and Mrs Barnett Legh inherited Adlington from her father in 1991 and are restoring the important 18th-century picturesque garden with a Palladian tea house, shell house and an arched Chinese bridge.

ARLEY HALL, Northwich.

The Hon Michael and Mrs Flower.
Tel: 0565 777353.

5 m north of Northwich, 6 m west of Knutsford and 7 m south of Warrington, juncs 9 and 10 M6, juncs 19 and 20 M56.
Open: April to Oct Tues to Sun and Bank Hols 12-5.
Gardens £2.80, house £1.60 (children half-price).

Cheshire abounds in Victorian country houses built on mercantile or industrial fortunes. Arley, one of the county's most imposing, was contrastingly the product of a long established landed estate and built by the personification of a serious-minded patrician Victorian landowner, Rowland Egerton-Warburton. In 1813 he inherited the estate from his great-uncle Sir Peter Warburton and during a long tenure from 1831 until his death in 1891 he rebuilt the house, with the help of his wife Mary created the outstanding gardens which have been immaculately maintained and improved by future generations.

Arley was a collaboration between Rowland and the Cheshire architect George Latham. Rowland decided that the house would be 'Elizabethan' and to guarantee authenticity the pair toured 16th-century houses noting architectural details. These were incorporated: swirling chimney stacks, pointed gables and Tudor heraldic beasts on the roofline (some now removed to the garden), stone-mullioned windows, decorative stonework and diapered brickwork.

Inside some panelling from the old house was re-used but Latham's new work predominated. The main rooms were all given elaborate ceilings, some barrel vaulted and the library and gallery in particular had tall 'Elizabethan' chimney-pieces. Latham's tour de force was the oak staircase, its strapwork and panelled plasterwork powefully authentic. Rowland and Mary's portraits hang in the drawing room which contains the set of Louis XV-style furniture they purchased for the room. Rowland's support of the Oxford Movement led him to commission Salvin to build the imposing chapel adjacent to the house.

The major features of the Arley garden all survive as important testimony to its original quality; the double herbaceous border laid out in 1846 is probably the oldest in England and was painted by George Elgood in 1889 and the series of individual gardens are as planned by Rowland and his wife. Their son Piers was a highly accomplished watercolourist and many charming scenes of the house and garden at Arley - and many picturesque Cheshire seats - hang in the house. Michael Flower and his wife, and his mother Lady Ashbrook (who had inherited Arley) before him, have all been devoted custodians of the garden and made important new contributions of their own.

CAPESTHORNE HALL, *Macclesfield.*

Mr and Mrs William Bromley-Davenport.
Tel: 0625 861221.

7 m south of Wilmslow on A34.
Open: April Sun, May, Aug, Sept Wed and Sun, June, July Tues, Wed, Thur and Sun, Bank Hols 1.30-3.30.
£3.50, children £1.50, concessions.
Tea room.

The Bromley-Davenport family's unusual crest, of a felon's head encircled by gold noose, tells of powerful positions held by ancestors during mediaeval times, since when they steadily acquired and consolidated their landed estates. The consolidation involved an unusual number of marriages within the family, so that when William Davenport wanted to marry his cousin Ellen Davenport in 1529 the Archbishop of York had to give special dispensation becuse they were, 'third and fourth degree of kindred.' This sense of accumulation is reflected in their home, Capesthorne, which surprises many visitors by its size and is the combination of three different architectural efforts.

Originally between 1719-31 William Smith of Warwick, elder brother of the better-known Francis, built a rectangular brick house with flanking wings for John Ward whose daughter and heiress married Davies Davenport. In 1837 their great-grandson, Edward Davenport decided to 'update' the house and commissioned the fashionable architect Edward Blore to carry out rebuilding and extension. It is Blore's style and broad expanse that really survives today; in 1861 a fire broke out and gutted all the central block, but when Anthony Salvin was commissioned to rebuild he was asked to keep to the style of Blore's original, although he did lower the central block between the great turreted towers from three storeys to two with an attic.

Inside Salvin's hand is more obvious as he planned the set of main rooms and their decoration. The prosperity and wide connections of the family through both 18th and 19th centuries are well demonstrated in the paintings and other works of art. The sculpture gallery contains the pieces collected in Italy by Edward Davenport while the American room contains fine collection of 18th and 19th-century furniture from the United States, from the present owner's mother's home, Villanova Pa. Among quantities of family portraits, a Lowry is a surprise discovery. He painted Capesthorne in 1954.

DORFOLD HALL, *Nantwich.*

R.C. Roundell Esq.
Tel: 0270 625245.

1 m west of Nantwich on A534.
Open: April to Oct Tues and Bank Hol Mon 2-5.
£2.50, children £1.50.

Dorfold is a fine, original Jacobean house in a county where there is a greater preponderence of Victorian replicas. Nonetheless, it was given a strong Victorian flavour by the garden designer William Nesfield, much of which greets the visitor in the balustraded, cobbled forecourt with low gabled buildings - some Jacobean, some dated 1824, as well as gates and a dog sculpture that Nesfield originally purchased at the Paris Exhibition of 1855.

In front is the handsome block of the main house, built of diapered brick with stone-mullioned windows, gables and octangular chimneys. The house was built in 1616 for Ralph Wilbraham whose portrait by Cornelius Johnson hangs in the dining room, but because of the Wilbrahams' Parliamentarian loyalty, the house suffered badly at the hands of Royalists during the Civil War. In 1754 it was bought by James Tomkinson (whose family, like the Wilbrahams, were lawyers), who began the garden and park that survive today and commissioned Samual Wyatt to remodel the downstairs rooms. Carved marble chimneypieces were introduced, but Wyatt's most enjoyable addition was the plaster ceiling in the library, done to commemorate a Tomkinson wedding in 1772 with a pair of doves in the centre and panels of the four seasons in the corners.

Fortunately, perhaps, the finest room, the upstairs drawing room, is part of the Jacobean original. The barrel vault ceiling is decorated with complex strapwork incorporating heraldic emblems and the high fireplace flanked by Doric columns also carries armorials. The panelling and freize are also original and the decorative mood is complimented by portraits of Sir Francis Bacon and Lord Burleigh.

Mr Roundell's family inherited Dorfold from the Tollemaches (who had married a Tomkinson and were descended from the Wilbrahams and therefore giving the house unexpected continuity), and among Roundell family portraits the most striking are of the present owners by Howard Morgan, which hang adventurously among the Jacobean splendours of the drawing room. Although the more intricate, labour-intensive parts of Nesfield's garden design have been simplified, it remains full of interest, the impressive lime avenue approach contrasting with the woodland and water gardens.

PEOVER HALL, *Knutsford.*

Randle Brooks Esq.
Tel: 0565 722404/722135.

4 m south of Knutsford off A50.
Open: May to end-Sept, except Bank Hols.
£2.50, children £1.50.

The flat Cheshire countryside lends itself to improvement and William Emes gave Peover Hall an expansive setting during the 18th century shortly after its owners, the Mainwaring family had added a new wing to their Tudor house. The Mainwarings lived at Peover from shortly after the Conquest until 1919, when the property was sold. Mr Brooks parents bought Peover in 1941.

The imposing austerity of dark brick house's entrance front, is enhanced by the sense that it ends abruptly which it does; during the 1960s the Georgian wing was demolished and the house returned to its original proportions. The panelling and timberwork in some rooms - in particular the beamed roof of the great hall - is original; in others it has been introduced, saved from country houses less fortunate that Peover: the panelling and Corinthian columns in the dining room and the carved cornice in the morning room are good examples. The most spectacular introductions are the three splendid Victorian bookcases, two in the upstairs drawing room and one in the morning room, which came from Oteley near Ellesmere, another Mainwaring set.

Throughout the house Mr Brooks has introduced a fine collection of furniture including important four-poster beds, bobbin and other unusual chairs and an immense sideboard, elaborately carved with John signing the Magna Carta, made for the 1851 Exhibition. The compact integration of rooms on three floors - the top floor gallery has a fine ceiling of arched trusses - combines with the oak furniture and panelling to give an atmosphere of warmth, into which the good collection of paintings fits well. Over the upstairs drawing room fireplace hang a distinguished double portrait of the ill-fated Earl of Strafford and his secretary, Sir Philip Mainwaring, after Van Dyck.

It is remarkable that the two most important Jacobean stable blocks to survive in England were both built by the Mainwaring family. Those at Peover are later - 1654 - than the ones at Whitmore Hall described elsewhere, but they are considerably grander, their merit reflected in their Grade I status as opposed to the house's Grade II*. The thirteen bays have wooden Tuscan columns and carved strapwork and stretching the length of the interior is a decorated plaster ceiling. The adjoining coach house is mid-18th century. These, the park and the garden which Mr and Mrs Brooks have greatly improved make Peover's surroundings as enjoyable as its interiors.

RODE HALL, *Stoke-on-Trent.*

Sir Richard Baker Wilbraham Bt.
Tel: 0270 882 961.

6 m north of Stoke-on-Trent, off A50 and A34.
Open: Easter Mon to end-Sept, Wed and Bank Hols, 2-5
£3.50.

On the map Rode Hall looks uncomfortably close to Stoke-on-Trent and its seemingly endless satellites. In reality, encircled by park bounded by a long lake on one side, it is remarkably secluded, a house which has evolved with distinction through successive generations of owners and which now presents a rewarding variety. Entering the walled forecourt the visitor is greeted by an architectural composition that suggests development in stages. Central in the arrangement is the long, plainly elegant building that was the original house completed in 1708. Adjoining it on the left is the far larger block that is now the main house, built in 1752. On the right, at right-angles is a handsome stable block built either shortly after the original house or during the ensuing decades.

The original house was built by Randle Wilbraham; his son also Randle, who Horace Walpole described as 'a very able lawyer' built the more substantial later block. As finished, his house had its entrance on the north side - now facing the garden. In 1799 his grandson, another Randle, commissioned John Hope to make alterations which included moving the entrance to its present position between the two tall semi-circular bays. It is likely that the house was stuccoed around this time. The stucco - as well as an ugly Victorian porte cochere - was happily removed during restoration in 1927 by the present owner's grandfather, Sir Philip Baker Wilbraham, when Darcy Braddell designed the present Ionic portico.

Inside the house illustrates these changes, as well as the contributions of succeeding generations. The entrance hall is part of Hope's Regency work - as are most of the interiors - but beyond, the fine staircase hall with delicate plaster decoration to its walls and ceiling survives from the mid-18th century work. So too does the adjoining plan of three rooms along what was the entrance front, a central octagonal hall with the library - originally the dining room - on one side and the drawing room on the other. They were redecorated by Hope but still present an immensely agreeable ensemble. The library bookcases - like those in the hall - are some of the fine Gillows furniture bought for the house during the Regency work.

During this period important changes took place. The dining room became the library and Rode's most impressive room, the present dining room was added, the work of Lewis Wyatt who took over after Hope's death in 1808. Wyatt extended the room into an apse at one end and gave it a vaulted ceiling whose two ribs stretch between pairs of green scagliola columns. With a black marble chimney-piece, green walls and more Gillows furniture, the room is memorably handsome.

Hudson's portrait of the lawyer Randle Wilbraham hangs over the dining room chimney-piece and among many other Wilbrahams, the delightful Beechey of Letitia Rudd whose husband commissioned Hope and Wyatt, hangs in the drawing room. But many other pictures date from the marriage in 1872 of Katharine Wilbraham, heiress of Rode, and Sir George Baker 5th Bt. of Loventor in Devon. Sir George Baker 1st Bt. was a physician of great distinction; head of the Royal College of Physicians he was doctor to George III and, like his son, a Fellow of the Royal Society. He was a friend of Reynolds whose portrait of his wife, as well as his self-portrait, hangs in the drawing room.

Sir Richard Baker Wilbraham has made his own particular contribution to Rode with a notable collection of early-English porcelain. His wife has carried out extensive restoration and replanting in the garden - of comparable historical interest to the house. Humphry Repton supplied designs for the park, which account for the delightful approach and, on the far side, moving the main road to accomodate the long boundary lake. These plans which were only later implemented by John Webb. This work was added to during the 1850s by William Nesfield whose design for the rose garden - along with Repton's Red Book - survives in the house.

BROWSHOLME HALL, *Clitheroe.*

Mr and Mrs Robert Parker.
Tel: 0254 826719.

5 m north-west of Clitheroe, off B6243.
Open: Easter, Spring and Aug Bank Hol Sun and Mon, Sat in July, Sat and Sun in Aug, 2-5.
£2.80, children £1.20, concessions.

The Forest of Bowland is among the most unspoilt and undiscovered pieces of countryside in Britain; among the wooded hills and valleys of the Ribble tributaries one gets the impression that human habitation has scarcely increased over the centuries. Into this romantic landscape Browsholme, pronounced Brusom, with its long pink-grey stone facade, fits with disarming ease; successive generations of Parkers have been involved in the forest and held the position of Bowbearer of the Forest of Bowland.

The house is Elizabethan with later additions such as the arrangement of the three classical orders rising up from the front door, a piece of early-17th century bravado by a local craftsman. The 18th century saw the addition of modest wings before the most important changes were wrought by Thomas Lister Parker, an intriguing connoisseur, who wished to return his home to its Elizabethan origins and commissioned Jeffry Wyatt (later Sir Jeffry Wyatville).

Wyatt's two main designs, for which the drawings remain at Browsholme, were the drawing room with its Elizabethan-revival decoration and the new dining room, built to display Parker's considerable collection of pictures. Among a total of 14 Northcotes the most distinguished are the large groups 'Grouse-shooting in the Forest of Bowland' and 'Scene in the Forest of Bowland'.

With his commissions of paintings, purchases of Regency furniture and lavishing of gifts on a young actor William Betty, Thomas Lister Parker overreached himself and had to sell Browsholme to his cousin and heir. Important contents date from other generations. In the library two fine Devis portraits are of Robert Parker and his cousin Edward (T.L.'s grandfather); Batoni's likeness of Daniel Wilson was a gift from the sitter to his friend Edward. Robert Parker, who married his cousin Elizabeth, Edward's sister, was a supporter of Prince Charles Edward, and gave the house its collection of rare Jacobite relics.

In recent years the most welcome addition was the watercolour of Browsholme by Turner. More crucial has been the demanding post-war restoration carried out by Christopher Parker and his son Robert, the present owner. Visitors are greeted by intriguing variety in the hall which carries echoes of the antiquarian Thomas Lister Parker, but the various rooms and Browsholme's superb setting reveal a family connection deep-rooted through many centuries.

HOGHTON TOWER, *Preston.*

Sir Bernard de Hoghton, Bt.
Tel: 0254 852986.

5 m east of Preston on A675.
Open: Easter, then Sun to end Oct, Tues, Wed, Thur in July and Aug.
£3.50, concessions.

De Hoghtons of Hoghton Tower boast descent from an illustrous companion of William the Conqueror and the notorious Lady Godiva of Coventry; the hill-top house is best known as the place where James I knighted the [sir] loin of beef during his visit of 1617. Such ancient and varied history whets the appetite of the visitor as he climbs towards the castellated building that looks as though it dates from early in the family occuption (unbroken male succession since the early-12th century), but is infact Tudor. Built around two courtyards, its walls uniform dark stone, the house is forbidding rather than welcoming and there is none of the decorative or achitectural relief one might expect in a building of the period.

Nonetheless, it was the pure mediaevalism which appealed to Sir Henry de Hoghton 9th Bt who, during the 1860s, returned to the house after over 150 years absence by the family and began extensive restoration of long-term decline. He employed the architects Paley and Austin and the work was completed by his younger brother Sir James, the 11th Baronet,in 1901. The work was of high standard; Gillows supplied furnishings such as the new panelling for the ballroom, and the house was successfully rejuvenated. Today it consciously evokes the period of its construction and the hey-day of the generations who followed until the death of Sir Gilbert de Hoghton 2nd Bt. The great hall still contains the oak table on which King James is reputed to have dubbed the privileged joint and a magnificent oak bed emphasises the 17th-century atmosphere. Most of all, however, it is the survival of the secluded courtyard character, in contrast to the austere exterior, which is the most evocative part of Hoghton's survival.

LEIGHTON HALL, *Carnforth.*

Mr and Mrs R.G. Reynolds.
Tel: 0524 734474.

2 m west of A6, exit 35 M6.
Open: May to Sept daily except Sat and Mon (open Bank Hols),
2-5 Aug 11.30-5.
£3.20, children £2, concessions.
Tea room.

It is heartening that Leighton's setting has not changed since William Linton's views were painted in 1825. Gates lead into the park at its highest point and the pale stone house appears at the foot of the bowl-shaped park, its roofscape silhouetted against a background of Lakeland peaks. Linton's views were done to record the Gothicization of the house, since when the only alteration has been the addition of the large west (left) wing and tower during the 1870s.

The architect's drawing of the 1763 Georgian house that was so enlivened half a century later, survives at Leighton. In 1822 the house was bought by Richard Gillow, grandson of Robert founder of the family furniture-making business, who went to Lancaster because his father was a prisoner in the castle.

The Gillows furniture is Leighton's highlight, much of it mid-18th century, considerably earlier than the period of the firm's greatest renown. The rarest item is the 1750 alterpiece in the family chapel, but all the main rooms have pieces which illustrate the furniture's unfussy, elegant quality. The Gothic character of the interiors is limited to fine windows, doorcases and occasional features such as the hall screen beyond which the cantilevered stone staircase curves gracefully upwards. The dining room's warm panelling incorporates a series of 18th-century romantic landscapes and the furniture is almost exclusively Gillows. In the drawing room notable Gillows pieces are the early-18th century games table, the satinwood writing table, and rare lady's work-box, their interest heightened by comparison with French furniture.

Three generations of Gillows spanned from 1822 when Richard bought Leighton to 1966 when his grandson's widow died aged 96. Her daughter had previously married James Reynolds and their son and family are the present owners. Through the 19th century the family enriched their home with the paintings, French clocks and many other works of art that remain today. The most striking Reynolds contribution is the portrait of Lady Reynolds and her daughter by Luke Fildes. Among the other pictures, some Gillow pastels reveal that they were not only furniture makers; Monseigneur Gillow was the finest sporting shot of any priest of any denomination in England and his sister Josephine became the all-England ladies billiards champion.

MEOLS HALL, *Southport.*

Mr and Mrs R. Hesketh.
Tel: 0704 28171.

5 m from Southport.
Open: Details on request.
Price available on request.

Meols is among the most distinguished post-war country houses. Although a surviving 17-century entrance block and wing provide the nucleus the most substantial parts are post-1950, designed and executed by the present owner's father, Colonel Roger Hesketh and his brother. There had been a house on the site of Meols since the early-13th century, but during the 18th-century the resident Hesketh married a Fleetwood heiress and they moved to her family home, Rossall Hall, Meols assuming a subsidiary position. Roger Hesketh inherited in 1938 but shortly afterwards the Second World War and subsequently restrictive building regulations delayed work until around 1950.

At a time when more country houses were being destroyed than rebuilt Meols benefitted from the outstanding old materials that were available. The bricks for the east front - the most substantial exterior - came from Tulketh Hall near Preston after its demolition in 1960. The fine doorcase whose rusticated style is perfect for the house's early 18th-century appearance, is the work of Giacomo Leoni and once adorned Lathom House, Lancashire's premier Palladian house that he designed, whose prolonged demolition ended in 1960.

Other materials were re-used inside, including marble chimney-pieces and a new balustrade for the stairs, but the major influence - and impetus for the rebuilding project - was the collection of Fleetwood-Hesketh furniture, paintings and works of art that Roger Hesketh had inherited from a cousin in 1938. Thus, for instance, the height between cornice and dado in the new library was dictated by the size of the early-19th century painting of Sir Peter Fleetwood-Hesketh's arab stallion by James Ward.

NORTHUMBRIA
Seaton Delaval

RABY CASTLE, *Staindrop.*

The Lord Barnard.
Tel: 0833 60202.

1 m north of Staindrop on A688.
Open: Easter Sat to following Wed, May to end-June Wed and Sun, July to end-Sept daily except Sat, Bank Hols (Sat to following Wed incl), 1-5.
£3.30, children £1.50, concessions.

Massive Raby Castle is testament to how far south Anglo-Scottish border struggles stretched; the Nevills who built and steadily extended the castle were Wardens of the Scottish Marches and a family of considerable power - one married Joan daughter of John of Gaunt and Joan's Tower is named after her. They became earls of Westmorland but fell from grace in 1569 when the 6th earl led the Rising of the North. Raby was confiscated by the Crown and acquired in 1626 by Sir Henry Vane whose descendants have lived here since.

The gateway survives from the old curtain wall which provided protection from the bleak surroundings, a far cry from today's parkland with large lake and sloping walled gardens. Many of the nine towers date from different periods of the castle's original construction - mainly during the 14th century; the twin-towered Nevill gateway was the only entrance to the inner courtyard and the castle walls retain large sections of monumental mediaeval masonry, thirty feet high and in places twelve feet thick.

The great kitchen was built in 1360 and in use until 1954. Otherwise Raby was remodelled during the 18th and 19th centuries. The 1st Lord Barnard, furious at his son's marriage determined to disinherit the miscreant and sold the contents, took off the roof and cut down most of the trees in the park. His son took his case to Chancery and won. Restoration was carried out with advice from James Paine, at the same time the park was replanted.

During the 1780s more alterations were carried out for the 2nd Earl of Darlington by Carr of York, in particular the creation of the present entrance hall. Carr raised the ceiling and made a new entrance large enough to accomodate a carriage (solving the problem of carriages turning in the inner court). The room became a striking example of Gothic revival on a huge scale, with its high vaulted ceiling supported on deep red scagliola pillars.

The most extensive changes came during the 1840s when the 1st Duke of Cleveland employed William Burn whose 'baronial' reputation was well suited to working at Raby. He transformed the old mediaeval hall into the enormous Barons' Hall extended to a length of 130 feet and given a new timber roof. The Chinese drawing room was remodelled into a dining room and given a 'Jacobean' strapwork ceiling and marble fireplace incorporation Hercules.

Considering its size, the ranks of portraits in the Barons' Hall give an indication of the array of works of art to be found at Raby. Family portraits by the leading artists of successive 16th, 17th, 18th and 19th century generations; Old Masters in the ante-library, and, in the small drawing room, outstanding English sporting paintings. Given the quantity of portraits it is a source of amusement that the family ancestor, Barbara Duchess of Cleveland does not hang at Raby while her rival Nell Gwyn painted by Lely does. The huge Kandler Meissen birds are a splendid adornment, while the marble statue by the American Hiram Powers in the entrance hall, of a manacled, nude Greek slave girl caused a sensation at the 1851 exhibition.

ROKEBY PARK, *Barnard Castle.*

Sir Andrew Morritt.
Tel: 0833 627268.

Near Barnard Castle.
Open: end-May to early-Sept, Mon and Tues, 2-5 (last admission 4.30).
Price available on request.

Rokeby is an important and little-known Palladian villa, built between 1725 and 1730 by the distinguished amateur architect Sir Thomas Robinson. Robinson was rebuilding his own family home which had been acquired by an ancestor c.1610 and he corresponded about his work with the leading exponents of Palladianism, his father-in-law Lord Carlisle at Castle Howard, Lord Burlington, and the architect William Wakefield. The delightful, chaste exterior introduces the series of fine interiors with many distinctive Palladian features including impressive doorcases with columns and pediments and fine carved marble chimney-pieces.

Robinson had no heir and 1769 sold Rokeby to J.S. Morritt whose family have lived in the house ever since. Morritt's portrait by Benjamin West hangs in the saloon, the house's most impressive room and originally Robinson's hall, with, among other Morritt paintings and Reynolds' 'Hope Nursing Love'. Above are a series of historical portraits that were some of the works of art included in Robinson's sale. Morritt's sister Anne was an artist of great talent and worked in needlework the copies of famous pictures which still hang in the house. The most important contribution to the collections, however, was made by Morritt's connoisseur son John, who collected during a grand tour of Europe and in 1813 purchased Velasquez's 'Rokeby Venus.' (The picture was sold in 1906 and hangs in the National Gallery.)

ALNWICK CASTLE, *Alnwick.*

The Duke of Northumberland.
Tel: 0665 510777.

In Alnwick, on north side of town centre.
Open: Easter to mid-Oct daily, 11-5, (last admissions 4.30).
£3.60. children £2.20, concessions.
Home-made teas.

The first view of Alnwick immediately conjures up images of the border struggles in which for centuries the castle was constantly embroiled. Some battlements and gatehouse turrets still bear the eerie stone figures put up to fool the Scots into thinking there were more men than in reality. Percys succeeded de Vescy's as hereditary Wardens of the Scottish Marches in 1309 and have been at Alnwick ever since. From undisputed masters of the region they progressed through more peaceful centuries to become cultivated, collecting grandees as befitted their dukedom to which the ancient earldom was elevated in 1766.

The rugged fortress, with its undulating levels of battlemented stone walls, became superbly picturesque during the 18th century with the landscaping of the surrounding park by 'Capability' Brown. Around the same time the interiors were transformed by Robert Adam who created a series of Gothick interiors, but they were swept away during the 1850s by the 4th duke, and it is his decorative work, consciously evoking the Italian Renaissance, that survives today: an abundance of richly carved and gilded ceilings, brilliant gold and scarlet damask walls, and monumental Carrera white marble chimney-pieces.

Paintings, furniture and works of art throughout illustrate the combination of distinguished family history and connoisseurship. There can be other English family whose three main houses; Alnwick, Northumberland House in London, and Syon House on the Thames, were all specially painted by Canaletto. All three paintings hang at Alnwick. Generations of Percys and their connections are matched by important Italian Old Masters, collected by the 4th duke for his newly decorated home. When Northumberland House was demolished in 1874 its superb English funiture - pieces by Kent, Addam and attributed to Linell - went to either Alnwick or Syon; but none rivals the castle's outstanding furniture, a pair of cabinets with Florentine 'pietra dura' made for Louis XIV by Domenico Cucci at the Gobelins factory, removed from the Tuileries during the French Revolution and bought by the 3rd duke in 1822.

The mixture of rugged mediaeval history and later cultivation and establishment is constantly evident to the visitor and illustrates with rare interest the progression of one of England's most senior families through successive centuries.

BAMBURGH CASTLE, *Bamburgh.*

Lady Armstrong.
Tel: 0668 214208.

On coast on B1340, 16 m north of Alnwick, 6 m from Belford.
Open: Easter to end-Oct daily, 1-5.
£2.50, £1.10.
Tea room.

High on a cliff dramatically overlooking its village to the west and the North Sea in the opposite direction, Bamburgh Castle conforms to every picturesque notion of an ancient impregnable stronghold. Vast and intimidating from the outside it is therefore surprising to enter a comfortable Victorian country house. The castle was restored by the 1st Lord Armstrong who purchased it in 1894 (after his even more ambitious work on the house and garden at Cragside, also in Northumberland.) At Cragside he transformed nearly a thousand acres of rough hillside into ornamental woods and gardens and built a house which he eventually extended by over one hundred rooms. He is estimated to have spent £1.5 million on the restoration of Bamburgh; the two projects together represent one of the great Victorian millionaire's follies.

While the interiors perpetuate the atmosphere of Lord Armstrong's period, strong echoes of Northumbrian wars and saints are also heard at Bamburgh. Lindisfarne is just across the water and it is impossible not to feel something of the Dark Ages when visiting the castle. Indeed the greatest period in its history was the 7th century when it was conquered by Edwin of Northumbria and became seat of the kings of Northumbria. Under King (Saint) Oswald the monastery on Holy Island or Lindisfarne was founded, before the castle was sacked by the Vikings.

For the tourist there are ghosts and tales and, of course, dungeons (with gruesome tableau vivant), There are fine contents, including the series of portraits, but they do not match the grandeur and quality of Lord Armstrong's restoration work.

CHILLINGHAM CASTLE, *Wooler*

Sir Humphrey Wakefield, Bt.
Tel: 06685 359.

12 m north of Alnwick off A1 and A697.
Open: Easter and May to end-Sept, daily except Tues, 1.30-5.
£3.30, children £2.50, concessions.
Tea room.

The recent restoration of Chillingham has been an heroic and serious undertaking by Sir Humphrey Wakefield. A grand and very handsome mediaeval border fortress, with "the true rust of the Barons' Wars" Chillingham has been saved with great panache. Famous for its wild cattle, a unique kind of safari, everything about a visit to Chillingham is out of the ordinary. Internally it is full of touches that leave one wondering how much Sir Humphrey is indulging his sense of humour. An enormous and highly erotic nude (Susannah and the Elders) forms a backdrop in the chapel. The arched stone alter had emerged from behind the rotten 19th-century plasterwork in a study. Here "Put out more Flags" seems to have done the trick with many a cherished battle banner given a last flourish.

The experience is akin to a visit to an eccentric Irish country house with a touch of "Carry on Castle". The scene of fun continues (with dire warning to the faint-hearted) in the Dungeon which has a connoisseurs' collection of instruments of torture any Inquisitor would be proud of. The gardens and grounds have been superbly restored and are immaculately maintained in intriguing counterpoint to the surrounding Cheviot Hills.

CHIPCHASE CASTLE, *Wark-on-Tyne.*

Mrs P. Torday.
Tel: 0434 230685.

10 m north of Hexham, off B6320 at Wark.
Open: mid-June to mid-July daily, 2-5.
£3.

Occupying a key strategic position in the North Tyne valley, Chipchase was for centuries involved in the roaming struggles and skirmishes of the the Scottish borders. The great pele tower with corner turrets perched against the skyline dates from the fourteenth century and must have provided wide observation over the surrounding country as well as secure defence; now it abuts the south-east corner of the more comfortable house built of similar stone in the 1620s and then altered during the mid-18th century.

At that time the south front overlooking parkland and the Tyne valley beyond was made symmetrical with an arrangement of sash windows - the geometry completed with dummy ones in the tower, string courses and a Doric doorway. The 1620 Jacobean entrance front retains its E shape, the two bays with battlemented two-storey window bays flanking the front door, above which are semi-hexagonal windows on two floors and the upper flourish of an armorial shield charger of the Heron family who built the Jacobean house. Today the arrangement of bays, battlements and generous fenestration presents an impressive picture on both main fronts.

Inside the central hall is flanked by dining and drawing rooms which extend into the two west-facing bays. James Paine is credited with designing the delicate plaster ceiling in the drawing room, but the most striking decorative feature is in the upstairs billiard room, the ornately carved oak overmantel supported on triple clusters of pillars, and incorporating the five senses, Time's winged chariot and the seven graces on armorial shields. The billiard room's lofty ceiling with plaster decoration contrasts with the cosy lower ones of the ground-floor rooms and two fine Aubusson tapestries hang on the walls. The dining room contains a fine set of mid-19th century furniture by James Mein of Kelso. Interesting paintings include Richardson's Wreckers off the Mouth of the Tyne in the entrance hall.

At a short distance from the entrance stands a small chapel of mediaeval origins, but rebuilt at the same time as the mid-18th century work on the house and of considerable note for the box-pews and choir stalls with Ionic pilasters and other furnishings which have no rival for the period in Northumberland.

MELDON PARK, *Morpeth.*

Michael Cookson Esq.
Tel: 0670 72661.

6 m west of Morpeth on B6343.
Open: late-May to late-June daily and Aug Bank Hol, 2-5.
£3.00, children 50p, concession.

Meldon is an important Greek Revival house by one of the leading figures in the early-19th century movement, John Dobson. The impact of the chaste stone exterior is heightened by the house's position overlooking the Wansbeck valley. Dobson spent a month inspecting the Meldon estate before choosing a picturesque spot that would best offset his planned house. The lack of decoration is severe and extends to the style of the Ionic entrance portico on the west side arranged like a Greek propylarum, but the proportions are so exact that the overall effect is one of satisfying quality.

Inside Dobson arranged the main rooms around a large two-storey staircase hall. The south front contains the library, central ante room with a bow, and drawing room. They interlink through sets of double mahogany doors so arranged that the first doorcase exactly frames the second and the second frames the windows on the east side. Internal decoration is restrained in the utmost; marble chimney-pieces - black in the library, austere white in the drawing room and the ceilings with restrained cornices and simple geometric patterns. The dining room ceiling is coffered with slightly more vigour, but the only room with any hint of theatre is the staircase hall, its single lower flight dividing into two returns. Ornament was limited to the ceiling and a delicate wrought iron handrail, but between the wars the composition was upset, albeit by a distinguished hand. Edwin Lutyens - who left his mark on a number of Northumberland houses after his daughter had married Viscount Ridley of Blagdon - replaced the handrails with mahogany ones, extended the plaster decoration to wall panels and set four columns in the upper landing.

Dobson's charming watercolours of the house survive at Meldon and his fastidious taste would have approved the other paintings and furniture that the main rooms contain. Successive generation of Cooksons hang in the dining room, their hunting attire suggesting an hereditary enthusiasm for the chase confirmed by the outstanding stables a short distance from the house. Horses are not the only animals to have been faithful friends; Isaac Cookson lost his dog while travelling in Maryland USA and it reappeared at Meldon some time after his return to England. The house is open to the public at the time when the woodland garden with its rhododendrons are at their best and the walled kitchen garden beyond should not be missed.

PRESTON TOWER, *Chathill.*

Major T.H. Baker-Cresswell.
Tel: 066 589227.

7 m north of Alnwick, 1 m from A1.
Open all year, daily during daylight.
£1, concessions.

Tall gaunt Preston Tower is evidence of the gruelling, violent life in mediaeval Northumberland. It was built by Robert Harbottle around 1392 after he had been promoted by Henry IV for good support in the border clashes. Contemporary with the dashing Harry Hotspur, Harbottle fought at the battles of Otterburn and Halidon Hill and his cousin, Sir Guiscard was slain at Flodden.

The battlemented stone turrets have only small arrow slits to give light although there is the surprising decoration of a large clock near the top of the centre block. The few rooms are deliberately stark and provide a vivid suggestion of life for those under the endless threat of 'Border Raids'; guard room and prison on the ground floor, primitive quarters above and an upper room with details of the Battle of Flodden. A far cry from later, more civilised country houses, it recreates history as enjoyed by generations of schoolchildren.

SEATON DELAVAL HALL, *Whitley Bay.*

The Lord Hastings.
Tel: 091 237 3040/237 1493.

Between Blyth and Whitley Bay, off A190.
Open: May to end-Sept Wed, Sun and Banks Hols 2-6.
£1.50, children 50p.
Tea room.

It is a tribute to the genius of Sir John Vanbrugh that the burnt-out shell of Seaton Delaval presents one of the most impressive visions among English country houses. The splendours of his other two masterpieces, Castle Howard and Blenheim, provide scant preparation although the scale is similarly monumental. The warm Oxfordshire countryside and rolling Howardian Hills are replaced by bleak, windswept Northumbrian coast. Deprived of its decoration by a catastrophic fire in 1822, its stone blackened by industrial pollution, the central block of the house stands stripped to the architectural skeleton that Vanbrugh conceived. The combination of the setting and the reputation of his patrons, the 'gay Delavals', who careered through life sometimes talented and worthy, more often reckless and dissipated, urged Vanbrugh to a design to match.

The purse of Admiral George Delaval - who commissioned the house in 1718, but who died in 1723 as a result of a riding accident before the building was complete - was not as large as those of Vanbrugh's patrons at Castle Howard and Blenheim. But any reduction in size is more than compensated for by the gargantuan scale of the detail and the extremes of the component parts. Certainly the vast courtyard facing north towards the sea one mile away and the port of Blythe beyond, makes no concessions.

On either side are the east and west wings, reminiscent of Castle Howard, with long two-storey facades with central pediments and elegant arcades which continue in curves to join the north-facing central block. The transfer from the horizontal proportions of the wings to the vigorous verticality of the central block is abrupt. Great ringed Doric columns - grouped in threes - stand on either side of the central door at the top of broad steps. Octagonal towers on the corners, of which there are a matching pair on the south front, are balanced by taller square towers that contain staircases, while across the centre extends the bizarrely tall attic storey topped by its pediment and chimney-cases. The overall impression is one of architectural metamorphosis, as though the house has thrust its way up out of the ground.

The restless movement is exaggerated by the rusticated stonework and other details and is equally evident on the south front dominated by an Ionic portico. Inside the heroic scale continues in two rooms that fill most of the space: the entrance hall - originally two-storey and open to the roof but retaining its symmetry in the arched recesses on two levels - and the saloon beyond which stretches the length of the south front. On both sides the staircases wind giddily up their towers.

After the fire in 1822 the central block was abandoned for nearly one hundred and fifty years and was open to the elements for much of that time. Only enlightened restoration by Lord Hastings, whose family inherited Seaton Delaval in 1814, having married the Delaval heiress, saved the house from total dereliction after requisition during World War Two. Neither wing was damaged in the fire and the west wing which once housed cavernous kitchens, is now the family home, its elegantly furnished rooms providing stark contrast to the adjacent shell. In the east wing Vanbrugh's stables survive as he built them; fit for horses that drew Apollo's chariot. Vanbrugh did not live to see Seaton Delaval completed in 1828, but the house strongly evokes the mood of a requiem and its idiosyncrasies present a suitable monument.

SOUTH EAST
Firle Place

BELMONT, *Faversham.*

The Harris (Belmont) Charity.
Tel: 0795 890202.

4 m south-west of Faversham, off A251 at Badlesmere.
Open: Easter to end-Sept Sat, Sun and Bank Hols, 2-4.30.
£3.80, children £2.20.
Tea room.

Belmont's inaccessability has contributed to its undeserving obscurity. Its architectural distinction is only one aspect of a rewarding ensemble with the splendid fortes of, empire, cricket and clocks. The house boasts the finest private clock collection in the country, assembled by the 5th Lord Harris. His father was a figure whose importance in the history of English cricket is second only to that of W.G. Grace. Generations of the family served with distinction as imperial soldiers and administrators.

Belmont has been the Harris home since it was bought at auction by the 1st lord - victor of Seringapatam - with the prize money from his Indian campaign. On the site of an existing 18th-century house, named Belmont because of its superb position overlooking the surrounding countryside, the present house was built for Colonel John Montresor by Samuel Wyatt between 1783-93. It remains one of the most unspoilt examples of Wyatt's work, as the authority on the family of architects, John Martin Robinson has noted. Samuel 'thought of himself as an engineer-architect rather than an artist-architect like his brother James and Belmont is a text-book example of his work.'

Floor-length windows to maximize the views combine with the bows and domes to give the house an attractively generous appearance while glass look-outs are a good example of Wyatt's ingenuity. The house was built of similar red brick to the stable courtyard on the west side but the main fronts were covered in pale mathematical tiles - another novelty as was the Coade Stone decoration that is the exterior's most attractive feature: the Ionic capitals and, more strikingly, the circular and square plaques set into the walls.

Wyatt's restrained but impeccable neo-Classicism continues inside, in the broad axial corridor off which the main drawing room, dining room and library open along the east front. The cantilevered stone staircase with a wrought-iron and lead balustrade and mahogany handrail rises the full height of the house to an oval skylight.

The contents compliment Wyatt's work. In the entrance hall three rare longcase clocks, including a Tompion and a Knibb set the standard for the array that follow throughout the house and provide a symphony of chimes on every hour. Much of the furniture is Regency, added by the 2nd Lord Harris, but there are earlier English pieces and French furniture in the drawing room. Among family portraits, many hanging on the various levels of the staircase hall, the outstanding work is the large group of the 1st Lord Harris and his family by Arthur Devis in the dining room. The most engaging is the 2nd Lord Harris as a boy, vaulting a gate in Richmond churchyard, by W.R. Bigg in the drawing room.

Fascinating memorabilia abounds such as the richly decorated sword presented to the 2nd lord by his fellow officers, 'in testimony of their respect for his highly meritorious conduct at the ever memorable battle of Waterloo;' and the exotic headdress of Tippoo Sultan who was defeated at Seringapatam. For clock enthusiasts in particular the top floor clock museum is absorbing.

BOUGHTON MONCHELSEA PLACE,
Maidstone.

Charles W. Gooch.
Tel: 0622 743120.

In Boughton Monchelsea, on B2163, 5 m south of Maidstone.
Open: Good Fri to early-Oct, Sun and Bank Hols, Wed in July and Aug.
£3.25, children £1.25, concessions.
Tea room.

Boughton Monchelsea enjoys a spectacular position on a south-facing ridge looking out over a vast expanse of the Kentish Weald. Not surprisingly the site had been built upon for some time in 1551 when Robert Rudston purchased the manor and began the changes which produced the present house; substantially built after 1567, of local Kentish ragstone dug from a quarry in Boughton, its entrance front with a distinctive two-storey porch and gables.

Most of the internal character dates from alterations by later generations of the family. The impressive staircase was built during the 1680s, nearly a century later the hall and dining room were given a Gothick appearance with vaulting and clusters of columns and the battlements were added to the parapet. Bold Regency furniture compliments the Gothick decoration while the drawing room retains the earlier combination of a delicate Rococo giltwood mirror over a marble chimney-piece of the same period. Good Mortlake tapestries hang over the stairs and in the dining room, while the parish church tucked into a corner where garden meets park should be visited for its unexpectedly splendid memorial to Sir Christopher Powell by Scheemakers.

CHIDDINGSTONE CASTLE, *Edenbridge.*

Trustees of the Denys Eyre Bower Bequest.
Tel: 0892 870347.

In Chiddingstone off B2027.
Open: April, May and Oct Wed, Sun and Bank Hols,
June to Sept Tues to Sun and Bank Hols 2-5.30.
(The Trustees reserve the right to close the castle for private functions).
£3.50, children £1.50.
Tea room.

The young architect William Atkinson was working on Scone Palace near Perth when, in 1805, he supplied designs for Squire Henry Streatfield to update his Carolean home, Chiddingstone. While Scone finished up a palace, one of the most prestigious commissions of Atkinson's career, at Chiddingstone his more humble client had been too ambitious. In 1807 building was stopped with only the north and south wings complete, the east range was left with its old dormer windows. When Streatfield's son continued the work he used the less competent Henry Kendall.

Streatfields lived at Chiddingstone for 450 yers from Henry VIII's reign; by the turn of this century the castle was let and sold in 1938. After a short spell as a school it was badly damaged during wartime occupation and then, in 1955, help arrived in the form of Denys Eyre Bower, penniless bank clerk and collector, who latterly turned art dealer, who bought Chiddingstone to display his collections, specialised and unusual: Stuart and Jacobite pictures and memorabilia; Egyptian antiquities; Japanese and Buddhist works of art.

Chiddingstone's most elegant room is the White Rose drawing room hung with a rare collection of Stuart portraits; as well as more familiar faces there are Prince Charles Edward's brother, Prince Henry Cardinal York, and Charles I's small children Princess Elizabeth and the Duke of Gloucester by Cornelius Johnson. Of similar quality is Samuel Cooper's miniature of Charles II; most exotic - but in another room -is the portrait of Nell Gwyn, draped but nude, representing Venus with her son the Duke of St Albans as Cupid. The picture is by Lely and Bower did not consider it suitable to hang with the royal Stuarts. Other rare items include Charles I's handkerchief and the letter from the Duke of Monmouth to James II written the night before his execution.

The Japanese collection contains superb laquer pieces, including the Beckford cabinet which Bower discovered in 1940, and exquisite carved ivory and lacquer Japanese ladies. Amongst the Egyptian antiquities is a mummified cat. With plenty of such oddities, the various collections are an intriguing discovery that also reflect the connoisseurship of their creator.

GODINTON PARK, *Ashford.*

Godinton House Preservation Trust/Alan Wyndham Green Esq.
Tel: 0233 620773.

1 m north-west of Ashford off A20.
Open: Easter Sat, Sun, Mon, June to Sept Sun and Bank Hols 2-5.
£2, children 70p.

Mellow brick gables beckon above yew hedges shaped to match as one approaches Godinton through its 18th-century park which disguises the house's proximity to Ashford. From around 1500 until 1895 it was home to the Toke family, Kentish squires who improved the house at different times - with the occasional flourish. Shortly after the turn of this century the then owner commissioned Sir Reginald Blomfield to lay out the present garden which so enhances the house's surroundings, and in 1919 Godinton was bought by Mr Wyndham Green's grandmother, The Hon Mrs Ward.

The east front is early 17th century when the present house was built to the surviving square-plan around a small courtyard; the south front which also overlooks the garden is 18th-century and the north-facing entrance front mainly early-19th century. In he great hall the magnificent tiebeam and kingpost are part of the 14th-century roof most of which is concealed behind a later ceiling. Beyond the hall the staircase with heraldic beasts was described by Christopher Hussey as 'overloaded with enrichment' and although dated 1628, could be in part 19th-century.

The 1635 upstairs great chamber is the finest room; created by Captain Nicholas Toke a rumbustuous soldier who had five wives and died in 1680 when en route to London looking for a sixth. He was responsible for the room's superb carved chimney-piece and panels with a frieze of military figures reflecting his own enthusiasm. Downstairs the chimney-piece in the library carved with symbolic figures commemorates one of his marriages. Here, as in the great chamber and hall, the fireplace is of unusual local Bethersden marble.

Toke portraits and some furniture, notably the fine Chippendale dining chairs remain at Godinton, but important additions have been made by both Mr Wyndham Green and his grandmother. The elegant white drawing room hung with a collection of watercolours (including Myles Birket Fosters) was her sitting room, outside which the garden hall is furnished and decorated with Chinese Chippendale chairs and Chinese ceramics. The library displays the majority of the house's important early-Worcester collection. Among many portraits, Wards in the dining room, Tokes and suitable royal Stuarts in the great hall, the pick are in the great chamber and the adjoining gallery; works by Raeburn, Reynolds, Cornelius Johnson and Van de Helst.

HEVER CASTLE, *Edenbridge.*

Broadland Properties Ltd.
Tel: 0732 865224.

3 m south-east of Edenbridge off B2026.
Open: Daily March to Nov 11-5.
Prices on application.
Restaurant.

The combination of Hever's appearance, its comet-like rise and fall during Henry VIII's reign and its transformation by one of the wealthiest of Edwardian plutocrats gives an air of unreality to the place; one might not be surprised to hear that it is all a lavish film set. But such hints of pastiche disguise important mediaeval architecture, absorbing history and restoration of unparalleled munificence and quality.

The moated mediaeval castle was bought in 1462 by Sir Geoffrey Bullen. His grandson Sir Thomas was father of Anne Boleyn who Henry VIII married having tried her elder sister Mary as a mistress first. Boleyn supremacy was brief and ended with Anne's execution on Tower Hill in 1536. Their demise was emphasised when Henry VIII later granted Hever to his divorced 4th wife, Anne of Cleves. The castle was occupied by three successive families from 1557 until 1903, when it was bought by William Waldorf Astor, who had settled in England in 1890 and would become a British citizen and peer.

It is his Hever that the visitor sees today and it is fortunate that when the Astor family sold the place in 1983 the major fittings and many contents remained in place. The unrivalled armour collection has gone, but Astor's series of immaculately precise and superbly worked Tudor interiors survive, notable in particular for their panelling and carving by W.S. Frith, as do much of the carefully chosen furniture and Astor's eclectic often fabulous collection of works of art and antiquities.

Astor made two major additions to Hever; the extraordinary 'Tudor village' which provided necessary extra rooms and service areas and continued the architectural quality of his work on the castle, and the Italian gardens. The latter, with its Pompeiian Wall displaying an astonishing array of antiquities, and classical architecture culminating in the loggia overlooking the lake created by damming the passing River Eden, is the most important Italianate garden in England.

LEEDS CASTLE, *Maidstone.*

Leeds Castle Foundation.
Tel: 0622 765400.

4 m east of Maidstone, off B2163, junc 8 M20.
Open: March to end-Oct daily 10-5, Nov to end-Feb (except Christmas Day) 10-3.
£7, children £4.80, concessions.
Restaurant.

Few castles can rival Leeds' reputation for antiquity and romance and its island position remains superb, evoking the times of the mediaeval kings and queens for whom it was a favourite haunt. The arrangement of pale stone buildings confirm that it was a place for enjoyment rather than a defensive fortress; they present a cross-section of periods from Norman to the 19th century.

Among the oldest are the keep or Gloriette on its own small island and reached by corridors over an arched stone bridge and the revetment wall with two drum bastions. The main body of the castle which extends from the corridor bridge onto the larger island was rebuilt as part of extensive restoration by Fiennes Wykeham-Martin during the 1820s. Facing across the castle's lawned courtyard is the Tudor Maiden's Tower while at the entrance to the castle is the largely 13th-century gatehouse.

In 1926, by which time Leeds was again in need of restoration, it was sold by the Wykeham-Martin family and bought by the Hon Olive Lady Baillie whose mother was a member of the American Whitney family and her father the grandson of the 1st Marquess of Anglesey who led the cavalry at Waterloo. Up to the Second World War Lady Baillie restored the buildings and redecorated the interiors, assisted by the French decorator Stephane Boudin.

The finished work combines suitability to the castle's ancient origins with the comforts of a country house and involved the introduction of many important works of art. Old Masters such as Tiepolo's The Pulchinello's Kitchen and modern paintings add distinguished variety to portraits of Leeds' royal occupants such as Henry VIII, and later non-royal owners, in particular the Culpepper and Fairfax families whose successive ownership spanned the 17th and 18th centuries. Other major additions by Lady Baillie include the 16th-century newel staircase and fireplace in the Henry VIII banqueting hall, both French, the 17th-century panelling from Thorpe Hall near Peterborough and an extensive collection of rare Chinese porcelain.

Lady Baillie's devoted and distinguished custodianship of Leeds was completed some time before her death in 1974, when she arranged for the property to pass into the ownership of a charitable foundation who would maintain it and enable it to provide wide public enjoyment.

LULLINGSTONE CASTLE, *Eynsford.*

Guy Hart Dyke Esq.
Tel: 0322 862114.

In Darenth valley via Eynsford on A225.
Open: Sat, Sun, Bank Hols April-Oct, 2-6.
£3.50, children £1.50.
Tea room.

North Kent, within walking distance of the M25 motorway, is not where one would expect to discover so secluded a piece of countryside as the small Darenth valley. Lullingstone Castle was recorded as Lullingstone Ros in Domesday with an estate of 120 acres. Today it is the same size; in between the estate swelled to 6,000 acres and Harts and Dykes occupied positions of power and entertained royalty.

Sir John Peche was one of Henry VII's most dashing knights and set about transforming Lullingstone after being knighted at the Battle of Blackheath in 1497. He added the battlemented gatehouse through which the visitor approaches, possibly the earliest brick gate-house in England. The house lies across expansive lawn with little St Botolph's church to the left, is deceptive; remodelling during Queen Anne's reign disguises the Tudor construction. In the hall a 1725 view shows both the original moat and a second gatehouse.

The expansive hall was the original great hall but remodelled with the other main apartments by Sir Thomas Dyke at the beginning of the 18th century. His portrait - and that of his son Sir John Dixon Dyke, unusual full-length works by Domenico van Schmissen - both hang in the room. The dining room to one side was panelled during the remodelling, and the staircase inserted, with its characteristic early-18th century balusters and deliberately shallow treads to assist the ascent of the portly Queen Anne.

Upstairs is Lullingstone's forte, the Elizabethan drawing room, which was retained by Sir Thomas in his remodelling. The barrel vault ceiling with sumptuous plasterwork is original but the panelling with pilasters and carved capitals was Sir Thomas's work. Anne in royal robes surveys the room from one end and a leather chest with her crown and monogram stands in the room.

The parish church should not be missed. It retains evidence of Norman origins and Edward III reconstruction. Its rood screen was inserted by Sir John Peche and the north chapel built for his splendid tomb. There are more tombs and wall memorials to Harts and Dykes, the plaster moulded ceiling was put in during the Queen Anne work, the windows contain stained glass from the 14th to the 18th centuries and the alter rail was added in the late 20th century by Sir Oliver Hart Dyke who also restored the gatehouse and much of the castle.

QUEX PARK, *Birchington.*

Trustees of the Powell-Cotton Museum.
Tel: 0843 42168.

In Birchington, off A28.
Open: Easter to end-Sept Wed, Thur, Sun (Fri in Aug), 2.15-6.
£2.50, children £1.80, concessions.
Tea room.

Quex Park is a curiosity among country houses. Marooned among cabbages and potatoes of the Isle of Thanet it hides strange surprises and unexpected treasures. A hint of what lies ahead comes as one approaches; from the woods that surround Quex a quaint white-painted metal tower points skyward. It turns out to surmount a Gothick folly called the Waterloo Tower built by John Powell Powell to celebrate the great victory and to accomodate his enthusiasm for campanology; it contains one of the few secular peals of twelve bells in England.

John Powell Powell was responsible for much of Quex's present appearance. Inheriting from an uncle in 1808, he demolished the delapidated old house, replaced it with the Regency one that largely survives, and planted the park that securely encloses it. From 1883 the house was extended by Henry Horace Powell Cotton and took on a Victorian appearance. His son, Major Percy Horace Gordon Powell-Cotton, made the most unusual - and distinguished - additions to Quex. Explorer, collector, hunter and naturalist, he was an authority on Indian and African fauna and ethnography and in 1896 begun the museum at Quex, adjoining the house, which now contains an astonishing array of dioramas, containing exhibitions of animals in their natural habitat.

Major Powell-Cotton also acquired the distinguished collection of Chinese Imperial and Taste porcelain which is the highlight of Quex's works of art, as well as the almost bewildering array of antiquities from many African and oriental countries and rare items of British archaeology. In the house panelling and other carved decoration is all Kashmir walnut, while much of the furniture is elaborately carved padouk wood from India. Three generations of Cottons served the East India Company and their portraits hang with other members of the family in the Armoury (whose weapons are now in the museum).

In addition to the main collections notable curiosities abound throughout the house: in the boudoir a pair of tortoiseshell and satinwood card tables; in the gallery an Italian 17th-century marble bust of The Laughing Philosopher which belonged to Henry Lord Holland who had a substantial house at Kingsgate near Broadstairs and who owned Quex for a time from 1767; and in the library the Congreve or rolling-ball clock, made for John Powell Powell by William Congreve, who made rocket batteries during the Napoleonic Wars.

SQUERRYES COURT, *Westerham.*

J. St A. Warde Esq.
Tel: 0959 562345.

In Westerham, off A25.
Open: Sun in March, April to end-Sept Wed, Sat, Sun, Bank Hols 2-6.
£3.50, children £1.60, concessions.
Home-made teas.

Carolean in date, William and Mary in appearance and satisfyingly symmetrical, Squerryes is the English country house of many people's imagination. The house was built in 1680 by Sir William Crisp. In 1700 Squerryes was sold to Edward Villiers, 1st Earl of Jersey and, in 1731, to John Warde whose family have lived here ever since.

John Warde brought to the house much of the fine early 18th-century furniture, including the upholstered chairs and giltwood mirrors in the dining room. He also commissioned the splendid armorial service from Canton, about 150 pieces in all, bearing the Warde arms impaling Bristow. He watched his racehorses exercising from the gazebo in the park and his sporting enthusiasm prompted the painting of him and his family at Squerryes by John Wootton.

His son, also John, was the family's most important collector and brought to Squerryes most of the distinguished paintings. In the dining room are Dutch cabinet paintings by Jacob Ruysdael, Van Goyen, Hondecoeter and Steenwyck, although the group by Van der Helst was acquired by the family at an earlier date. Other paintings acquired by John Warde II are by Peter de Ring, Luca Giordano and Rubens and include Van Dyck's Martydom of San Sebastian.

John Warde I was responsible for the tapestry room. The three Soho arabesque tapestries were specially woven around 1720 by Joshua Morris and incorporate the Warde arms, as do the settees and stools in the room. Very different is the Wolfe room, a sanctuary to the general who was born and brought up in Westerham and was a close friend of George Warde, for whom Benjamin West painted the arresting posthumous portrait of Wolfe as a boy.

The Warde sporting enthusiasm remained strong. John Warde II commissioned Stubbs to paint his Arab horse. His son, also John holds the horse in Stubbs' painting but achieved more lasting fame as the 'Father of Foxhunting'. He is credited with being the first man to keep hounds excusively for fox-hunting, was master of the Pytchley for eleven seasons, founded the West Kent hunt and continued to ride to hounds when weighing well over 20 stone. His picture by Barraud hangs in the drawing room, with the Wootton and other enjoyable family paintings, not least a Zuccharelli of Harleyford Manor near Marlow, married home of a Warde daughter and Toad Hall in Wind in the Willows.

SOUTHSIDE HOUSE, *Wimbledon.*

The Pennington-Mellor-Munthe Trust.
Tel: 081 947 2491/946 7643.

On south side of Wimbledon Common, on B281.
Open: Oct until end-May, Tues, Thur, Sat and Bank Hols 2-5.
£5.

There is a stirring story that at the height of the London Blitz Mrs Hilda Pennington-Mellor-Munthe left Southside House after it had suffered a number of direct hits from German bombs and set off in the family carriage, the horses steered by an alcoholic Irish riding master, to the safety of her Herefordshire home Hellens. She and her maid clasped jewellery, silver and other valuables they were able to carry to safety and which she returned after the end of the war when the War Damage Commission voted to assist the extensive rebuilding that was required at Southside.

The house has passed - via occasionally tortuous routes by descent or marriage from Charles Pennington who developed a modest farmhouse into the present William and Mary house. It continued to be known as Holme Farm until the early 20th-century when it became Southside House. Pennington had sent his wife and daughter to the house from the city of London after their son had died in the plague; his affection for his surviving family is shown by the two statues of 'Plenty' and 'Spring' set in niches on either side of the front door. Ensuing generations made considerable changes to the house's interiors; at one time it was divided into two dwellings, but the post-war restoration returned it as faithfully as possible to the late 17th-century original, the period emphasised by interior fittings such as large classical doorcases and deep carved freizes.

As at the family's home at Hellens Southside's greatest attraction is the distinguished picture collection which illustrates the lively family history and introduces the characters with whom they were associated. The dining room contains an impressive number which include a full length of James Stuart, Charles I's nephew, attributed to Van Dyck, Hogarth's portrait of Sir Charles Kemeys-Tynte and St George by Edward Burne-Jones. A number of portraits in the house illustrate the family's close Connection with the dukes of Wharton and it was from the Whartons that the collection of small portraits by Rouselle showing various relations of the 4th Lord Wharton.

LOSELEY HOUSE, *Guildford.*

Mr and Mrs James More-Molyneux.
Tel: 0483 304440.

3 m south-west of Guildford via A3 and B3000.
Open: May Bank Hol to end-Sept, Wed, Thur, Fri, Sat and Aug Bank Hol Mon 2-5.
£3.50, children £2.
Tea room.

Set in parkland inhabited by its famous herd of Jersey cows, Loseley House evokes the reigns of Elizabeth I and James I, both of whom visited the house. Sir William More was one of Elizabeth's most trusted advisors and he built the house between 1562-68. The Bargate stone came from the ruins of Cistercian Waverley Abbey and the sense of movement given to the entrance front by tall gables is emphasised by the chalk clunch window dressings and quoins.

The Tudor atmosphere is immediate as one enters the great hall, with panelling from Henry VIII's Nonsuch Palace. Decorative panels along the minstrels' gallery above one end of the hall were painted by an Italian Toto del Nunziata to adorn Henry VIII's banqueting tents. After James I visited Loseley he presented the full-length portraits of himself and Queen Anne by John de Critz, but the most distinguished royal portrait is Edward VI wearing his father's royal collar; it is the first painting of the young boy after his accession. Family portraits in the hall are dominated by the splendid group of Sir More Molyneux, his wife and eight of their eleven children, by Somers.

From the expansive hall the mood is immediately intimate in the small library, enclosed by bookcases and panelling. The panel over the chimney-piece bearing the arms of Elizabeth I commemorates her visits. Sir William More began the collection of books that was continued by later generations.

The drawing room beyond has a richly worked plaster ceiling inserted and gilded for James I's visit as was the delightful frieze incorporating family emblems of the moorhen, cockatrix and mulberry tree. But its most astonishing decoration is the chimneypiece carved out of a massive single block of chalk. Sir William More's portrait hangs in this room, a distinguished old man by Lucas de Here; as do his son's (whose daughter eloped with the poet John Donne) and those of other descendants.

The Tudor atmosphere continues in the bedrooms, while throughout the house there is a rich variety of furniture. The most interesting piece is the 16th-century inlaid Wrangelschrank cabinet collected by Sir Poynings More which is in the drawing room along with an inlaid Queen Anne cabinet decorated with seaweed design.

ARUNDEL CASTLE, *Arundel.*

Arundel Castle Trustees Ltd.
Tel: 0903 883136.

In Arundel north of A27.
Open: April to end-Oct daily except Sat 11-5.
£4.50, children £3.50, concessions.
Restaurant.

Arundel Castle is entirely suitable a home for England's senior dukes; its walls encapsulate the vicissitudes of their progress. Shortly after the Conquest William I granted lands in Sussex to Roger de Montgomery who built the original castle. His Fitzalan Earls of Surrey descendants extended it and, like the Howard dukes of Norfolk, were in the mainstream of English history throughout the turbulent mediaeval and Tudor centuries. Only years after the two families were joined in 1556 by the marriage of Lady Mary Fitzalan and Thomas 4th Duke of Norfolk, he was beheaded by Elizabeth I for plotting to marry Mary Queen of Scots. Such brushes with royalty were commonplace and the family history is dotted with attainders, executions and martyrs.

Head of the peerage and Roman Catholic to boot, the Norfolks were a likely target during the Civil War and in 1643 parliamentary forces destroyed much of the existing castle. For over a century the semi-ruined buildings were hardly occupied, the family lived in splendour at 18th-century Norfolk House in London and at Worksop Manor. Occasional restoration was begun, but nothing serious until the late-18th century when the 11th duke set about the work. He restored some buildings round the quadrangle but his main contribution was to lay out the park that stretches away from the castle on the other sides from the town.

Henry the 15th duke between 1875 and the First World War, was largely responsible for the castle as it is today. He was advised by C.A. Buckler who fused architecture with genealogy and antiquarianism and Arundel emerged as a celebration of Roman Catholic mediaevalism.

The scale is impressive: the entire complex of towers, turrets and walls was refaced with ashlar stone and cavernous rooms were given church-like interiors - at times it seems that you are never out of a chapel. The dining room was one, the private chapel is one of the two most exhilarating Gothick revival interiors along with the library, whose vaulted ceiling was designed to look like a church; down the hill from the main body of the castle the Fitzalan chapel forms one end of the parish church. The vast proportions reach a climax in the barons' hall.

As much as in the architecture and fabric of the castle, family history is told by the sumptuous array of portraits: Stretes' of the poet Earl of Arundel, beheaded by Henry VIII; his father the ruthless 3rd duke who encouraged two successive nieces, Anne Boleyn and Katherine Howard, to become wives of Henry VIII and subsequently lose their heads, who only avoided his son's fate because the king died, by Mytens; and the collector 14th earl of Arundel, many of whose treasures were destroyed by the parliamentary sacking, by Van Dyke - once with his Talbot heiress wife and once with his son. If the Mytenses and Van Dycks are outstanding, the picture gallery rivals any in England for historical importance, and later additions came from Worksop Manor and, after 1938, Norfolk House. The London home also provided much of the outstanding 18th-century furniture. While most houses have their particular 'keepsakes' few are of the importance of Mary Queen of Scots' rosary, a gift from the 4th duke.

Today, displaying its pageant of history in immaculate style, it is hard to imagine Arundel at the end of the 18th century when the 11th duke deliberately retained some of the mediaeval ruins and kept a rare breed of enormous American owls in the deserted keep.

FIRLE PLACE, *Lewes.*

Viscount Gage.
Tel: 0273 858335.

5 m south-east of Lewes on A27.
Open: May to Sept inc, Wed, Thur, Sun, and Bank Hols Sun and Mon, 2-5.
£3.50, children £2, concessions.
Restaurant/Tea room.

A warm, unassuming 18th-century house of manorial proportions, Firle has a cloak of intimacy which initially disguises the quality and richness of its contents. Georgian over early-Tudor, the rooms are pleasing unpredictable in their arrangement and in a sense reflect that it is a house built by great artisans and unknown architects. From being recusant Elizabethan Catholics, the Gage family grew to 18th-century prosperity through conformity and marriage and in the process Firle became fabulously enriched with art treasures. Old Master paintings - largely from the Cowper Collection - by Van Dyck, Rubens, Fra Bartolemo and de Koninck, range alongside a fine collection of English portraits by Reynolds, Zoffany, Gainsborough and Lawrence.

Exceptional English and French furniture and Sevres porcelain complete the astonishing collection. The visitor is left ruminating where, outside England, one would discover such treasures shrouded by such modest understatement. On departure the church with its brasses, and unspoilt village should not be missed.

GLYNDE PLACE, *Lewes.*

Viscount and Viscountess Hampden.
Tel: 0273 858337/858224.

In Glynde 4 m south-east of Lewes of A27.
Open: June to Sept Wed, Thur and 1st and last Sun of month, Bank Hols.
£3, children free with adult.
Tea room.

An Elizabethan flint house, built around a courtyard on the edge of the South Downs, Glynde has passed through three families on its way to the present occupants, the Brands, Lords Hampden. The atmosphere is a blend of the 16th and 17th centuries with a element of 18th-century tidying up. Only the 19th century is nowhere visible. Built by the Morleys, a Civil War family who inherited the house from the Waleys, it passed to the Trevors. The Trevors included a Bishop of Durham who lived in the house, enriched and improved Glynde during the 17th and 18th centuries, notably adding the fine staircase and grand panelled portrait gallery. Full of good country house furnishings and a score of fine Old Master paintings, Glynde is first and foremost a family home, inasmuch agreeable informal. The appearance of public visitors rarely disturbs the slumbers of the family dog who is usually ensconced on the drawing room sofa.

GOODWOOD HOUSE, *Chichester.*

The Duke of Richmond.
Tel: 0243 774107.

3 m north-east of Chichester off A285, A286 and A27.
Open: Easter Sun and Mon to end-Sept, Sun and Mon (Tues, Wed and Thur in Aug) 2-5. Closed on event days.
Price available on request.
Tea room.

The French spy Louise de Keroualle, Duchess of Portsmouth could probably claim the distinction of being Charles II's most beautiful mistress. Her son was made Duke of Richmond and given the usual fistful of additional titles and Goodwood House was his hunting lodge. Its incomparable setting on the South Downs inspired the 3rd duke to build the race course and during his long life he transformed both the house and its surroundings. William Chambers built the stables for him during the 1750s, demonstrating his mastery of pure classical architecture. Towards the end of the century the 3rd duke turned to James Wyatt to execute a scheme of monumental grandeur; an octagon with a series of classical facades and a domed tower at each corner. The present house is the three sides of the octagon that were completed.

Only from the air does the house have a peculiar appearance; from the ground the combination of the flint walls, two-storey colonnade on the entrance front and the green-domed towers presents a harmonious whole. Inside Wyatt's marvellous tapestry room survives intact with its Gobelins tapestries of Don Quixote, rich neo-classical decoration and white marble chimney-piece. Here successive monarchs from Edward VII have held meetings of the Privy Council while in residence for Goodwood races.

Other rooms display the treasures acquired or collected by generations of the family. Not surprisingly there are outstanding royal Carolean portraits by Van Dyck, Lely, Wissing and Kneller which hang in the ballroom - planned as a gallery by the 3rd duke. His patronage of the arts is constantly evident. The receipt of payment for his superb portrait by Reynolds is preserved in the house; his portrait by Romney is of similar quality and he collected much of the French furniture and porcelain. Other highlights include paintings by Canaletto, the best being the famous commissioned pair of Whitehall and the Thames painted from the windows of Richmond House in London, and, as one might expect, a Stubbs of the 3rd duke's horses training on the Downs. Preservation and additions by later generations have ensured that Goodwood retains its rich history and collections.

GREAT DIXTER, *Northiam.*

Quentin Lloyd Esq.
Tel: 0797 253160.

½ m north of Northiam, off A28.
Open: April to mid-Oct, daily except Mon (open Bank Hols) 2-5.
£3.50, children 50p, concessions.

Great Dixter was bought in 1910 by Nathaniel Lloyd, architectural historian and Arts and Crafts connoisseur. At that time it was a mediaeval hall house with subsequent alterations. Almost immediately Lloyd commissioned his friend Edwin Lutyens to assist with restoration and improvement of the house. At the time Lutyens was arguably at the zenith of his career in English domestic architecture; his most delightful houses were built and the grandeur of New Delhi and post-war commissions lay ahead.

The work at Great Dixter must have greatly appealed and he carried it out with consummate skill and sensitivity. The oldest part of the house was built between 1450-64, timbered and tile-roofed, entered through a gabled two-storey porch and containing a great hall with parlour and solar beyond in a tall barge-boarded gable. Floors and partitions had been inserted around 1595. Lutyens removed these to open up the hall to its two-storey height and timbered roof with the rare combination of king-posts and hammerbeams. On the other side of the entrance porch he built on a tile-hung addition and supervised the linking on to the back of the house of a timbered yeoman's cottage which Nathaniel Lloyd had found derelict in Benenden and moved to Northiam.

The garden at Great Dixter was always an important priority for Lloyd and part of Lutyens' achievement was the restoration of the barn, oast and other farm buildings which became features of the garden and, with thond Burton, the or ginality by the ceiling of the top-floor gallery painted by Oliver Messel. T e work revealed some hidden original features such as thgree; where Lutyens suggested brick walls Lloyd insisted on the yew hedges which, with the topiary, are now such a feature of Great Dixter's appearance. Lloyd's son Christopher has brought fame to the Great Dixter garden and made it a mecca for rare-plant enthusiasts, while his other son Quentin looks after the house and estate.

HAMMERWOOD PARK, *East Grinstead.*

David Pinnegar.
Tel: 0342 850594.

3 m east of East Grinstead on A264.
Open: Easter Mon to end-Sept Wed, Sat and Bank Hols 2-5.30.
£3.50, children £1.50.
Home-made teas.

David Pinnegar bought Hammerwood Park in 1982 in an advanced state of dereliction; evidence remains today in the unrestored parts of the house where ceilings are still eerily missing. But much was achieved with commendable speed so that in 1992 the house's bi-centenary could be celebrated with genuine pride.

Hammerwood is of considerable importance as the first major house designed by the Yorkshireman Benjamin Latrobe. Four years later he emigrated to the United States where he was responsible for the White House, the Capitol and a selection of other major American buildings. Latrobe studied under S.R. Cockerell with whom he developed an enthusiasm for Greek revival architecture which he put into practice at Hammerwood built as a hunting lodge, dedicated to the god Apollo, for John Sperling, and inspired by original details at Paestum which Latrobe had visited.

The main front faces south, a restrained composition of five-bay central block with tall Doric pilasters and flanking lower wings which have one of the house's many architecturally innovative features, matching Greek Doric temple porches. Another novelty was the use of Coade stone for the limited amount of decoration, notably the Bacchic plaques above the doorways in the two porticos, their partying figures copied from the Borghese Vase. Any doubt about Latrobe's Greek inspiration is dispelled by an insription in Greek on one of the Coade stone capitals; 'This is the first portico of John Sperling's mansion. The architect is B.H. Latrobe. He made it in the 1792 year of Jesus Christ and the second year of the 642nd Olympiad.'

Inside some of Latrobe's plaster cornices and ceilings have been restored and - with the exception of the huge dining room and rooms above - most of the main rooms painstakingly redecorated and furnished. In addition to the dereliction restoration was hampered by earlier division of the house into flats. The most impressive flourish is the allegorical trompe l'oeil mural which now decorates the entire staircase hall, completed for the 1992 celebrations. It is no surprise that the restoration has won a number of awards and David Pinnegar and his family have worked tirelessly, against considerable odds and hostile local opposition to the house being given extensive public access.

HAREMERE HALL, *Etchingham.*

Jacqueline, Lady Killearn.
Tel: 0580 819245.

Off A265, 1 mile from Hurst Green.
Open: Details on application.
Price details on application.

Where the land drops steeply from the edge of the Weald down to the Rother valley, Haremere Hall sits tucked underneath the scarp with views over the gentle landscape beyond. No doubt this position was one of the attractions to Lord and Lady Killearn when they bought Haremere in 1948 after his retirement from a distinguished ambassadorial career. The two main fronts of the ragstone house are both handsome and immediately tell of their different dates. Facing west the 1616 main front has two delightful projecting bays with Dutch gables of theatrical height. The south front has a 19th-century broad gable over an unusual two-storey mullioned bay window but the neat symmetry of the rest of the range immediately suggests its 1682 period.

The panelling in the great hall is probably contemporary with this later period, but the ceiling is more likely to date from the earlier work. There are striking carved fireplaces and overmantels, some original, others introduced by different owners - of which Haremere has had a regular succession. The most colourful was the Regency Sir John Lade, who inherited a considerable forture and spent a large amount of it entertaining his friend the Regent or in various reckless schemes. His consuming passion was driving and he once steered a four-horse phaeton from Bath to London in eight hours. His lowly-born wife Letty used such language that the Regent often commented 'he swears like Letty Lade'.

Lampson - Lord Lillearn's family name - portraits alternate with other decorative pictures recalling his successions diplomatic postings such as Egypt and the decoration and furnishing of the house is their work, as is the attractive terraced garden.

MICHELHAM PRIORY, *Hailsham.*

Sussex Archaelogical Society.
Tel: 0323 844224.

1 m east of Upper Dicker, off A22.
Open: end-March to end-Oct daily 11-5.30.
£3.30, children £1.90, concessions.

Michelham Priory comprises the surviving buildings from the Augustinian priory founded in 1229. After suppression during the dissolution and subsequent sale the priory passed through successive owners, the earliest of whom added to the buildings, but by the beginning of the 20th century much of the priory was derelict. In 1924 it was bought by Mr and Mrs Richard Beresford-Wright who carried out extensive restoration, continued by their successor Mrs Hotblack who in 1959 bequeathed the property in trust to the Sussex Archaelogicial Society.

The expansive moat which provides an ideally gentle atmosphere, gives an indication of the priory's former substance, four ranges of buildings enclosing a square cloister and incorporating a large church. This and much of another range has gone and the surviving buildings - occupied as a house after the dissolution - comprise part mediaeval with Tudor additions. A bridge over the moat leads through the tall 14th-century gatehouse and of the main priory buildings the south range is the most intact with warm sandstone walls, mullioned windows and deep tiled roofs. In the remainder of the west range is the fine 13th-century undercroft through which visitors enter the house and many other rooms contain exhibitions of monastic life and museums. Detached from the priory buildings is a 16th-century barn with an impressive timber roof, a timbered water-mill and there has been extensive restoration of the gardens.

PARHAM HOUSE, *Pulborough.*

Tel: 0903 744888.

2 m west of Storrington off A283.
Open: Easter to Oct Wed, Thur, Sun and Bank Hols 2-6 (last entry 5).
£4, children £2, concessions.
Home-made teas.

Situated idyllically beneath the South Downs Parham is an Elizabethan house of distinction. In 1922 it was acquired by Clive Pearson and his wife, who restored and adorned it with outstanding works of art, notably Tudor and Stuart paintings. Their devoted work was continued by their daughter, Mrs Tritton, until her death in 1993. Built in 1557, in 1601 Parham was sold to the Bysshopp family whose descendants lived in the house until the Pearsons. Bysshopps became baronets and, in 1816, revived the ancient barony of Zouche. The 17th Baroness Zouche sold Parham in 1922, when it lacked water, drains or electricity and alarming amounts of the roof.

The 1557 house was built of local grey stone with Horsham 'slabs' on the roof. The traditional E-plan has gabled wings and a central porch while the entrance front's most striking feature is the towering mullioned and transomed windows of the great hall. Under the Pearsons the existing parkland setting was greatly enhanced with delightful replanted and extended gardens.

The Pearson's restoration revealed some hidden original features such as the stone fireplace in the great hall, and returned others to their original state such as the ceiling of the parlour which had been removed and the room incorporated with the great chamber above. Among the most important fittings in the house is the Renaissance carved oak screen at one end of the hall.

For many visitors, however, it is the works of art at Parham, notably the historical portraits collected by Clive Pearson, that are the highlight. Tudor monarchs and leading members of ther courts look down from walls throughout the house, familiar faces such as Charles II (by Verelst) and some less familiar, such as Edward VI by Stretes, with the occasional flourish such as Robert Peake's large portrait of James I's eldest son Henry Frederick Prince of Wales, riding a white charger. His younger brother Charles was painted when he had taken over as Prince of Wales by Mytens. The royal figures are not only English; in the parlour hangs Claude Deruet's double equestrian portrait of Louis XIII and his wife and a portrait of his father, Henry IV, Elizabeth of Bohemia and her husband and the Spanish princess Anna Maria. There are many Bysshopp faces and Knatchbulls (Mrs Pearson's family). For anyone looking for variety from the portraits there are seascapes, a kangaroo painted by Stubbs and a mouth-watering view of Venice by Bellotto.

Needlework is second only to the paintings and is predominantly Jacobean and Stuart; the furniture is equally suitable, extending from fine Tudor oak to early-Georgian walnut and a few excursions into later 18th-century mahogany. There is much else besides, not least a room devoted to Sir Joseph Banks, connected to the Knatchbulls by marriage.

ST. MARY'S, *Bramber.*

Peter Thorogood Esq.
Tel: 0903 816205.

In Bramber, 10 m north-west of Brighton off A283.
Open: Easter to end-Sept, Sun, Thur and Bank Hols,
Mon in July, Aug, Sept, 2-6.
£3.30, children £2, concessions.

After wartime occupation which included being driven into by a tank St Mary's seemed doomed and was only saved by Dorothy Ellis outbidding a reclamation merchant who wanted the timbers and stone. She began the restoration which, in more recent years has been carried on by Peter Thorogood, to celebrate the house's 15th-century origins and distinguished features.

The quality of the building with its roof of Horsham stone and closely timbered overhanging upper storey is easily explained; it originally formed one side of a courtyard built during the 1470s for William of Waynfleet, a cleric of substance, Bishop of Winchester and founder of Magdalen College Oxford. St Mary's was built on a site that had been granted to the Knights Templar during the 12th century, when Bramber was a thriving port on the River Adur.

Now the restoration has removed some of the more intrusive alterations that took place once St Mary's ceased to be a monastic hostelry and eventually descended to a rough farmhouse, and has made the best of the panelled rooms. Highlights throughout are carved oak doors and fireplaces (the Gothick stone ones were introduced around 1896 by the Hon Algernon Bourke who restored the house at that time). In the parlour there is a Dutch-style wainscot with ebony panels, while the gilt and flower-painted leather wall-covering along the passage has been expertly restored, as have the arched panels of the painted room, each with a landscape or seascape. Probably early-17th century they represent a rare early example of tromple l'oeil. Among Peter Thorogoods major additions is the unrivalled collection of work by the 19th-century comic artist and poet Thomas Hood and the delightfully rejuvenated house is the more interesting for fresh interests enhancing those long-established.

Thames
&
Chilterns
Chicheley Hall

LUTON HOO, *Luton.*

The Wernher Family.
Tel: 0582 22955.

South of Luton off A6129.
Open: Details by request.
Price available by request.

Edwardians were exacting in their demands for quality and comfort, but not necessarily purist over architecture or decorative styles. When the South African diamond magnate, Sir Julius Wernher, bought Luton Hoo in 1904 he commissioned C.F. Mewes, the architect of the Ritz Hotel, to completely remodel the house, but retain the austere Greek Ionic portico that was the only surviving feature of earlier work by Sir Robert Smirke. The result may have been architecturally curious but it was undeniably splendid in the lush Francophile Beaux-Arts style so favoured by American contempories of Wernher.

Luton Hoo already had a long distinguished history of occupation for seven hundred years, with an 18th-century zenith when the Marquess of Bute bought the estate and made his new Adam house and its contents universally admired. In 1843 the house was destroyed by fire, only Smirke's portico survived. It was subsequently rebuilt by a Victorian industrialist who sold Luton Hoo to Wernher. All that remained from the Bute hey-day was - and is - 'Capability' Brown's expansive park where he created some of the skilfully serpentine lakes for which he was renowned.

For Wernher Luton Hoo was to be a place of luxury and display; the interior decoration achieved its peak in the circular main staircase which ascends round the white marble group L'Amore degli Angeli by Borgonzoli, but most rewarding are the collections built up by Sir Julius and continued by his son Sir Harold (who divided the house into private residence and public museum). Sir Julius's forte was European works of art, Sir Harold brought in most of the outstanding 18th-century English furniture, his mother the equally distinguished English porcelain of the same period and his wife, Lady Zia, daughter of Grand Duke Michael of Russia, the Faberge collection for which Luton Hoo is perhaps best known. All contributed to the picture collection, among whose Old Masters are rarities such as the 15th-century Spaniard Bartolome Bermejo's St Michael.

WOBURN ABBEY, *Woburn.*

Marquess of Tavistock and Trustees of the Bedford Estates.
Tel: 0525 290666.

In Woburn 8 m north of Dunstable on A4012, junc 12 and 13 M1.
Open: Jan to end-March Sat and Sun 11-4.00; March to end-Oct daily 11-5.45 (last admission 5).
£6, children £2, concessions.

A pioneer of commercial opening to the public, which began in 1955 in response to the death duties facing the present 13th Duke of Bedford, Woburn's high public profile occasionally hides the distinguished history of its family and the wonderful works of art with which it is filled. Crammed might be more accurate, for in 1950 extensive dry rot demanded that two sides of the quadrangle, whose plan had survived from the old Cistercian monastery, should be demolished and the available room space was halved.

Russells have been collecting and commissioning for generations, since John, 1st Earl of Bedford brought them to prominence during Henry VIII's reign. They were later assisted by judicious marriages to heiresses, notably Rachel daughter of the Earl of Southampton. Although her husband was executed after being implicated in the Rye House Plot of 1683 her fortune including the Bloomsbury estate, passed to their son who became the 2nd duke.

The 4th duke was the outstanding statesman of the politically distinguished family. He commissioned Henry Flitcroft to build the Palladian west wing which presents its confident facade to the park, and to design the wing's interiors. After 1786 the 6th duke commissioned Henry Holland to rebuild the south and east wings (the latter was part of the 1950 demolition). Holland also designed the Chinese Dairy that is shown as a Chinese Temple in Humphry Repton's 'Red Book' for the park that he laid out for the 6th duke. Holland's riding school and tennis court were demolished; his conservatory was transformed by the 6th duke and Jeffry Wyatville into a scuplture gallery.

Woburn contains one of England's foremost picture collections. They present an education to both scholar and less expert enthusiasts. The state dining room is devoted to Van Dyck, another to Reynolds and the smaller dining room to twenty-two Canalettos all commissioned by the 4th duke. Other highlights are works by Velasquez, Lorrain and Cuyp. Flitcroft's long gallery contains George Gower's celebrated Armada Portrait of Queen Elizabeth I. Holland's library contains superb volumes on natural history and horticulture that reflect successive Russells pioneering interest in gardening and farming. The English and French furniture and works of art provide an intriguing insight into the connoisseurship and changing taste of different generations.

DORNEY COURT, *Windsor.*

Mr and Mrs Peregrine Palmer.
Tel: 0628 604638.

In Dorney, 2 m west of Eton and Windsor on B3026.
Open: Easter week-end, Sun and Bank Hols in May, Sun, Mon, Tues June to end-Sept, 2-5.3- (last admission 5).
£3.50, children £1.75, concessions.
Home-made teas.

The 20th century has often conspired against England's country houses, not least those close to London. Dorney Court is a short distance from sprawling Slough and tourist-ridden Windsor and within earshot of the M4 and Heathrow flight-paths. All this can be forgotten as one approaches to a memorable first view; a symphony of patterned rose brick, leaded windows barge-boarded gables and towering chimneys, all rising above clipped yew hedges.

It is as authentically mediaeval as it looks and, as such, a rarity. In 1924 Country Life called it 'one of the finest Tudor manor houses in England.' But the house was substantially built before Henry Tudor ascended the throne and it is the craftsmanship of transition from basic mediaeval to more decorative Tudor that is most fascinating, both inside and out.

In 1537 the wealthy grocer Sir William Gerrard (or Garrard) who was Lord Mayor of London bought the Dorney Court estate and established 450 years of unbroken continuity. His daughter married Sir James Palmer from Kent and they inherited Dorney. From 1620 the succession has been unbroken from father to son. 17th-century Palmers were distinguished royalists; Sir James was knighted by his friend Charles I and his son was Charles II's cupbearer. More personal service was provided by Sir Roger Palmer whose wife Barbara was the king's mistress and eventually Duchess of Cleveland. Sir Roger was a skilful ambassador for the king and made Earl of Castlemaine, but more probably in recognition of his wife's contribution than his diplomatic prowess.

This period is wonderfully evoked in the great hall where, above the linenfold panelling, Tudor, Stuart and 18th-century portraits line the walls. Over the fireplace are Sir Roger and Barbara by Lely and the other portraits include works by Johnson and Kneller. A shrewd looking Sir James, an outstanding miniaturist, his likeness complete with earring, looks down from the gallery at one end where there are also a rare group of seven eminent Turks presented to Lord Castlemaine when he was in the Levant. Across the hall the irregular octagonal parlour has a low timbered ceiling and a striking carved chimneypiece. The Chinese lacquered bureau is one of the most interesting pieces of furniture in the house.

Above the parlour the great chamber is now the principle bedroom. This and the other oak panelled bedrooms continue the same mood as the main rooms downstairs. The exception is the dining room, decorated in William and Mary style with a patterned plaster ceiling and painted and gilded panels. On the stairs hangs one of the heroes of the British Raj, Field Marshal Sir Donald Stewart, the first man into Delhi after the Mutiny and eventually commander-in-chief in India.

The brick-towered church is adjacent, as one might expect of a mediaeval manor and contains an amazing Gerrard tomb dated 1620. The gardens around the house add greatly to the overall picture and recall Dorney's most distinguished horticultural incumbant, John Rose, the Palmer's gardener who grew the first pineapple in England and was immortalised in the painting by Danckerts, presenting it to Charles II who made him gardener at St James's Palace.

HIGHCLERE CASTLE, *Newbury*.

The Earl of Carnarvon.
Tel: 0635 253210.

4 m south of Newbury on A34.
Open: July, Aug, Sept, Wed to Sun inc, Bank Hols Sun and Mon 2-5.
£5, children £2.50, concessions.
Tea room.

Highclere is a vast and impressive 19th-century nobleman's house designed by Charles Barry, standing on the crest of a superb Capability Brown park. The castle, which stands at the centre of one of the country's great sporting estates, is the finest neo-Elizabethan house in England and a worthy precursor to Barry's Houses of Parliament.

The elaborate interior is a mixture of Baronial, Gothic, Italianate and Rococo revival of considerable opulence and character. A good collection of European furniture and mostly English paintings reflect a long family history at Highclere dating from the 17th century. The most unusual contents - and most celebrated - are the remaining part of the Egyptian collection of the fifth earl, of Tutankhamun fame. These were dramatically rediscovered in 1987 by his grandson the present earl and are shown in an imaginative pictorial reconstruction of the earl's patronage of Howard Carter's excavations.

STRATFIELD SAYE HOUSE, *Reading.*

The Duke of Wellington.
Tel: 0256 882882.

1 m west of A33, between Reading and Basingstoke.
Open: May to end-Sept, daily except Fri, 11.30-4.
Price available on request.
Restaurant.

The nation proferred £600,000 to the victor of Waterloo to purchase a suitable country house and estate. The Duke of Wellington settled on Stratfield Saye because of its surroundings and the warmth of the house. A plan by Benjamin Wyatt for a grandiose Waterloo Palace shows what might have been. Instead the duke remained at Stratfield Saye, adorning the house with trophies from his campaigns, and stampingeach room with his personality. The long facade with embracing wings is immediately welcoming and remains faithful to its original date of 1630 when commissioned by Sir William Pitt, James I's Comptroller.

In all the rooms the Duke of Wellington's additions account for Stratfield Saye's memorable atmosphere. He himself planned the water-closets and central heating system which were pioneering luxuries during the early-19th century. The library bookcases were filled with his own leather-bound volumes of history and many others that came from Napoleon's library.

Indeed the presence of the duke's great rival and his family are ever-present, from the tricolour banners in the hall, to the busts along the gallery and the important collection of Dutch and Flemish paintings in the drawing room. They were part of the baggage captured from Joseph Bonaparte after his defeat by Wellington at Vitoria in 1813, which the French general had himself acquired from the Spanish royal collection. On discovering their identity Wellington immediately offered them back to King Ferdinand VII of Spain, to which the king graciously replied; 'His Majesty, touched by your delicacy, does not wish to deprive you of that which has come into your possession by means as just as they are honourable.' The greater part of the collection is at Apsley House and was presented with the house to the nation by the 7th duke in 1947.

The duke so enjoyed the effect of the gallery, lined with prints, that he created a print room of his own next door and decorated other rooms in a similar manner. The music room is dedicated to the memory of Wellington's charger at Waterloo, Copenhagen (who is buried in the grounds). Amongst all the trophies and memories of the duke's military glories, and the impressive family portraits, Stratfield Saye never loses the sense of being the duke's home. Nothing confirms this more than the charming picture of him by Robert Thorburn in the last year of his life with his grandchildren.

CHENIES MANOR HOUSE, *Chenies.*

Lieut Colonel and Mrs Macleod Matthews.
Tel: 0494 762888.

In Chenies off A404, junc 18 M25.
Open: April to end-Oct Bank Hol Mon, Wed, Thur 2-5.
£3.50, children £1.75. Gardens only half-price.
Home-made teas.

The village of Chenies has well resisted the urban and motorway encroachment around it, the tranquil manor house tells of past grandeur and adoption by the present owners to being a characterful family home. John Russell, who became 1st Earl of Bedford and founded the distinguished dynasty, acquired the manor by marriage and expanded it to suit his position of importance within Henry VIII's court and to entertain his monarch. Elizabeth I was staying here while signing papers regulating the imprisonment of Mary Queen of Scots and both monarchs held privy councils in the house.

Building on the existing manor Russell's house extended to two courtyards, the inner of which enclosed the present buildings and others that were reduced c.1750 to a garden wall. What remains today is the 15th-century gatehouse that he altered and the 'new wing' that he added to provide extra lodgings. The deep-toned brick has an immediately Tudor feel, as do the crow-stepped gables, but the best feature are the superb chimneys whose builders were later taken by Henry VIII to work at Hampton Court; the similarity is clearly evident. A visit by the King to Chenies was one of the occasions of the adultery by his feckless wife, Katherine Howard which led to her execution.

During the civil war a garrison of parliamentary soldiers was kept at Chenies in the upper armoury which is a fine early example of a long gallery, stretching over the lodgings of the new wing. The Russells did not occupy Chenies after 1627 and following deterioration during the occupancy of successive tenants, alterations in the 18th and 19th centuries reduced the house to its present size. The second period of alteration witnessed the remodelling of many rooms, which was the basis for the restoration carried out by the present owners from 1955 when they bought the house. Surviving old details in parts of the lodgings wing, and 16th-century furniture and tapestries successfully perpetuate the Tudor atmosphere while the main dining room and drawing room have a later more airy feel.

During their time at Chenies the Macleod Matthews have developed a widely-admired garden, whose flower borders and the formal sunken garden are perfectly in keeping with the Tudor period of the house. An interesting recent addition is the Chenies hedge maze.

CHICHELEY HALL, *Newport Pagnell.*

Trustees of the Hon Nicholas Beatty.
Tel: 0234 391252.

2 m east of Newport Pagnell on A422, junc 14 M1.
Open: mid-April to end-May and May and Aug, Sun and Bank Hols 2.30-6.
£3, children £1.50.
Tea room.

Photographs do not do justice to Chicheley Hall and it is only when visiting that the Baroque vigour and vertical ingenuity of the house's exterior are fully appreciated, facing the lime avenue that makes for an ideal approach. The brickwork is of a glorious deep hue and the succession of main facades present carefully planned architectural variety.

The house was long attributed to Thomas Archer, its bravado suited his individual style of Baroque. Infact it was designed between 1719-23 (two decades later than originally thought) by Francis Smith of Warwick for Sir John Chester. The move from exterior facades to interior rooms marks an intriguing progression from Baroque to Palladian illustrating what was happening in fashionable circles at the time. Sir John Chester was one of the first patrons of the darling of English Palladianism, William Kent; he and other friends funded Kent's fist visit to Italy, during which the young Kent painted the ceiling of Chicheley's hall, a room designed by another emerging Palladian, Henry Flitcroft. With the elegant staircase beyond, it makes a memorable introduction.

The architectural note continues in the panelled drawing room and through the house the ensemble of rooms are intimate but faultlessly proportioned. Hudson's portrait of Sir John clearly indicates that he was a man of taste, but does not reveal his obvious sense of humour; his upstairs library appears to be another elegant but conventional panelled room until it is discovered that the panels swing open to reveal hidden bookshelves.

Furniture and other contents confirm that Sir John was a discerning collector; good examples are the set of four gilt mirrors in the drawing room. His family continued to own Chicheley leaving his work remarkably untouched until 1952 when the house was bought by the 2nd Earl Beatty, son of the distinguished admiral, who introduced a rich new vein of interest. The house now contains many memories of his naval career, especially in the top floor Beatty museum and in his sitting room, elsewhere are stirring paintings by W.L. Wyllie of Jutland and Beatty's flagship the Lion being towed past the Forth Bridge; The admiral's personality is impressed by portraits by Sargeant and de Lazlo.

Chicheley's gardens retain a rare feature of early 18th century formality in the three-sided canal designed by George London.

NETHER WINCHENDON HOUSE,
Aylesbury.

Trustees of Will Trust of J.G.C. Spencer Bernard.
Tel: 0353 290101.

6 m south-west of Aylesbury, off A418.
Open: May and Aug Bank Hol 2.30-5.30.
£1.75, children £1.25.

Set in peaceful water meadows around the River Thame, Nether Winchendon's first impression is both curious and intriguing. An avenue of Dawn Redwood trees - a first example of the rarities elsewhere in the garden - leads towards an imposing battlemented screen of Gothick arches; beyond is a courtyard enclosed on two sides by the house. The initial impression that the house is 18th-century Gothick, albeit of a charmingly unorthodox style, is correct. It was the work of Sir Scrope Bernard, a clever 18th-century politician who took on the house from his brother Sir Francis, Governor of New Jersey and then of Massachussetts at the outgreak of the War of Independence.

Hints of an older house in the entrance front become strong suspicion at the east end and are confirmed along the south-facing garden front. Scrope's Gothick accounts for the castellated towers, theatrical gable and arched windows, but above are swirling Tudor chimneys pointing to the older building which Bernard extended and remodelled. From the 12th century Nether Winchendon belonged to Notley Abbey, during the latter decades before Henry VIII's dissolution it was let and one tenant, Sir John Daunce, a prominent civil servant during Henry VIII's reign left a strong stamp on the house. He added a parlour, now the drawing room, on the east end and the carving of the freize and ceiling is sophisticated Renaissance work and includes Sir John's portrait in profile. He also brought to the house the rare tapestry in the dining room (formerly the great hall), depicting Henry VIII being confirmed as Defender of the Faith.

In 1559 the house was bought by William Goodwin who was probably responsible for the chimneys and the Elizabethan west wing. Descent went by marriage to the Tyringhams who were in occupation for some two centuries and added the cupola to the heterogeneous skyline and, early in the 18th century passed to Bernard cousins whose family have remained in occupation. Most of the portraits are Bernards and they are responsible for other interesting contents. The dining room contains Romney's portrait of the philanthropist Thomas Bernard, nephew of Sir Scrope, whose wife Harriet commissioned the unusual early Worcester, Barr, Flight and Barr porcelain.

STOWE, *Buckingham.*

House only: Stowe School.
Tel: 0280 813650

4 m north of Buckingham.
Open: July to late-Aug.
£2, children £1.

The pleasure grounds and their buildings at Stowe have been much in the public eye since being given to the National Trust in 1989; so much so that the house has assumed a secondary position. At the same time visitors might suspect that the series of sales from the collections of the dukes of Buckingham, and the occupation of the mansion by Stowe School together mean that there is little to see. They would be wrong to make this assumption. This palace is full of echoes and evidence of its past grandeur. The architecture survives as do the interiors, notably te series of state rooms herladed by Vanbrugh's north hall and Borra's Pantheonic south hall.

An excellent guide book fleshs out the history and gives a good impression of what the roooms would have looked like when fully furnished. The remaining chimney-pieces, full length portraits by Beechey, a pair of Atheniennes, dated c.1780 and attributed to Valdre, scuplture by Veyrier, Banks and Trentanove, together hint at the splendours that have gone.

The grounds are administered by the National Trust who are carrying out an ambitious programme of restoration to the various temples an other buildings by 18th-century architects; Vanbrugh, Kent and Gibbs.

WOTTON HOUSE, *Aylesbury.*

Mrs Patrick Brunner.

In Wotton Underwood, 2 m south of A41 between Aylesbury and Bicester.
Open: Wed in Aug and Sept.
Price available on request.

The fact that a house of Wotton's distinction was within a fortnight of demolition when saved by Mrs Brunner and her husband speaks loudly of the architectural travesties that have plagued the 20th century. Wotton's quality is immediately obvious; its history tells of superior patrons, architects and craftsmen. Grenvilles had lived at Wotton for centuries when Richard Grenville built the house in 1704. There seems little doubt that it was a direct precursor for the original Buckingham House in London, begun a year later: certainly the plans of an imposing central block flanked by pavilions are identical, Wotton's pavilions with lanterns which survive were more attractive.

Grenville married into the midst of political and artistic fashion; his wife was Hester Temple who inherited Stowe in 1749 in the midst of the evolution of this supreme early-Georgian house and landscape. Grenville employed the leading craftsmen of the day, Tijou supplied wrought-ironwork and Sir James Thornhill painted ceilings (destroyed by fire in 1820).

Equally important, the connection with Stowe came at the time when the head-gardener there was a certain Lancelot Brown. Wotton's park is one of his earliest independent commissions, probably carried out between 1742-46 and as such of great historical importance. Careful restoration by the Brunners has revealed the supreme confidence which was to characterize all his later work, as well as a quantity of garden architecture that was fashionable at the time - and in the Stowe style - but which Brown would steadily reduce in most of his later commissions.

As a result of the 1820 fire the Grenville/Temple descendant, the 2nd Marquess of Buckingham introduced Wotton's second phase of architectural distinction, remodelling of the interiors by Sir John Soane in what proved to be one of his last country house commissions. The impressive vertical thrust, characteristic of the house's original Baroque style and enforced by the giant Corinthian pilasters was diminished but by no means destroyed when he remoed the attic floor. Despite changes in the 1920s his arched hall survives leading to the tall oval staircase which reused Tijou's original ironwork in its balustrade. The Brunner's painstaking restoration preserved the characteristically restrained details of Soane's work in the main rooms and their decoration is entirely harmonious with the house's character.

GORHAMBURY, *St Albans.*

The Earl of Verulam.
Tel: 0727 854051.

2 m west of St Albans, off A4147.
Open: May to Sept Thur 2-5.
£3, children £2, concessions.

Proximity to London was an important priority for Tudor courtiers and among the quantity of seats in Essex and Hertfordshire Gorhambury occupied a distinguished place as the home of Sir Nicholas Bacon Lord Keeper of the Great Seal (who Elizabeth I visited and chided 'my lord, what a little house you have gotten!'), and subsequently his more famous son, Sir Francis. During the 17th century Gorhambury passed to the Grimstons, who became baronets, viscounts and, at the beginning of the 19th century, earls.

The ruins of the Bacon home make a picturesque folly in the park, but the present house is radically different, an impressive Palladian villa with broad steps leading up to a monumental portico, the whole building austerely white since refacing with Portland stone during the 1950s. The entrance hall is equally imposing and here one is introduced to Gorhambury's historically important collection of portraits, Bacons and Grimstons, relations and marital connections, alongside monarchs and other leading figures, particularly from the 16th and 17th centuries. Sir Francis is represented as Lord Chancellor by Van Somer, and his nephew Sir Nathaniel, probably the best amateur painter of the 17th century, shows his skill with two large still lives and a rakish self-portrait complete with earring; the Grimstons begin with Edward Grimston dated 1446.

If the 18th century is not so densely illustrated it provides the house's visual highlight in the drawing room, Reynolds' conversation piece of the four children of the 2nd Viscount Grimston (one of whom rebuilt the house), a worthy compliment to the group by Van Dyck in the dining room of the Earl of Northumberland with his wife and daughter. The library is arranged in Sir Francis's 'divisions of knowledge' and the two splendid marble chimneypieces designed by Piranesi and brought in Rome are rare trophies of the rebuilder Grimston's grand tour.

KNEBWORTH HOUSE, *Knebworth.*

The Lord Cobbold.
Tel: 0438 812661.

Off A1M junc 7.
Open: April, May and Sept week-ends, June to end-Aug daily except Mon 12-5.
£4.50, children £4, concessions.

There is more than a hint of imperial fantasy about the glimpse of Knebworth from the passing road that says much about the house's long, eventful and occasionally eccentric history. A medley of towers, turrets, heraldic beasts and battlements dance between trees. They beckon enticingly and confirm on closer inspection that Knebworth is a Victorian revival of Henry VII's period. Not just a revival, however, for Sir Robert Lytton fought at Bosworth with King Henry, became a confidant, bought Knebworth in 1492 and altered the old manor into a square around a courtyard. Externally little changed until the early-19th century when it was Gothicised by the redoubtable Elizabeth Bulwer-Lytton.

Her son Edward Bulwer-Lytton wrote distinguished but now unfashionable historical novels extolling the period when his home was originally built. He set about remodelling it in suitable style with the help of the architect John Crace. Bulwer-Lytton's later political career brought him a peerage which was elevated to an earldom in the next generation when his son was Viceroy of India. The 2nd earl continued the imperial Connection of service in India and these three generations brought to Knebworth a rich and dinstinctly Victorian mixture of the arts, politics and society. Tragically two sons of the 2nd earl died as successive Viscount Knebworths; the eldest in a flying accident in 1933, the younger at El Alemain in 1942 and thus Knebworth passed to their sister Lady Hermione who married the 1st Lord Cobbold, parents of the present owner.

There is important early-classical 17th-century panelling in the banqueting hall. Crace's work is particularly evident in the fantastical state drawing room, while the entrance hall and Bulwer-Lytton's library were among alterations by Edwin Lutyens who married Emily, daughter of the 1st earl. Family portraits span the centuries from Sir Robert the original builder to Lord Cobbold in his garter robes. Bulwer-Lytton was painted in his study by E.M. Ward, in Byronesque pose by Van Holst, and by his friend Daniel Maclise, whose important historical picture 'Edward IV visiting Caxton's Printing Press', hangs in the drawing room.

Distinguished friends and acquaintances also appear; Sir Philip Sydney painted by Jan de Critz; Disraeli hangs in the drawing room; there are quantities of letters from Dickens to his friend Bulwer-Lytton; Churchill's 1930s painting of the banqueting hall survives, as does a slightly earlier humourous sketch by Rex Whistler for remodelling the exterior.

SYON HOUSE, *Brentford.*

The Duke of Northumberland.
Tel: 081 5560 0881/3.

On north bank of River Thames, between Brentford and Isleworth.
Open: April to end-Sept, Wed to Sun inclusive and Bank Hols,
Sun only in Oct; 11-5 (last admission 4.30).
Price available on request.

The square castellated exterior of Syon which remains largely as built by Lord Protector Somerset during the reign of Edward VI gives little hint of the superb suite of interiors created over three hundred years later by Robert Adam for the 1st Duke of Northumberland. The Brentford gate built by Adam announces the Percy seat in emphatic style with the ducal lion on top of the tall arched gateway and his decoration of the interiors is of a grandeur to match.

In 1750 the properties of the 'proud' Duke of Somerset - which inluded all the Percy estates - were divided and Syon, with Alnwick Castle and Northumberland House in London were inherited by the duke's only child, Lady Elizabeth Seymour. She married Sir Hugh Smithson who acknowledged his wife's legacy by assuming the name of Percy. By special remainder he was able to inherit the earldom of Northumberland and in 1766 he was elevated to a dukedom.

Four years earlier he commissioned Adam to work on all three houses: Syon, Alnwich and Northumberland; beginning at Syon. Adam's work was a masterly combination of the atmosphere of a classical villa and elements that hinted at Syon's past and incorporated the social requirements of his patron. The great hall which greets the visitor is one of his most successful and imnpressive essays in Roman classical; beyond the ante room is decorated in richer style and leads to the dining room. The drawing room was for ladies, but mainly an introduction to the gallery beyond which he made out of the old long gallery.

Throughout the rooms the standards of decoration and fittings are unfailingly high. Joseph Rose executed plasterwork and the splendid gilded figures and panels of trophies in the ante room; Francisco Zuccarelli painted the exquisite lunette portraits which line the long gallery between Adam's groups of Corinthian pilasters. Adam himself designed much of the furniture, designed the Roman statues in the hall, ordered the figures and busts in the dining room, and designed the black and white marble floor in the hall whose pattern lines are mirrored in the ceiling. The composition of detail which was his superlative quality when planning interiors is fully revealed. In the drawing room the collection of royal Stuart portraits match the decorative quality and in the rest of the rooms open to the public, not designed by Adam, if the decorative quality is not so prominent the paintings and works of art amply compensate.

ARDINGTON HOUSE, *Wantage.*

Mrs Desmond Baring.
Tel: 0235 833244.

In Ardington off A417, 2 m east of Wantage.
Open: May to Sept Mon and Bank Hols 2.30-4.30.
£2. Home-made tea by arrangement.

John Betjeman was a regular visitor to Ardington and considered the dining room 'the nicest in Oxfordshire'. Certainly its warm panelling and cheerful plaster decoration encourage conviviality but it does not begin to rival the staircase hall which is the Ardington's glorious forte. Its quality was no doubt partly responsible for the rueful comment by a descendant of the house's builder, Edward Clarke that the house had been 'the proximate cause of the ruin of the family.'

Clarke may have over-reached himself but he did so in style. Gervase Jackson-Stops has recently attributed Ardington to one of the Strong family of master-masons who worked, among other places, at Blenheim and Greenwich. Ardington was built in 1719-20 and is both ambitious and assured; the main south and north facing facades were precisely symmetrical and identical and the detail of the three different shades of brickwork speak of superior craftsmanship.

If the main facades are indentical the staircase hall provides their link, stretching from one side of the house to the other. The 'imperial' staircase rises in two flights to a half-landing and returns via a central 'flying' flight to the first floor. The twisted oak balusters continue the vein of craftsmanship; for the staircase enthusiast it is heady stuff, hardly less impressive to the ordinary visitor.

Despite Edward's extravagance the family stayed on at Ardington until 1831 when it was sold to Robert Vernon whose collection of pictures now hang in the Tate and National Galleries. After a period as a subsidiary house of the Lockinge estate in 1939 it was rented by Mr and Mrs Baring. They bought the house in 1960 and since then have carried out discerning restoration such as removing stone-rendering applied by Vernon which detracted from the brick-work. Barings now look down on the elegantly furnished rooms, including Batoni's portrait of John Baring whose son Francis established the bank, while Lance's painting of Ardington in 1845 provides a happy link with the past - showing the house to be unchanged since then.

BLENHEIM PALACE, *Woodstock.*

The Duke of Marlborough.
Tel: 0993 811325.

In Woodstock on A44.
Open: mid-March to end-Oct daily 10.30-5.30 (last admission 4.45).
£6.50. Restaurant/Tea room.

Blenheim is England's most monumental palace, and one can only understand its scale by knowing the unique set of circumstances that produced it. Marlborough's victories needed to be celebrated. At the time his wilful wife Sarah was at the height of her influence over Queen Anne whose favourite she had long been. When the decision had been made to present the victorious duke with a royal estate where the nation would build him a suitable seat, Vanbrugh was chosen as architect, rather than the more senior Wren.

While the construction of Vanbrugh's exteriors are consummate Baroque architecture Blenheim was always going to be 'first a monument and only second a house.' Originally it ws surrounded by formal gardens but 'Capability' Brown's park which was laid out later is more suitable landscape and the lake that he created by damming the River Glyme achieved lofty fusion between palace, Vanbrugh's bridge, and landscape.

Vanbrugh's heroic scale extended into the entrance hall which is so large that it not really a room in the conventional sense. From here the decorative variety and quality continue majestically. Alterations have been made, in particular by the 9th duke, but they make no appreciable impression on the original effect. Marble doorcases surmounted by the Marlborough arms as Prince of the Holy Roman Empire are more to be expected in some great German or Austrian Baroque palace. There are tapestries illustrating Marlborough's campaigns and ceilings depicting him kneeling to Britannia.

Blenheim was sumptuous when Duchess Sarah eventually died in 1744 after a lifetime of quarrelling - Vanbrugh was eventually banned from Blenheim following their running battles - but future generations of Marlboroughs appear to have lived easily within the vast portals and made important additions. Much came to Blenheim from the Sunderland inheritance, although the famous Sunderland library was sold in the 1880s, and the house has assumed an additional mantle to the 1st duke's as the birthplace of an even more revered Englishman, Winston Churchill. Amidst all the splendour it is difficult to imagine Blenheim as occupied by any one family, but two superb groups from different periods, Reynolds's of the 4th duke and family and Sargents' of the 9th duke and family face each other across the red drawing room and seem to convey the ducal inheritance from generation to generation.

BROUGHTON CASTLE, *Banbury.*

Lord Saye and Sele.
Tel: 0295 262624.

2 m south-west of Banbury on B4035.
Open: mid-May to mid-Sept Wed, Sun also Thur in July and Aug and Bank Hol Sun and Mon, 2-5.
£3.20, children £1.50, concessions.
Tea room.

Broughton's placid stone facades reflected on all sides by its broad moat are a memorial to the mediaeval and Tudor status of its owners but conceal conflict and violence. The 1st Lord Saye and Sele was dragged from the Tower of London by Jack Cade's revolting mob and beheaded by them in 1451. His son died fighting for Edward IV at the battle of Barnet. A century and a half later the 8th baron gathered at Broughton those leaders opposed to Charles I's determination to rule without parliament to discuss opposition to the king, although he deplored the later execution. Thereafter family history was quieter, Broughton abandoned for long periods for a more fashionable home in Kent. The extravagence of the Regency 15th baron dissipated the family fortunes and at the same time allowed their home to slumber on without damaging alteration.

The original moated house was built around 1300, a century later, when Broughton was owned by the great William of Wykeham, the license to crenellate produced extensions and the gatehouse through which one still approaches Broughton having crossed the bridge over the moat. The 2nd Lord Saye and Sele married Margaret Wykeham in 1451 and thus Broughton passed to the family who have lived there ever since. The mediaeval house was incorporated into the present Tudor building, completed in 1554 by the 6th lord whose son was responsible for much of the interior work.

The chapel, the vaulted undercroft now the dining room and the groined passage with a similar vaulted ceiling are mediaeval. The more extensive Tudor rooms are invitingly domestic if expansive. As was usual, the great hall was made out of the old mediaeval hall, although its Gothick ceiling is one of the few 18th-century features in the house and may easily have been the work of the gentleman-architect who was a near neighbour. At the same time the long gallery was also Gothicised and today the predominance of Tudor and Stuart family portraits along its spacious length retain the feel of its original period.

The most important Tudor features inside Broughton are chimney-pieces and overmantels, in particular the stone columned chimney-piece in the bedroom slept in by Queen Anne in 1604 and the stucco overmantel in the King's Chamber where James I slept on the same occasion. The overmantel is unique in England and contemporary work of the most comparable style is at Fontainbleau in France. An interior porch dates from the Restoration of Charles II, celebrated with vigour by Lord Saye and Sele during the last two yeas of his life, to atone for his earlier parliamentary loyalty. No doubt the same sentiments inspired him to purchase the fine seascape by Peeters set in a panel over the fireplace, showing Charles II setting sail for England from Scheveningen.

KINGSTON BAGPUIZE HOUSE,
Abingdon.

Lady Tweedsmuir.
Tel: 0865 820259.

5 m west of Abingdon off A415 and A420.
Open: April to end-Sept Sun and Bank Hols 2.30-5.30.
£2.50, children £1.50, concession.
Teas.

Although its architect is not known Kingston House is confidently dated 1670; while there is not firm reason to dispute this it makes the house precociously advanced in style and the more intriguing for having been built for modest squires, the Latton family. Today from the passing road its tall symmetry and warm balance of brick with stone quoining and window dressing is immediately impressive. It must have been more so when one approached along a formal avenue to gates and a paved forecourt; today the drive leads through the park at an angle to a front door on the side.

Many of the architectural features are unusual for the period, but the overall effect presents a house far more imposing than its size would suggest. Inside the same feeling of transition from a Restoration house towards more spacious William and Mary and 18th-century style is equally strong; the rooms are a symmetrical progression focusing on the grand saloon that was the entrance hall, the interior's best feature, the cantilevered staircase, is beyond and other main rooms on either side.

Lady Tweedsmuir inherited Kingston from her aunt Miss Marlie Raphael who had bought it in 1939. There is a delightful portrait of Miss Raphael as a child in the dining room, her main contribution at Kingston was the garden where a fine raised terrace walk is surviving evidence of the Tudor house that was replaced. At one end of the terrace a gazebo is built over a Tudor cockpit and beyond the terrace is Miss Raphael's woodland garden.

STANTON HARCOURT MANOR,
Stanton Harcourt.

Mr Crispin and the Hon Mrs Gascoine.
Tel: 0865 881928.

9 m west of Oxford, on B4449.
Open: Selected days April to end-Sept, 2-6.
£3, children £2.
Teas on Sun and Bank Hols.

Harcourts trace their lineage back a thousand years to Normandy and they have been at Stanton Harcourt since the end of the 12th century. Such ancient families who later prospered - as did the Harcourts - often forsook their old mediaeval manorial homes, which may possibly have been enlarged during Tudor times, for a grand new seat elsewhere in their estates, only to return this century to more manageable and domestic circumstances.

Stanton Harcourt dates from 1380. Some of the original parts survive as rare mediaeval buildings and the house expanded through the next two centuries, at its peak enclosing an inner and outer courtyard. After 1688 the family departed. Simon Harcourt became the most distinguished lawyer of Queen Anne's reign, was Lord Chancellor and was made a viscount. He was described by one contemporary as 'a second Cicero'. He built a new house at nearby Cokethorpe. It was his grandson the 1st earl, however, who established the family in even greater style at Palladian Newnham whose foundations were built with stone from the now ruinous Stanton Harcourt and which became a renowned 18th-century seat especially admired for its park and gardens developed by the 2nd earl.

Nuneham remained the family seat until the mid-20th century but after wartime requisition the last Viscount Harcourt (Mrs Gascoine's father) decided to return to Stanton Harcourt, restoring the parts that remain today and creating the romantic gardens around the old buildings and mediaeval moat, ponds and stews.

The main house is the 1540 gatehouse extended by Lord Harcourt but historically the most important part is the detached great kitchen, a square building with an octagonal timbered roof shaped like a cone to collect smoke which was released by opening wooden louvres. There is no other surviving kitchen like it in England. Also detached from the main house is Pope's Tower which was the chapel of the mediaeval manor, but derives its name from occupation by the distinguished poet in 1717-18, when it was semi-ruined but habitable. Pope completed the translation of some of Homer's Iliad during his stay and his message on a pane of glass survives 'In the year 1718 I

Alexander Pope finished here the fifth volume of Homer.'

Nuneham may have gone but the paintings and works of art that graced its rooms are now at Stanton Harcourt and views by Sandby confirm the house's graceful situation. If the portraits of the Lord Chancellor and his ambassador grandson, as well as other distinguised Harcourts hang in less spacious surroundings than originally envisaged for them, they are no less suitable and combine with 18th-century furniture in particular to perpetuate the family's distinguished patronage.

STONOR PARK, *Henley-on-Thames.*

Lord and Lady Camoys.
Tel: 0491 638587.

5 m north of Henley on B480.
Open: April Sun and Bank Hol only, May, June and Sept Wed, Sun and Bank Hols, July Wed, Thur, Sun, Aug Wed, Thur, Sat, Sun and Bank Hol, 2-5.30 (Bank Hols 12.30-5.30).
£3.50, children free.

Hidden halfway up one of the most stunning valleys in the Chilterns, Stonor has been the home of the Stonor family for more than eight centuries. As befits its age and distinguished length of unbroken occupation, it evolved like so many English country houses, from the mediaeval hall to the Elizabethan 'E'-shaped house. Its present mellow facades, surrounded by deer park with noble trees perpetuate an atmosphere of antiquity.

During the 18th century decorations such as glazing-bars for the windows were added and interiors remodelled, many with a Gothick flavour. Stonor is the classic recusant house with its chapel, strong Catholic traditions and memories of Edmund Campion, who was hidden here and kept a clandestine printing press. During the 20th century the addition of Francis Stonor's collection of Italian Baroque paintings, drawings and works of art greatly enriched the more traditional country house furniture and family portraits. The deeply embedded Catholicism notwithstanding, the collection has brought a very Roman and slightly exotic feeling to the house.

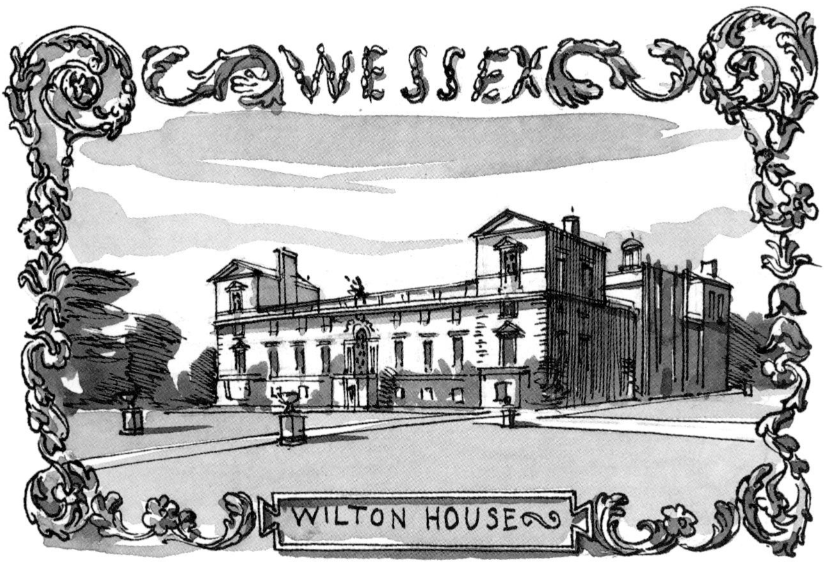
WESSEX
WILTON HOUSE

GODOLPHIN HOUSE, *Breage.*

Mrs S.E. Schofield.
Tel: 0736 762409

5 m north-west of Helston.
Open: Thur in May and June, Tues and Thur in July, Aug, Sept and Bank Hols, 2-5 (10-5 Thur in Aug).
£3, children £1.

Even in days of lengthy travel Godolphin was too remote to be the main seat of great men and tucked below wooded Godolphin Hill it perpetuates an atmosphere of rarely disturbed slumber. The Godolphins prosperity was built on tin mining and at the end of the 17th century a family meteor appeared in the form of Sidney, 1st Earl of Godolphin who served Charles II, James II, and William III before becoming Anne's Lord High Treasurer and the most important man in England, His son married the 1st Duke of Marlborough's daughter who became duchess in her own right, but their only son died childless and Godolphin passed to the Dukes of Leeds who added the name to their own but never occupied the house.

Much was demolished at the beginning of the 19th century, the rest became a farm and was sold in 1921. The future looked bleak when in 1937, Mrs Schofield's husband bought the property and carried out commendable restoration. Godolphin as originally built was most interesting for its use of local granite and other materials and Mr Schofield followed this example in every aspect of his work. The main front is as welcoming as unusual, very long and low its 17th-century colonnade with pillars of local granite stretches between identical 15th-century towers. The Schofields also hunted down a number of the most interesting original contents, pride of place going to Wootton's painting of the Godolphin Arab, one of three 18th-century stallions from which all British racehorses descend. Charles II is reputed to have slept in the king's room when as Prince of Wales he was escaping to the Scilly Isles.

PENCARROW, *Bodmin.*

Molesworth-St Aubyn Family.
Tel: 020 884 369.

4 m north-west of Bodmin off A389 and B3266.
Open: Easter to mid-Oct daily except Fri and Sat 1.30-5.30.
£3, children £1.50, concessions.
Home-made teas, light lunches.

Pencarrow's ochre-stuccoed Palladianism is a cheerful contrast to the granite houses and windswept landscape of Bodmin Moor. Only one side facing a courtyard and roofed with grey Delabole slate confirms that the mid-18th century house was built around an older one. If the house is mainly 18th-century its surroundings are a fine example of Cornish Victorian planting which has been steadily renewed and extended by successive generations, not least the present occupant Sir Arscott.

Financial stewardship of the Duchy of Cornwall during Elizabeth I's reign founded the Molesworth fortunes which prospered through the 17th and 18th centuries. Sir John Molesworth, 4th Bt began remodelling the house, the work was finished by his son. Pencarrow was one of the few houses by the architect Robert Allanson, who died aged only thirty-eight. The rooms retain high quality Georgian interiors: elegant marble chimney-pieces and doors surmounted by broken pediments. The oustanding decorative feature is the rococo stucco ceiling in the music room depicting the Four Seasons. Such details and the hall where marble pillars support a vaulted ceiling with a cantilevered stone staircase beyond, confirm Allanson's talent in the best 18th-century tradition.

During the 1830s Sir William Molesworth made the entrance hall into a library with bookcases below panels carrying a series of family portraits and panelled the music room where the major addition was the early-Georgian carved wood alcove that he inserted to contain an Italian marble figure of the Borghese Venus. Sir Williams' additions give the house greater depth of interest.

The Molesworths - and, from 1839 Molesworth-St Aubyns - have been discerning commissioners and collectors as the portraits and other works of art at Pencarrow confirm. The dining room portraits are - except for one by his 'master' Hudson - exclusively by Reynolds and demonstrate how a privileged selection of Cornish houses benefitted from his being a 'local' artist. The most delightful 18th-century family picture , however, is the Arthur Devis conversation piece of the Four Misses St Aubyn in the ante room.

The Pencarrow bowl, containing a Chinese artist's impression of the house, is the charming highlight of a good collection of Oriental porcelain and the furniture throughout - English, French and Italian - is of equal quality.

PRIDEAUX PLACE, *Padstow.*

The Prideaux-Brune Family.
Tel: 0841 532411.

On edge of Padstow, 7 m from Wadebridge.
Open: Easter Sun for two weeks then Spring Bank Hol to end-Sept Sun to Thur 1.30-5.
£3.50, accompanied children (14 and under) £1, group rates.
Tea room.

Prideaux's first impression is almost military; battlemented terrace walls with toy-fort like little towers flanking steps up to the long front of the house whose age is not immedately obvious. The visitor is left guessing throughout most of their tour and none would predict the variety that appears. For Prideaux is an originally Tudor house altered during the 18th century, given Strawberry Hill Gothick additions during the early-19th and full of other unexpected treats. Its immaculate appearance is thanks to dedicated restoration carried out since 1988 by the present owners and still continuing.

Shrewd Tudor Prideauxs did well out of the Dissolution, gained the property which had belonged to the Priory of Bodmin and in 1592 Nicholas Prideaux had completed his 'new house', built on the Elizabethan E-plan with gables and castellated bays. New, but not the first, during the restoration work a few years ago a slate panel of the original 13th-century building was revealed. Sir Nicholas's portrait hangs over the fireplace in the dining room where part of the dark panelling is his work, but his most sensational interior was the great chamber with its richly-worked ceiling depicting the story of Susannah and the Elders, concealed by an 18th-century ceiling inserted below until a few years ago when it was opened up and restored.

His house was altered by Edmund Prideaux after his Grand Tour in 1739, who removed the gables from the entrance front and inserted the Georgian sash windows. His most dramatic additions, however, and the house's most surprising contents, were from the nearby house of Stow, Restoration home of the Grenville family, earls of Bath, demolished only a generation after it was built. The panelled Grenville room contains carving by Gibbons sumptuously regilded during recent restoration, three inset paintings by Verrio and the earl's vast wine cooler. The shallow rising cantilevered staircase also came from Stow. In 1799 the Rev Charles Prideaux married a Brune heiress and celebrated the match by adding the Gothick wing and rooms which complete the house's development. The Gothick exteriors face south and inside the cleric's tour-de-force was the library where Gothick furniture compliments the lofty arched window with heraldic glass and the ribbed ceiling.

Charles Prideaux-Brune also commissioned one of the most interesting groups among the house's fine paintings, all by the Cornish artist John Opie who was born and brought up on the estate and was paid 20 guineas and a suit for five pictures. These hang in the morning room with the most romantic of the family portraits - both in looks and story. It is Humphrey Prideaux painted on his Grand tour by Rosalba Carriera who became so enamoured with her sitter that she slid a love letter into the portrait's frame; sadly it lay undiscovered for over two hundred years. The Grenville room contains an important collection of royalist Caroline portraits and generations of the family hang in the hall. Among a host of fine works of art one of the most intriguing is an astrological clock made in 1800 by a Padstow craftsman, which shows the position of the stars and other details all in relation to Padstow.

Impressive evidence of the on-going work can be found at Prideaux inside and out. Alec Cobbe is redecorating the drawing room with a series of panels containing Cornish scenes; the Gothick dairy is undergoing complete restoration and Edmund Prideaux's 18th-century garden, with an Ionic temple built with stone from Ralph Allen's quarries at Bath, is being extensively restored.

TREWITHEN, *Grampound Road.*

Mr and Mrs Michael Galsworthy.
Tel: 0726 882763.

On A390 between Probus and Grampound.
Open: Mon and Tues April to July and Bank Hol Mon 2-4.30.
£2.80.
Tea room.

Visitors approach Trewithen through undulating parkland containing venerable holm oaks and arrive at the forecourt enclosed by the house's trim north facade and flanking cupola-topped stable blocks. It is a welcoming arrival, but the house's tour de force lies on the other, south-facing side. Tree felling in the protective beech wood by governemnt order during World War One inspired George Johnstone to open up a broad 200-yard lawn stretching away from the house; today to look back to the pink-tinted stone facade, the view flanked by towering tree magnolias, banks of rhododendrons - many raised by Johnstone - and other woodland plants is one the most memorable house and garden vistas in England.

The present Trewithen was built by Philip Hawkins shortly after he purchased the estate in 1715. His ancestor John had left the family's native Kent as a recusant Catholic during the troubled reign of Mary Tudor and sought peace in distant Cornwall. By the early 18th-century the family were prosperously established in Cornwall and Philip employed the London architect Thomas Edwards who designed the neat Palladian house that survives hardly altered today. After his death in 1738 Philip's work was continued by his nephew Thomas Hawkins who had married a sophisticated London heiress Anne Heywood; they employed Sir Robert Taylor who designed the saloon, now the dining room, with fine rococo plasterwork and imposing colonnaded arcades with vaulted alcoves at both ends. Anne's indulgent father regularly produced presents for the new house, their correspondence mentions a set of six Chippendale dining chairs still in the house.

The other main rooms are warmly panelled and retain furniture and pictures from Thomas and Anne Hawkins' time as well as additions by later generations. The last Hawkins was always called C.H.T., whose father John, a distinguished horticulturalist and Fellow of the Royal Society, planted the Holm oak acorns from his Sussex estate Bignor Park. C.H.T.'s sister married a Johnstone and the family descent continued to George Johnstone, grandfather of the present owner. Among the Hawkins portraits there are others to tell of these family Connections; Raffles - including Sir Stamford - ancestors of George Johnstone's wife whose connexion also brought the Reynolds portraits of Zachariah Mudge and his wife (whose son Thomas became the famous clockmaker).

In 1991 Patsy and Janet Swanborough completed a delightful bird's-eye view of Trewithen showing the house in its garden setting, the combination which quite rightly draws most visitors. Despite being paralysed from the waist down following a hunting accident in 1932 George Johnstone continued to expand the garden. One of his rhododendrons was named after his wife, Alison, and a further, quite famous cultivar was produced under the name of 'Trewithen Orange'. An equally well known variety of camellia was named Glenn's Orbit by his widow, Alison, in 1962 because it was forwarded for its Award of Merit on the day that the American astronaut completed his space orbit of earth. First his daughter Elizabeth and subsequently his grandson Michael Galsworthy have maintained and built on the his garden.

BICKLEIGH CASTLE, *Tiverton.*

Mr O.N. Boxall.
Tel: 0884 855 363.

4 m south of Tiverton A396, off A3072.
Open: Easter week, then Wed, Sun, Bank Hols in May then daily except Sat to end-Oct 2-5.30.
£3.20, children £1.60.
Tea room.

Bickleigh Castle's thatched Norman chapel is probably the oldest complete building in the county, its main body dating from 1100. It survives from the period when the castle was orginally built, in a then strategic and now picturesque position on the wooded slopes of the River Exe. From 1410 it belonged to the Courtenays of Powderham who rebuilt the castle as a fortified manor, but of their home only the gatehouse survived from the Civil War when General Fairfax 'sleighted' the castle, demolishing the two main wings. By this time Bickleigh had passed by marriage to the Carew family; Thomas Carew eloped with Anne Courtenay but was forgiven after brave service at Flodden and other battles and Bickleigh was Anne's dowry when they married.

After Fairfax's devastation Sir Henry Carew restored the gatehouse and built the thatched farmhouse which became the main dwelling. But after his death with no heirs in 1681 the place fell into disrepair until this century when successive owners have carried out restoration, and this work has beencarrie on by the present owners since purchasing the property in 1970. The arrangement of the buildings: chapel gatehouse, farmhouse, cottages and barns makes a harmonious vernacular group and the old moat is the focus of the garden.

The gatehouse retains its vaulted entry with armoury and guard room on the ground floor and great hall stretching over both on the first floor. The armour has a suitable feel as does the Tudor furniture in the guard room, all added by the present owners. The most prized survivor from the Civil War is a carved stone overmantel in the farmhouse's garden room. The dining room contains samplers collected by Mrs Boxall and the watercolours, plaster reliefs and charcoal studies in the farmhouse were done by her mother and sisters. The thatched barn contains an enjoyable museum and exhibition of the Mary Rose, Henry VIII's ill-fated warship of which Sir George Carew was vice-admiral, and a later collection of World War II spy and escape gadgets.

CADHAY, *Ottery St Mary.*

Lady William-Powlett.
Tel: 0404 812432.

1 m north-west of Ottery St Mary on B3176.
Open: Spring and August Bank Hols Sun and Mon and Tues, Wed, Thur in July and Aug, 2-6 (last admission 5.30).
£2.50, children £1.

Following the lime avenue that leads to Cadhay one gets an impression of approaching an undiscovered house, a feeling that strengthens as the warm stone gables first appear. Undiscovered and long-established; John Haydon's 'fair new house', built between 1546 and 1550, infact extended an existing house incorporating a mediaeval great hall dating from 1470 or earlier. Sometime after 1587 (when he married Joan Poulett) John's great-nephew Robert filled in the empty south side to link the house around its central courtyard, and made the long gallery on the first floor of the new wing.

The timber roof of the great hall survives in one upstairs room but the courtyard plan is certainly later, confirmed by the sophisticated pattern of flint and sandstone on the internal walls of the courtyard. It is called the court of the Sovereigns because of its stone figures of Henry VIII, Edward VI, Mary Tudor and Elizabeth positioned at first-floor level over doorways. Dating from 1617 (carved beneath Elizabeth with Robert Haydon's initials) and set in niches flanked by classical columns and other decoration, they would appear to be a local craftsman's Renaissance flourish.

After two centuries of occupation the Haydons sold Cadhay in 1736 and thereafter it belonged to a number of owners. In 1910 it was bought by W.C. Dampler Whetham (who became Sir William Dampier) and he carried out extensive and careful restoration. The house's plan makes for an easy progression of rooms around the courtyard; the dining room to one side of the entrance hall leads to an adjoining trio of sitting room, living hall and drawing room along one side and above eac corner of the house contains a main bedroom. Some of Cadhay's most interesting paintings are the fine portraits of Lady William Powlett and her husband and daughter, by the little-known Australian artist M. Cohen.

FURSDON, *Thorverton.*

E.D. Fursdon Esq.
Tel: 0392 860860.

9 m north of Exeter, off A3072.
Open: Easter Mon to end-Sept, Thur and Bank Hols only 2-4.30.
£2.75.
Home-made teas.

For some seven centuries generations of Fursdons have occupied the area by continuous male succession, but not always on the well-chosen site of the present house, perched overlooking its terrace garden which projects the view south over the undulating, wooded valley below. The house was built during the 18th century retaining the shell of an older building and around 1815 the present appearance was completed with the addition of the library wing and central colonnade which both links the two slightly projecting wings and adds an agreeable note of decoration to the unpretentious entrance facade.

Although, like the exterior, Fursdon's interiors are principally 18th-century in appearance, evidence of the older house has appeared on a number of occasions. In the drawing room on one side of the entrance hall the field panelling with a frieze and Corinthian columns is c.1732, but two archways in the oak screen in the dining room were recently discovered to be early-Tudor doorways, probably leading into the original house's great hall. The dining room has pale panelling and an atmosphere that has changed little; which indeed it has not done in much of the house. A watercolour of the interior dated 1860 shows a sofa table in the library in the same position as today and the Lely portrait of Fursdon's most formidable chateline, Grace Fursdon, hanging over the same doorway. While she stirred strong likes and dislikes, her grand-daughter, another Grace, drove a rejected lover to fire a pistol at her own portrait which hangs nearby; the shot-hole is still visible in the back of the canvas.

An adventurous recent addition - part of admirable rejuvenation through much of the house - is the fine Axminster carpet, specially woven and incorporating the Fursdon crest of five feathers into its pattern. The distinctive crest also adorns a George III gilt mirror in the hall. But the most delightful exhibit in the house, ideally displayed in rooms of intimate size, is the costume collection. Among 18th-century pieces are a rare mantua or court-dress, worn once in 1753 by Elizabeth Fursdon and a tiny pair of child's shoes dated 1772, that belonged to George Fursdon aged one.

HARTLAND ABBEY, *Bideford.*

Sir Hugh Stucley, Bt.
Tel: 02374 41264.

At Hartland Point, 15 m west of Bideford, 5 m from A39.
Open: May to end-Sept Wed, Sun in July and Aug and Sept,
Bank Hol Sun and Mon Easter to Aug, 2-5.30.
£3, children £1.50, concessions.

Hartland Abbey is reputed to have been the last in England to fall during Henry VIII's dissolution, no doubt because of its remote, secluded position in a narrow wooded valley that runs inland from the dramatic Atlantic coastline at Hartland Point. The superb setting survives and the abbey has become one of the county's most atmospheric houses.

As one approaches Hartland the tower of St Nectan's Church stands loftily on the seaward hill beyond, a reminder of the original reason for the abbey's foundation in 1160. Part of the old building is incorporated into the present house, the remodelling beginning in 1704, an unusually long time after the dissolution, when an heiress of the Luttrell family who had been in occupation for a century, married Paul Orchard. Their work is commemorated in a stone in the south wall inscribed 'P.O. & M 1705'. More extensive work was carried out by their son, also Paul, who removed the abbey's great hall and chapel, rebuilt in the Gothick style and finished in 1779.

The outside is Orchard work, the inside substantially Stucley, carried out by Sir George Stucley (his great-grandmother was an Orchard). The drawing room linenfold panelling was copied from the House of Lords and an Exeter artist painted a series of panels showing Stucleys in heroic role at successive mediaeval events. Sir George employed Sir G.G. Scott and the most dramatic addition was the Alhambra corridor which he carried out in 1862 after Sir George had visited and been inspired by the Moorish original in Granada.

Good family portraits include works by Reynolds, Hudson, Northcote and Beechey all of whom were West Country artists by origin. Hudson (Reynolds' tutor) lived in Bideford and the house contains his fine full-length of Catherine, Lady Bampfylde. She was an ancestor of the Hon Lady Stucley, daughter of Lord Poltimore. The impressive 1835 group of six coach horses by Davis in the inner hall belonged to the Lord Poltimore of the day.

An exhibition of documents dates from the founding of the abbey and includes the seals of most English kings and queens since the early-13th century. The sporting parson Jack Russell's hunting equipment hangs on one wall and a photograph of Emperor Haile Salasse opening Hartland fete in 1938 adds an exotic note.

HEMERDON HOUSE, *Plymouth.*

J.H.G. Woollcombe Esq.
Tel: 0752 223816/337350.

2 m from Plympton, 5 m from Plymouth north of A38.
Open: Selected days in May and Aug 2-5.30.
£2.

The austerity of Hemerdon's neatly rendered Georgian exterior is quickly dispelled as one enters the hall where family history combine with welcoming rooms and interesting works of art. To the plan of main rooms: hall, library, drawing room and dining room which is contemporary with the house's construction, subsequent generations have added an overlay of character so that the library has a mellow Victorian air and throughout, the house is a family home - as it always has been.

Woollcombes have given fine service on many occasions. In the hall is a perfectly-crafted model of HMS Victor commanded by George Woollcombe 1824-27; also in the hall the highlight of a collection of swords is the one belonging to Lieutenant William Woollcombe of the Light Infantry, which he used at Waterloo. The upstairs landing is dominated by the powerful Victorian portrait by J.C. Horsley of Thomas Woollcombe, a moving figure in the extension of the Great Western Railway to nearby Plymouth and beyond. An unexpected discovery is the version of Reynolds' portrait of the Earl of Bath. But without doubt Hemerdon's outstanding painting, purchased in 1828, is the large Northcote in the drawing room of The Worthies of Devon, a distinguished group all originating from the county comprising Reynolds, John Gay, Lord Ashburton, George Monk, the Duke of Albemarle, Drake, Raleigh, Marlborough, Sir Richard Grenville and John Mudge.

The antiquarian enthusiasm of one member of the family is hinted at by Hamilton Smith's watercolour of the Landing of the Black Prince with Prisoners including the King of France, 5.5.1359 which also hangs in the drawing room but more immediately at home are the charming Devon landscapes executed during the 1820s and 1820s by William Bath, which compliment the four watercolours of Dartmoor by C.H. Smith in the first-floor passage. In a house where interior decorative features were used sparingly the handsome double arch in the hall is especially effective, as are the large Regency bookcases in the library which also contains good Chinese porcelain.

POWDERHAM CASTLE, *Kenton.*

Lord and Lady Courtenay.
Tel: 0626 890243.

In Kenton, 8 m south of Exeter off A379.
Open: Easter to Oct daily (ex Sat) 10-6.
£3.95, children £2.95, concessions.

Few families are more suited to live in a castle than the Devon Courtenays; described in Burke's Peerage as 'one of the most illustrous races among the nobility.' During the Middle Ages they married into both French and English royal families, and the English family descends from a Courtenay who accompanied Eleanor of Aquitaine for her marriage to Henry II. During the crusades they provided three emperors of Constantinople. The earldom of Devon was conferred in 1293, although between 1556 and 1831 it fell into abeyance.

Today the skyline of turrets and battlements evoke memories of Sir Philip Courtenay (knighted by the Black Prince after Poitiers), who built the original castle between 1390-1420. But almost all exterior and interior are later. Damage suffered during the Civil War forced the family to depart until 1740 when they returned after renovation by Sir William Courtenay. His son was created Viscount Courtenay and he ushered in the century which witnessed Powderham's elevation to a house of wide-ranging artistic quality.

Portraits by Thomas Hudson hang in many houses in the county, but few rival his work at Powderham; especially the group of the 1st viscount and his wife and children. Hudson's group was emulated for the next generation by Maatthew Peters who painted the 2nd viscount with his wife and twelve children - eleven girls and one boy. Two more girls were subsequently added.

The son who inherited as 3rd viscount and revived the Devon earldom was the family's most flamboyant character. As a young man he became embroiled in a scandal with William Beckford, later in life debts and his reputation forced him to leave England for America and Paris where he died in 1835.

The grand staircase hall was made in 1750 and rises through two storeys with memorable rococo plasterwork. The sombre dining hall was added in 1837 and subsequently decorated with panels of arms tracing the long family history; the 3rd viscount's music room designed by James Wyatt. It still has its organ at one end, the 3rd viscount himself painted the circular wall panels and his portrait - one of a number by Richard Cosway, better known as a miniaturist, hangs over the fireplace. The pink drawing room added during the 1760s exemplifies the 18th-century grace successfully married to Powderham's ancient, warring origins. Its bow windows look out across the deer park to the River Exe, a vew enjoyed by Courtenays for six hundred years.

S A N D, *Sidbury*.

Lieut Colonel P.V. Huyshe.
Tel: 0395 597230.

1 m north-east of Sidbury off A375.
Open: Bank Hol Sun and Mon in April, May and Aug and last week-end in July, 2-5.30 (last entry 4.45).
£2.50, children/students 50p, concessions.
Tea room.

Sand is an ideal example of a largely Tudor house so expertly restored during the early-20th century that this later work is difficult for the casual observer to detect. It is the more enjoyable in that the Huyshe family rebuilt Sand during the 1590s shortly after they acquired the property in 1560 and have retained ownership ever since. Between 1908-09 Rowlnd Huyshe, assisted by the architect E.H. Harbottle, carried out the restoration, which included rebuilding a wing demolished early in the 19th century, thereby restoring the house's satisfying harmony.

Rowland's work is part of the stone entrance front that greets visitors but the effect is pure Tudor; the cross-gabled wings embrace the central portion with mullioned and transomed windows for the hall and the two-storey gabled porch set to one side. Small gables over the upper windows stick up from the parapet in front of the roof. Tudor details continue inside; the newel stair, doorways and chimneypieces but most decorative is stained glass in the hall which includes a panel of a crowned pomegranate, possibly the badge of Philip II of Spain.

Close to the present house is the old hall house that was superceded, which retains its fine timber roof and in the gardens is a rare 1600 thatched summer-house with Tuscan columns, which carries the arms of Rowland and Anne Huyshe, who built the house, and a part-Greek part-Latin which, translated is admirably pious; 'the fountain of true fragrance is to be in fellowship with God.'

TAPELEY PARK, *Bideford.*

Hector Christie.
Tel: 0271 860528.

Off A39 between Barnstaple and Bideford.
Open: Easter to end-Sept, daily except Sat (open Bank Hol Sat), 10-6.
Admission: £3.50, £2.
Restaurant/Tea room.

The house stands proudly above the Torridge estuary looking across to Bideford. The drive leads dramatically up from the water's edge. Passing a blasted obelisk, you ascent to an elevated plateau with spectacular views out to sea. The plain 18th-century house of the Cleveland family was imaginatively reclad by John Belcher at the turn of the century. Inside his work is even more apparent. He remodelled the interior for Lady Rosamund Christie, whose husband inherited the house through his mother. It is her collection that gives the interior its distinctive character. She had a passion for grand 18th-century furniture and late 19th-century works of art. Here are to be discovered marvellous pieces of French and Italian 18th-century furniture nestling beside particularly fine inlaid cabinets from the Morris workshop at Merton. Late 19th-century paintings by Leighton and Richmond hang near good 18th-century family portraits. Bronzes by Leighton amd marlbes by Gibson and Benzoni give the interiors an aesthetic period flavour enhanced by he sumptuous collection of Pate sur Pate Minton china arranged in the hall.

Outside the Italian gardens are early-20th century. In front of the main house, beyond the gaggle of geese, are regular displays of jousting. As the delightfully idiosyncratic guide book hints, this a house well worth crossing North Devon to see.

TIVERTON CASTLE, *Tiverton.*

Mr and Mrs A.K. Gordon.
Tel: 0884 253200.

In Tiverton.
Open: Good Fri to end-Sept, Sun to Thur 2.30-5.30.
£2,75, children free/£1.75.
Tea room.

In one corner of the main courtyard of Tiverton Castle an unmistakeably Norman tower stands as testament to the place's ancient history stretching back to the reign of Henry I. On his orders Richard de Redvers built a castle to command the strategic crossing-point of the River Exe and Redfers remained until 1262 when Tiverton and its lands passed to their kinsmen, the Courtenays. Much of the castle was built by Hugh de Courtenay around the turn of the 14th century, during the Wars of the Roses its fortune followed the ups and downs of the its owners until Sir Edward Courtenay wasreinstated in the family honours by Henry VII. His son William married Katherine, daughter of Edward IV and, in her own description, 'daughter, sister and aunt of kings.' The connection was too close to her nephew Henry VIII and their son, who had been made Marquess of Exeter, was beheaded in 1539. Katherine had died in 1527; her funeral was probably the most sumptous event in the town's history.

Alterations were made during Elizabeth I's reign by the Giffard family who were still in occupation during the Civil War when the castle was destroyed by Fairfax and his Parliamentary army. Ruined sections, the old tower and 14th-century Courtenay gatehouse survived but the main house today was built during the late-17th century by a wealthy Tiverton merchant.

The present owner inherited from his uncle, Ivar Campbell who had bought Tiverton in 1960, restored many of the buildings and decorated and furnished the interiors. Their collection of paintings, furniture and clocks remain and their work on the castle has been continued by the Gordons. Suitably there is a collection of Civil War armour; few other places offer holiday accomodation in surroundings with such an ancient history.

UGBROOKE HOUSE, *Chudleigh.*

Lord Cifford of Chudleigh.
Tel: 0626 852179.

In Chudleigh.
Open: mid-July to early-Sept, Sun, Tues, Wed and Thur, 2.
£3.80, children £1.90, concessions.
Tea room.

Ugbrooke is a four-square castellated 18th-century house, mostly designed by Robert Adam but altered later. It has been the seat of the Lord Clifford of Chudleigh since the first of their title, Charles II's great minister Clifford of the Cabal.

Set in beautiful rolling Devon countryside, the house's exterior is impressively simple, a contrast to the pretty suite of Adam rooms and a rich marble Catholic chapel. The 1st Lord Clifford's Dutch paintings (of which he was a pioneering collector) are on view along with his portrait, one of Sir Peter Lely's masterpieces, and a great many other portraits of the family and their various relations. Francis Towne was a drawing master here and there are unusually intersting watercolours and pastels.

Capability Brown gave Ugbrooke a suitable parkland setting, with lakes and majestic trees. Around the castle terraced gardens make the most of views out to Dartmoor.

ATHELHAMPTON HOUSE, *Puddletown.*

Patrick Cooke.
Tel: 0305 848363.

1 m east of Puddletown on A35.
Open: Easter to end-Oct Wed, Thur, Sun and Bank Hols,
Tues from May to Sept and Mon and Fri in July and Aug, 12-5.
£4.20, children £1.70.

It was one the great country house escapes of recent years that Athelhampton was not destroyed by a potentially disastrous fire in 1992; it says much for the determination of the owners that the house re-opened to the public the following season. The fire was the latest in a series of challenges that have faced the ancient manor and make its survival the more to be enjoyed; especially by the enthusaist for mediaeval and early-Tudor architecture which make up the two wings enclosing the forecourt described by Robin Feddon as 'one of the most picturesque sights of Dorset.'

The central battlemented part of the entrance facade was built by Sir William Martyn to reflect his position as Lord Mayor of London. His oriel bay with three-tier windows is superbly delicate. The other wing is early-Tudor where Ham stone window mullions shine out from the grey walls and the height of gables topped by heraldic beasts are theatrically Renaissance in style. The most important room of Martyn's wing is the hall with its unique timbered roof.

19th-century decay was followed by restoration, first after 1848 but later and more substantially from 1891, by Alfred Cart de Lafontaine. His work was typical of the high standard displayed by Edwardian enthusiasts for the Mediaeval and Tudor and linenfold panelling ws introduced to many of the many rooms including the hall and King's room. Perhaps Lafontaine's most telling addition was to commission F. Inigo Jones to lay out the gardens whose water features, clipped yew and stone architecture perfectly compliment the house.

Lafontaine's work lasted half-a-century but when Robert Cooke bought Athelhampton in 1957 decay had once again set in. He, followed by his son, the MP Sir Robin and since his death his widow Lady du Cann and her son Patrick Cooke, have once again rejuvenated the old manor. In the process new touches were added; Robin Cooke's expert knowledge of the Palace of Westminster accounted for wallpaper whose pattern reproduced that designed by Pugin for the House of Lords. The most notable additions to the house have been the furniture while the gardens have been both restored and extended. The restoration works following the fire were completed in February 1994 and the house will be fully re-opened for the 1994 season.

ILSINGTON MANOR, *Puddletown.*

Mr and Mrs P. Duff.
Tel: 0305 848454.

In Puddletown 4 m from Dorchester on A35.
Open: May to end-Sept Wed, Thur, Sun and Bank Hols 2-6.
£3.
Lunch and tea by prior arrangement.

Ilsington Manor was built by the splendidly named Theophilus, 7t Earl of Huntingdon in 1690; its symmetrical facade in pure William and Mary style hides an intriguing past and evidence of rejuvenation since being bought by Mr and Mrs Duff in 1977. The house passed to the Walpole family when the Prime Minister's son (who succeeded his father as Earl of Orford) married Huntingdon's granddaughter Margaret and the Orfords retained ownership until 1862. For most of this period the house was let, between 1780 and 1830 to General Garth equerry to George III, as the king paid annual visits to Weymouth. Garth added marble chimneypieces and the plasterwork in the upstairs long library, but his period of occupation also produced a long-suppressed scandal. George III's Daughter, Sophia, gave birth to a child at Gloucester Lodge, Weymouth in complete secrecy. General Garth formally adopted the boy and brought him up at Ilsington as his son. Sophia died unmarried but the boy grew up to be troublesome and attempted to blackmail the royal family.

The story adds a enjoyable element to the house and gardens which the Duffs have extensively restored. The important entrance hall that Huntingdon modelled exactly on the one at Kensington Palace is one of their main successes with the original oak panelling being uncovered, while the house's most impressive room is the upstairs long library, whose balcony overlooks the garden. As well as their restoration the Duffs have brought to Ilsington a collection of paintings, scuplture and ceramics of considerable distinction; as well as many modern works the 'ruralist' and Pre-Raphaelite schools are well represented.

PARNHAM HOUSE, *Beaminster.*

Mr and Mrs John Makepeace.
Tel: 0308 862204.

On A3066 1 m south of Beaminster.
Open: April to end-Oct Wed, Sun and Bank Hols 10-5.
£4, children £2/free.
Restaurant.

As with many country houses, Parnham's history is one of centuries-long ownership by one family, followed by a rapid succession of owners through the 20th century. Happily in 1976 stability was brought by John Makepeace who established his distinguished furniture design-and-making workshop at the house, its craftsmanship well suited to the architectural setting.

From all sides, whether across the entrance forecourt or from the gardens where balustrading and yew topiary extend the house's gabled and battlemented architecture, Parnham presents an immensely satisfying combination of mellow Ham stone arched mullioned windows and turreted gables.

The house was extended from a mediaeval building in two stages during the 16th century and retains a strongly Tudor appearance and character, not least because the subsequent period of major alteration was the early-19th century when John Nash remodelled the garden facades, added the theatrical element of pinnacles and battlements to the original gables and designed a Gothick dining room inside. In 1896 the house was sold for the first time in its history; early in the 20th century Dr Han Sauer, advised by Colonel Lindsay who helped the Duke of Rutland restore Haddon Hall in Derbyshire, consciously evoked the house's mediaeval and Tudor origins, bringing in fine panelling and Renaissance plasterwork, and making the architectural additions to the garden that blend so well with the house.

During the Second World War the American generals Patton and Eisenhower planned the D-Day invasions in the same hall where three hundred years earlier the unfortunate royalist Lady Strode was summarily beheaded by a violently Cromwellian relation. All such violent scenes are now remote from the atmosphere that the Makepeaces have successfully created. While the contemporary furniture and college have given Parnham its reputation the combination of house and garden alone is of considerable merit.

PURSE CAUNDLE MANOR, *Sherborne.*

Mr and Mrs Michael de Pelet.
Tel: 0963 250400.

In Purse Caundle, 4 m east of Sherborne off A30.
Open: Easter Mon, May to Sept Thur, Sun and Bank Hols 2-5.
£2, children free.

Dorset is richly endowed with gabled village manor houses, but few rival Purse Caundle which has all the essentialy manorial elements: mediaeval origins; an initial impression of architectural modesty disguises one or two expansive flourishes; variety in interior scale and atmosphere; and retained connexions with the village surrounding it. The latter could hardly be more emphasised, Purse Caundle village hall is a ground floor room. The manor also gives one of its best features, a delicate oriel window dating from 1480 with Gothic carving on its stone exterior to the gable end overlooking the passing village lane.

On most sides the arrangement of gables seems irregular and only from the garden is an impression of symmetry given by the long Tudor wing with a deliberate E-shape of three gables. The irregularity confirms that the house evolved from the initial mid-15th century building put up by the Long family through a series of Tudor additions by their cousins the Hanhams. Admirable but expensive Royalist support during the Civil War impoverished the Hanhams, the manor was originaly sold to a cousin and then, in 1648, away from the family to John Hoskins. Mr and Mrs de Pelet bought the manor in 1984, becoming the sixth owners since 1900, some of whom had carried out important and often urgent restoration; in 1959 a large section of the roof collapsed and had to be rebuilt.

The house's centrepiece is the 15th-century great hall, its timber roof original except for Tudor tiebeams. It is unusually light for such a room, thanks to a tall five-bay mullioned window inserted by Lady Victoria Herbert during the 1920s. Above a panelled screen at one end is a balustraded minstrels' gallery, at the other the contrastingly intimate parlour has 17th-century panelling decorated with Corinthian pilasters. Upstairs the rooms boast a total of seven barrel ceilings, all inserted by the Hanhams during the late-16th century the most splendid of which is in the great chamber which has the oriel window at one end. Lady Victoria Herbert decorated the great chamber with its Wiliam Morris wallpaper, but otherwise the manor is greatly enhanced by the de Pelet's decoration, pictures and furniture and, not least, the atmosphere of an established family home.

SHERBORNE CASTLE, *Sherborne.*

Simon Wingfield Digby.
Tel: 0935 813182.

1 m south of Sherborne and 5 m east of Yeovil off A30.
Open: Easter Sat to end-Sept, Thur, Sat, Sun and Bank Hols 2-5.30.
Price available on request.
Tea room.

Sherborne Castle faces its ruined Norman predecessor across the lake of its expansive park, laid out by Capability Brown, which belies the proximity of the eponymous town. Sir Walter Raleigh acquired Sherborne at the height of his popularity with Elizabeth I and transformed a hunting lodge into an impressive Elizabethan house. After his disgrace it was granted by James I to John Digby who became Earl of Bristol. That title died out but the Digbys have remained. The name became Digby Wingfield and subsequently Wingfield Digby after the marriage in 1796 of Lady Charlotte Digby and William Wingfield.

Inside and out Sherborne bears witness to successive generations. Raleigh's Elizabethan house was extended by Lord Bristol with four wings ending in towers and the interiors combine remaining features of their work such as decorative ceilings and doorways, with later Georgian and - more particularly - Victorian alterations. The decorative riches are more than matched by the array of paintings, furniture and works of art. The Strawberry Hill Gothic survives intact while the Victorian alterations echo the earlier Elizabethan and Jacobean styles. Digby portraits through more than two centuries include many distinguished works by artists including Cornelius Johnson, Van Dyck and Lely, Reynolds, Gainsborough anda Batoni, Landseer and Sir Francis Grant. The range of English furniture is equally impressive; the French furniture is one of Sherborne's many rewarding surprises as are the outstanding collections of Kakiemon Japanese porcelain, Japanese lacquer and English, Chinese and Continental porcelain.

Although the old terraced gardens that Raleigh would have known were swept away by Capability Brown the visitor can still enjoy 'Raleigh's Seat' where he sat smoking his pipe until a servant - to whom the habit was unknown - threw a bucket of water over his master whom he feared was on fire.

WOLVETON HOUSE, *Dorchester.*

Capt N.T.L. Thimbleby.
Tel: 0305 263500.

1 m west of Dorchester on A37.
Open: May to Sept Tues, Thur and Bank Hol Mon 2-6.
Price available on request.

Approaching Wolveton to be confronted by the formidable gatehouse the visitor could be forgiven uncertainty about what to expect. Thomas Trenchard's house built at the turn of the 16th century - of which the gatehouse is the major surviving part - became a grand twin-courtyard Tudor house at the hands of his grandson George. Towards the end of the 18th century, however, the family had effectively deserted Wolveton for another home and thereafter the great majority was neglected, partly ruined and contents and fittings removed. Only in the time of Captain Thimbleby has restoration made the best of the many outstanding features that somehow survive.

In 1506 came Wolveton's most illustrous visitors, Archduke Philip of Austria and his Spanish wife Joanna daughter of Ferdinand and Isabella. En route from the Netherlands to claim the throne of Castile a storm inconveniently forced them into Weymouth harbour and they accepted Trenchard's hospitality before travelling to Windsor to visit her sister Catherine of Aragon who was waiting to marry the future King Henry VIII. The gatehouse's defensive purpose is recalled in the guardroom on one side, on the other is the chapel replacing the free-standing chapel that formed one side of George Trenchard's main courtyard.

The south front of the house that overlooks the garden is principally Elizabethan but the stair turret at one end is part of Sir Thomas's house. The north front has been considerably altered at diferent times and the porch is Victorian. Inside the great hall has lost all its original decoration and the outstanding Elizabethan rooms are the dining room and parlour, both with plaster ceilings. The former has a plaster overmantel while the parlour has a notable carved oak overmantel and doorcase which extends to the ceiling.

A stone groin vaulted passage contains carving of unusual quality and the monumental stone staircase with a pierced balustrade of open arches is both impressive and rare. The classical stone doorcase at the top of the stairs confirms the refinement of detail as well as a distinctly Renaissance style and leads into the great chamber which retains its fine carved fireplace the height of the room. It is an enjoyable idea that among the carved figures the Red Indians may have been described by Sir Walter Raleigh who often visited Wolveton. The garden retains a Tudor bowling green and the Norman church to which Sir Thomas added the west tower is worth a visit.

AVINGTON PARK, *Winchester.*

Mr and Mrs J.B. Hickson.
Tel: 0962 779260.

4 m north-east of Winchester off B3047.
Open: May to Sept Sun and Bank Hols 2.30-5.30.
£2.50.

Avington's handsome entrance facade, its monumental white Doric portico recessed between rich brick wings and flamboyantly surmonted by lead statues of Minerva, Juno and Ceres, as well as its lavishly decorated state rooms survive as evidence of the house's rollicking Restoration and indulgent 18th-century past. They are maintained by the dedicated enthusiasm of the Hicksons who have owned the house for some forty years, and are happily preserved despite the house being divided into eight units.

George Brydges was Charles II's groom of the bedchamber and rebuilt Avington to accomodate Charles on his frequent visits to Winchester; the cathedral prebendar refused to allow the king's mistress to stay in the hallowed close and Charles later referred to him as 'the ugly little man who would not give poor Nelly [Gwynne] lodgings.' Brydges' rebuilding was greatly assisted by the fortunes of his wife the notorious Anna-Maria Countess of Shrewsbury who attended a duel between her first husband Shrewsbury and her lover the Duke of Buckingham disguised as a page, when her husband was killed.

Brydges died in the lake at Avington trying to save his pet dog. He was succeeded by his son who in turn was succeeded by his cousin, James Brydges, Marquess of Caernarvon who became 3rd Duke of Chandos and a man of legendary wealth and extravagance. His wife built the wonderful church at Avington completed in 1771 which retains its Georgian box-pews and other furnishings. Her husband's improvements were more lavish. The main staircase was inserted with an inlaid handrail and lead balusters carved in Grecian honeysuckle and the main rooms were given their outstanding painted decoration. The most sumptuous room is the ballroom or great saloon with its lofty painted and gilded ceiling over a deep gilded frieze.

Chandos was succeeded by his only child Lady Anne whose husband Richard Earl Temple of Stowe became 2nd Marquess of Buckingham and was created Duke of Buckingham and Chandos by his friend George IV who stayed at Avington with Mrs Fitzherbert. The Chandos-Buckingham era ended in 1848 when the family's hereditary extravagance became ruinous and the estates were sold. Avington was bought by Sir John Shelly, brother of the poet and the family retained ownership until 1952 when Avington's contents were sold and the estate dismembered, when the Hicksons bought the house and grounds.

BREAMORE HOUSE, *Fordingbridge.*

Sir Westrow Hulse, Bt.
Tel: 0725 512468.

3 m north of Fordingbridge off A338.
Open: Easter, Tues, Wed, Sun in April, daily except Mon and Fri May, June, July and Sept, daily in Aug 2-5.30.
£4, children £2.50, concessions.
Home-made teas.

Breamore's imposing position on the western slopes of the Avon valley, with protective woodlands rising behind leads one to expect a house from the 18th century when the marriage of architecture and landscape was such a priority. Instead the visitor looks up to the austere gabled front of an Elizabethan house, the deep-red brick decorated with stone quoining but devoid of anything more fanciful; it is the carefuly arranged symmetry of gables and mullioned and transomed windows which creats the desired effect.

The house was built by William Dodington, whose duties as Elizabeth I's chancellor were obviously too onerous; he threw himself off the tower of St Sepulchre's Holborn in 1600. The house passed by marriage to the Grevilles and then, in 1748, was bought by Sir Edward Hulse 1st Bt. His father was physician to William III and son outdid father by holding the same office for the three subsequent monarchs. A fire in 1856 destroyed the Tudor interiors - only fireplaces and overmantels survived. The plaster ceilings are 19th century and the panelling was also put in.

Fortunately most of the contents were saved; benefitting from a series of judicious marriages to heiresses, the Hulse's built up exceptional collections which survive in the house today. There is a rich variety of furniture, including high-backed Charles II dining chairs, a set of Queen Anne chairs made with American walnut and a number of Dutch marquetry pieces. The pictures are the primary feature, however. The great hall, the largest and most impressive room contains a representative selection including the children of Charles I by Van Dyck, a full length by Cornelius Johnson of Sir Norton Knatchbull, the Holy Family by Benvenuto Tisio and an important Teniers, 'The Coming of the Storm'. The Teniers is one of number of Dutch paintings in the house collected by virtue of the family's Dutch origins and the marrige of the 2nd baronet to a Dutch wife; there are others in the dining room including four large still lives by Peter Andreas Rysbrach.

The two drawing rooms are 18th-century in style, both have gilt Chippendale overmantel mirrors. The portraits are of Hulses and their connexions by marriage. Francis Cotes painted the two Sir Edward Hulses, 1st and 2nd baronets in oils, and pastels of the 1st baronet and his family which hang in a bedroom. George II gave the portrait of his father in garter robes by Kneller to the 1st baronet in gratitude for his service as physician. Sir Samuel Hulse was ADC to the Prince Regent and became Field Marshal; Beech's portrait of the Regent hangs in the west drawing room and Sir Samuel acquired the set of Napoleonic battle scenes by Napoleon's travelling artist Beaufort and the sensitive head of the Duke of Wellington by J. Lucas. Hudson painted Sir Samuel and his brother Edward as children but in the same room is many visitors' favourite picture at Breamore, known as the Boy with the Bat. One of the earliest and finest portraits of a cricketer it came to the Hulses with Catherine Hamilton who married the 5th baronet.

The first Edward Hulse married Dorothy Westrow and this connexion brought Braemore's most unusual contents. Her uncle Admiral Hulse was one of Charles I's sailors who harried the Spanish galleons. Among his plunder was the set of fourteen paintings by an illegitimate son of Murillo called 'The Races of Mexico' destined for Philip IV of Spain but seized by Westrow en route. He also produced the rare Mexican fan which, with the English pile carpet dating from 1614 that hangs on the stairs, is one of a number of rare specialities that Breamore produces. Further variety is provided by the unusually evocative museum of rural life and old agricultural machinery and implements which is being expanded and provides a fascinating insight into long-gone ways of life.

PALACE HOUSE, *Beaulieu.*

The Lord Montagu of Beaulieu.
Tel: 0590 612345.

In Beaulieu, 7 m south-east of Lyndhurst, 14 m south of Southampton.
Open: Easter to end-Sept daily 10-6, Oct to Easter daily 10-5.
Price available on request.

Beaulieu is famous for its motor museum and Lord Montagu has been in the vanguard of country-house opening since 1952. Palace House is an interesting candidate for the success story that followed for it is not a stately home of great rank, filled with fabulous collections, but an idyllically positioned place of mediaeval monastic origins that evolved gently into a family home and whose contents illustrate that family's often distinguished history.

The Cistercian abbey was founded by King John in an uncharacteristically fulsome gesture; surrounded by spreading estates it flourished until the Dissolution following which it was bought by Henry VIII's future Lord Chancellor, Thomas Wriothesley, Earl of Southampton. The last Southampton daughter married Ralph 1st Duke of Montagu and thence Beaulieu passed with the glittering Montagu possessions to the Dukes of Buccleuch, the 5th of whom gave Beaulieu to his second son, Lord Henry Scott, as a wedding present. The fortunate son was subsequently created Lord Montagu of Beaulieu.

He employed the architect Arthur Blomfield to remodel and extend the abbey Great Gatehouse into a home. It had in fact been extended earlier and the tall twin gables facing the river are Elizabethan. Blomfield's work expanded the house's friendly rambling appearance while preserving the most interesting of its surviving monastic features; the old gateway and the 14th-century vaulting in the inner hall. Portraits begin with Chancellor Wriothesley and include the Montagu dukes as well as the Marquess of Monthermer whose early death ended the male Montagu line, but who brought to Beaulieu the Italian views by Antonio Joli which are the house's outstanding paintings.

The present Lord Montagu's father was painted in uniform reflecting the position he held of Inspector of Mechanised Transport to the Government of India during the First World War - an early indication of his son's enthusiasm to found the now renowned National Motor Museum in his father's memory. The series is brought up to date by a John Ward conversation piece of the present Lord Montagu and his family in the snow outside the house.

ROTHERFIELD PARK, *Alton.*

Sir James and Lady Scott.
Tel: 042 058 207.

On A32 at East Tisted, 4 m south of Alton.
Open: usually selected weeks in June, July and Aug.
£2.50, children free.

The Scott family could be considered fortunate to have purchased Rotherfield shortly after the turn of the 19th century. In 1801 the Marquess of Winchester was accompanying his recently acquired bride to the house when their coach stuck in the mud on the steep hill up from the main road. The enraged bride told him that he could 'sell dirty Rotherfield' because she would never live there and a few years later he dutifully did so - to James Scott.

The slope may make for troublesome approach but its elevated position greatly enhances Rotherfield's imposing nature and presents a series of impressive outward views focusing on the parish church. Scott's family business was brick-making and building so not surprisingly he set to work on his newly acquired home. With the help of the architect Joseph Parkinson he transformed it into a picturesque Gothick mansion. The cupola-topped turrets that enliven the skyline were added in the 1880s.

Inside the ambitious scale of Scott's work is most emphatic in the towering hall with its grand staircase. The decoration of the hall and other main rooms open to visitors - the drawing rooms and dining room - dates largely from the 1880s, the time of Arthur Scott and his wife Lady Mary, a granddaughter of the 1st Duke of Wellington, whose bust surveys the hall from the stair half-landing. Also in the hall are an attractive pair of watercolours by Lionel Edwards of the Scott boys in Plashwood during the 1930s and other family portraits hang in the dining room. The ensemble of good furniture, porcelain, and startling hunting trophies in the hall has remained largely unchanged since the 19th century and adds to the house's feeling of inviting family establishment.

The 1987 hurricane wrought havoc in the park and woods so carefully planted by James Scott as part of his picturesque essay at Rotherfield but considerable restoration and replanting has been carried out and the gardens continue to be an enjoyable feature for visitors.

STANSTED PARK, *Rowlands Castle.*

Stansted Park Foundation.
Tel: 0705 412265.

East of Rowlands Castle, off B2148.
Open: Easter and Sun, Mon, Tues May to end-Sept 2-5.30.
£3.50, children £1.50.
Tea room.

In 1924 the present Lord Bessborough's father bought Stansted Park which had been rebuilt in 1903 after a fire in 1900. The rebuilding, carried out for the Wilder family by Sir Arthur Blomfield, carefully preserved the Georgian character and appearance of the house which had been built by James Wyatt, with assistance from Joseph Bonomi, for an Indian nabob Richard Barwell. For the approaching visitor the house's red-brick with stone dressing, the low roof disguised behind a stone balustrade with a central pediment above the one-storey blustraded portico, could be unchanged Georgian and is given considerable stature by the view across the expansive cricket ground immediately in front.

Stansted was an ideal house to display the family's important collection of pictures which were saved from the fire at their family home in Ireland. In the staircase hall hang Dutch bird pictures and beyond, the main hall contains portraits among which the most interesting are by Angelica Kauffmann of the two Spencer sisters, Henrietta Frances who married the 3rd Earl of Bessborough and Georgiana who married the Duke of Devonshire. Henrietta, with her two small sons is the subject of possibly the house's most delightful portrait and arguably Hoppner's best work, which hangs in the dining room. A collection of late-19th and early-20th century portraits dominated by the full length by Philpot of Leolia Ponsonby who became Duchess of Westminster and the more arresting Birley of Roberte, the French mother of the present Lord Bessborough and her three children give this room an evocative period atmosphere.

Roberte Bessborough's French influence is most striking in the blue drawing room, decorated for her by Goodhart-Rendel who also redecorated the chapel in the style of the Sainte Chapelle in Paris. In the drawing room French silk covers the walls between blue and gilded woodwork and there is outstanding French furniture. The pictures are a variety and include Van Loo's portrait of the Marquis de Brienne, a stormy seascape by Claude Vernet and four fine landscapes by Dirk Dalens. The porcelain in this room and the dining room originates from the collection of Lady Charlotte Schreiber whose first husband Sir John Guest was South Wales's largest iron-making magnate. Their daughter married the 8th Lord Bessborough. Many other works of art contribute to the house's perpetuated air of classical Edwardian grandeur.

NUNWELL HOUSE, *Brading.*

Colonel and Mrs J.A. Aylmer.
Tel: 0983 407240.

1 m from Brading, off A3055, 3 m south of Ryde.
Open: July to end-Sept Sun to Thur 10-4.
£2.30, accompanied children 60p, concessions.

Sir John Oglander, the engaging Carolean diarist whose family accompanied the Conqueror and were established at Nunwell from the 12th century until 1982, wrote to his son, 'Fear God as we did; marry a wife thou can'st love; keep out of debt; see thy grounds well-stocked; and thou mayest live as happily at Nunwell as any Prince in the World.' Sir John was proud of his home where in 1647 he entertained his beloved Charles I the night before the king's imprisonment at Carisbrooke Castle and subsequent execution. Its original shape and one wing remains with enjoyable Queen Anne and Georgian additions.

His west wing lies on one side of the central block which was given a Queen Anne front with a handsome rusticated stone arched doorway, faced in mathematical tiles - an early example of their use. The other side was given altogether grander treatment during the 1760s and its symmetrical facade with a central bow overlooks the garden. The addition of the dining room in 1896 and the music room in 1906 have done nothing to upset the harmony of the house, greatly enhanced by its gardens and splendid views across the Solent.

Although the Oglander family sold Nunwell in 1982 their connexion is still evident as some of the house's contents remained to be mixed with those of Colonel Aylmer's family and that of his wife Shaunagh. Together they make for an enjoyable ensemble. Victorian Oglander portraits hang in the dining room along with John Aylmer driving his coach and four in 1821 and portraits of Colonel Aylmer and his son. There is Venetian furniture and glass in the panelled morning room that was Sir John Oglander's library. The drawing room in the centre of the Georgian wing benefits from the handsome bow and contains a fine Thomas Allen seascape of the English fleet leaving Harwich to collect George III's Queen Charlotte and French faience plaques from Castletown near the Guinness home in County Kildare. The library is the most impressively decorated room with with a typically mid-18th century plaster decoration to the ceiling and fireplace, and good mahogany bookcases of the period.

In the older part of the house a Jacobean oak-panelled staircase leads up to the bedrom where Charles I slept, and elsewhere the Aylmer family's distinguished record of military service is illustrated in a series of exhibitions while the home guard museum recalls the importance of this body for the small island which would have been in the front line of any threatened German invasion.

THE BISHOP'S PALACE, *Wells.*

The Church Commissioners.
Tel: 0749 678691.

In Wells at end of Market Place.
Open: Easter to end of Oct, Tues, Thur, Sun and Bank Hols, daily in Aug, 2-6.
£2.00, children free, concessions.
Restaurant.

The Bishop of Bath and Wells has stood on one side of the monarch at coronations since Richard I was crowned in 1189; the historical seniority of the see of Bath and Wells is amply confirmed by the seat of successive bishops since first built by Bishop Jocelin Trotman in the early-13th century. The only walled and moated palace other than arch-episcopal York the whole area covers thirteen acres within the lozenge-shaped moat fed with millions of gallons of water a day by the springs or wells which give the city its name. From the town the approach across Bishop's Green towards the bridge and gatehouse is the perfect cloistered introduction; from the gatehouse the expansive main court opens out, the palace buildings and chapel to the left, the ruined great hall and gardens in front.

The bishops live in the most modern, 15th-century wing that faces the cathedral across the moat. During the 1960s Bishop Henderson decided to open the other rooms which as a result bear his name. The vaulted entrance hall and undercroft are splendidly mediaeval. A Jacobean oak staircase leads up to the main rooms which were refurbished throughout - notably with plaster ceilings and panelling - during the 19th century. Pious prelates gaze down from one end of the long gallery to the other while Bishop Jocelin's solar and great hall have are the panelled room and - out of the hall -the drawing room and conference room. The latter contains an impressive 19th-century Wilton carpet originally made for Windsor Castle and all rooms contain portraits of successive bishops.

Linked to the Henderson rooms is the bishops' private chapel whose intimacy is superbly balanced with its lofty vaulted roof and broad arched windows with fine tracery and stained glass which give the chapel almost radiant lightness. The pews are Victorian and were carved in various Somerset parishes and along the back rows runs a frieze bearing the bishops' arms from 1275 to the most most recently translated, George Carey Archbishop of Canterbury.

COMBE SYDENHAM HALL, *Monksilver.*

Mr and Mrs W. Theed.
Tel: 0984 56284.

3 m south of Watchet on B3188.
Open: March to Oct Sun to Fri 10-5.
£4.
Restaurant/Home-made teas.

Although just in Somerset Combe Sydenham Country Park lies in a hidden valley within Exmoor's National Park. Sir George Sydenham's house was probably built to celebrate his knighthood in 1583, but the gatehouse through which visitors approach beneath its handsome tower belonged to an older house with defence an obvious priority. Sir George's house was built on the Tudor 'E'-plan and its character is best preserved in the elegant porch. The house was substantially rebuilt following the Restoration in 1660, although by this time it had been reduced to the surviving west wing which forms the main portion of the present house. Without doubt the most unusual feature were the four towers which marked the corners of Sir George Sydenham's courtyard, one survives with its gabled top to increase the hall's appearance of intriguing irregularity.

The estate is currently undera 40-year restoration plan, initiated by the The Theeds after they purchased Combe Sydenham in 1964. The house contains reminders of Sir Francis Drake's marriage to Sir George Sydenham's daughter - although not before he had been firmly rejected once by the family as a lowly sailor. The Elizabethan court room, originally a range of monastic cells, has been recently restored with a 16th-century style ceiling and heraldic stone floor. Work still to be carried out, especially in the west wing, will do more to unveil the surviving features of Combe Sydenham's Elizabethan and 17h-century past, as well as enhancing the house's inviting surroundings.

FORDE ABBEY, *Chard.*

Trustees of Forde Abbey.
Tel: 0460 20231.

1 m east of Chard junction off A30.
Open: April to end-Oct Sun, Wed and Bank Hols 1-4.30 (gardens daily).
Price available on request.
Restaurant.

'Nobody that could stay here would go from hence. Nobody is so well anywhere else as everybody is here.' Jeremy Bentham's remark made in 1814 is as true today. Forde is a beautiful house set in a remote, fruitful valley south of Chard. The Cistercians who came here in the 12th century, established a great abbey complete with church, cloisters and accomodation; it achieved its final monastic glory in the early-16th century under Abbot Chard. He was responsible for the Tudor-Gothic architecture reminiscent both in style and quality of the chapel at King's College Cambridge.

Unfinished at the dissolution, the abbey estates were leased and the buildings plundered. All was not lost, however, and after a century what remained was brought in 1649 by Sir Edward Prideaux, Oliver Cromwell's attorney-general. He made good the structure, retained some of the best early workr and remodelled the remaining building in a rich cosmopolitan style. Prideaux's rooms are beautifully panelled and have lively plaster-work ceilings. His splendid staircase richly carved with flowers, the tops punctuated with decorated urns, is a great showpiece leading from the great hall to the great chamber or saloon. The visitor is still overwhelmed on arrival in the saloon, exactly as Prideaux intended, for here are the house's main treasure, the great set of Mortlake tapestries of Raphael's Acts of the Apostles, astonishingly little faded.

Abbot Chard and Prideaux left their mark on Forde's architecture and interiors. The Evans family and their descendants the Ropers added significantly to the collection of furniture and paintings - notably an interesting group of old master paintings. More recently the 18th-century garden has been replanted and extended, including a luxuriant bog garden ful of horticultural rarities, and in 1993 won the HHA/Christie's Garden of the Year prize. House and garden together have the grandeur of an Oxbridge college, a rarity among country houses.

GAULDEN MANOR, *Tolland.*

Mr and Mrs James LeGendre Starkie.
Tel: 09847 213.

Off A358, 9 m north-west of Taunton, 1 m east of Tolland church.
Open: May to 1st Sun in Sept Sun and Thur, Easter Sun and Mon and Bank Hol Mon 2-5.
£2.80, children £1.25.
Tea room.

The sleepy manor of Gaulden is exactly what one would expect to find in the remote valleys of north Somerset that undulate between the Brendon and Quantock Hills. Robin Feddon called it 'ageless vernacular' and it is hard to think of a better description; part mediaeval, with a Tudor addition an 17th-century embellishments - notably inside - it is built of the local red sandstone and blends with the landscape.

Not least because of the unassuming exterior the plasterwork in the great hall is a revelation. In 1559 James Turberville, Bishop of Exeter was imprisoned in the Tower for refusing to take the Oath of Supremacy. He was released in 1563 and two years later retired to a secluded life at Gaulden. He was responsible for the frieze, which carrys his image and supposedly tells of his life with its images that include the scales of justice, a tower, the virgin and child and its Latin texts. He may have been responsible for the overmantel bearing the Turberville arms between the figures of Peace and Plenty but it is more likely to have been the work of his great-nephew John Turberville who bought Gaulden in 1615 - the bishop having only been a tenant. John was certainly responsible for the two ceiling panels depicting an angel blowing the last trump and King David, betwen a decorated plaster drop of exaggerated size.

The hall frieze extends into the small room beyond a 17th-century oak screen which was probably the chapel. The other notable Turberville feature is their coat of arms over the fireplace in the main bedroom. After the Turbervilles Gaulden became a farmhouse of varying fortune, at one time the hall was used as a barn to store straw, and the Starkies have done much restoration since they came here in 1966. A major addition is the garden they have created leading up to and round the old fish ponds.

HATCH COURT, *Hatch Beauchamp.*

Dr and Mrs Robin Odgers.
Tel: 0823 480120.

6 m south-east of Taunton, off A358.
Open: mid-June to mid-Sept Thur and Bank Hol Mon 2.30-5.30.
£3.00.
Home-made teas.

Hatch Court is a rarity; an 18th-century architectural masterpiece recast in the 1930s. The house's fascination lies in the marriage of these two periods. The house was designed in 1755 for John Collins by his friend Thomas Prowse, a remarkable gentleman all-rounder: member of parliament, lawyer, amateur artist and architect. He created a sophisticated Palladian villa with a central block topped by four towers, with an open arcade on the ground floor. The exterior is immediately reminiscent of Hagley Hall in Worcestershire, for which Prowse executed a design. The layout has remained unchanged apart from the delightful curved wings, one containing the orangery.

Inside the plan is assuredly Palladian, a spacious central hall with a spectacular double cantilevered staircase. The sequence of surrounding rooms contain good architectural fittings - bookcases and chimneypieces. On the staircase hang the Shuckburgh portraits from Bourton in Warwickshire including two imposing full lengths by Sir Martin Archer Shee.

The house was acquired in 1931 by Brigadier Hamilton Gault and his wife. They carried out stylish redecoration and discerningly introduced a group of contemporary works of art: portraits by Glynn Philpots; breezing equestrian paintings by Munnings; and sculpture. The rooms evince a strong period mood; the characters in Noel Coward musicals would have felt at home in the drawing room.

At the back of the house is a well laid out museum to Princess Patricia's Canadian Light Infantry which Gault, who came from Montreal, raised in seventeen days at the outbreak of the First World War. Adjacent to the museum is an 18th-century china room whiere the family collection of porcelain is still displayed. The other delight at Hatch is the spacious deer park through which one approaches the house perched on its eminence below a typical Somerset wooded hill, as well as the gardens, in particular the walled garden, recently restored by Dr Odgers and his wife who is Mrs Gault's great-niece.

BOWOOD HOUSE, *Calne.*

The Earl and Countess of Shelburne.
Tel: 0249 812102.

2 m west of Calne, 5 m south-east of Chippenham off A4.
Open: April to end-Oct daily 11-6.
£4.50, children £2.30, concessions.
Restaurant/Tea room.

Set in one of Capability Brown's most superlative and largest parks and overlooking broad descending terraces added in the 19th century, Bowood's long low classical facades complete a harmonious whole. Or so it seems; in fact the house has been called the grandest stable conversion in England and once formed two courtyards to one side of a palatial classical mansion, improved by Keene and Adam, whose size more truly fitted the surrounding landscape.

In 1955 the present Marquess of Lansdowne took the painful, unpopular decision that was necessary to the survival of Bowood as a viable estate, to demolish the big house and convert the twin courtyards built by Keene, which form the present house. Keene's work is best seen in the two-storey east front that stretches between matching pavilions, but the better-known front is Adam's south-facing range overlooking the terraces which was originally built as an orangery to close the courtyards on this side. The third and fourth architects to make important contributions to the present house was C.R. Cockerell who built the chapel in the arm that divides Keene's courtyards early in the 19th century, and Charles Barry who built the dizzily high clock-tower over the chapel and the ornate Italianate main entrance to the park with gilded gates.

It was important that the new house would be able to display the family's art collection - from Lansdowne House in London as well as the big house - and the success is immediately clear to visitors. Conversion work has continued in stages since 1955 and in recent years Lord Shelburne carried out work that has produced the sculpture gallery, shop and restaurant on the ground floor and exhibition rooms above.

Looking along Adam's orangery, or Diocletian wing as it is sometimes known, it is hard to imagine that following the 1st marquess's death almost all his extensive art collection was sold - the remainder including the busts and classical marbles that he assembled from Italy. Today they form one of Bowood's most important treasures. The orangery has become a picture gallery, its walls hung with fine family portraits and a rich variety of other paintings; it makes an absorbing introduction to the other main rooms beyond, including the laboratory where Dr Joseph Priestley discovered oxygen in 1774, Cockerell's chapel, the Adam library and the new sculpture gallery. Family history is constantly evident for almost all successive Lansdownes from the prime minister 1st marquess have held public office. There are items collected by the 5th marquess when Viceroy of India and the chair and footstool used by Queen Victoria at her marriage when the 3rd marquess attended as Lord President.

The house itself is only a part of Bowood's appeal, much of which lies outside in the Brown park with its expansive lake fed by a cascade at one end and overlooked by the Doric Temple, the larger gardens, the pleasure grounds and rhododendron walks, and - for younger visitors or intrepid adults - a state of the art adventure playground. On one edge of the rhododendron walks overlooking the Wiltshire countryside stands Adam's sombre mausoleum, his most distinguished contribution to Bowood. It was commissioned by the dowager Countess of Shelburne in memory of her husband who purchased Bowood in 1754 and whose son became the 1st marquess.

CORSHAM COURT, *Corsham.*

The Lord Methuen.
Tel: 0249 712214.

In Corsham 4 m west of Chippenham by A4.
Open: Jan to end-Nov daily except Mon and Fri 2-4.30,
Good Fri to End-Sept inc Fri and Bank Hols 2-6.
£3.50, children £2.00, concessions.

Methuen eldest sons have failed to inherit on three occasions and the present Lord Methuen only did so when his elder brother died after being hit on tho hoad by a cricket ball at his prep school. Happily these accidents have not affected the continuity or preservation of Corsham; the house's picture collection remains among the half-dozen best in an English house, its Old Masters with few if any rivals. A large number were assembled during the 18th century by Sir Paul Methuen and inherited by his cousin also Paul who purchased the Elizabethan manor of Corsham in 1745. In 1844 Frederick Methuen married Anna, only child of the Rev John Sanford, who brought to Corsham the rest of the Old Master collection.

The house saw many architectural changes from 1745. Paul Methuen retained the inviting Elizabethan south front that still faces the village and church across its broad courtyard, but gave the north front a Palladian look. In 1760 he commissioned 'Capability' Brown to design the park and enlarge the house, which Brown did by doubling the size of the Elizabethan wings on the south side and making the east wing into a set of state rooms to display the pictures. In 1800 John Nash carried out ambitious further work, adding pinnacles, buttresses and battlements and transforming the north front into Strawberry Hill Gothick. This did not last, however, and in the middle of the 19th century Thomas Bellamy replaced the north front with the present sombre, monumental design.

Brown's park was later altered by Humphry Repton who added the lake planned but not executed by his predecessor; but Brown's Gothic bath house remains one of the best garden buildings he - or any other English architect - designed.

His major interior was the picture gallery, a triple cube with a coffered and coved plaster ceiling originally designed by Burton Constable but rejected. The room was almost certainly planned with the major pictures in mind, this accounting for the powerful unity of the display: at one end Van Dyck's equestrian portrait of Charles I is central, on the main wall Van Dyck's 'Betrayal of Christ' to one side of the Scheemakers chimneypiece is balanced by Guido Reni's 'Baptism of Christ' of similar size in a matching carved frame. Over the fireplace is 'The Wolf Hunt' by Rubens. These are the largest but the other Old Masters and 18th-century landscapes that line the walls from above the furniture to ceiling are no less absorbing in quality and subject.

Brown's other state rooms are the cabinet room, the state bedroom and the octagon room. The first contains Filippo Lippi's 'Annunciation'; the highlight of the state bedrom is 'The Infant Christ' by Guernico; the octagon room contains forty paintings with a rare portrait of Elizabeth I in old age more than holding its own amongst works by Claude, Poussin, Breughel the elder and Teniers. The collection extends into the hall - where Bellamy's cold and cavernous staircase temporarily dampens the spirits - and corridors and the music room and dining room on the south front both of which he redesigned. Reynolds' vivacious quality at portraying children is superbly demonstrated in the two pictures of Paul Methuen's children in the dining room.

The quality continues in the furniture: in the picture gallery Adam pier glasses over side tables - a set of four - and the enormous suite of Chippendale furniture covered in crimson damask to match the walls; best of all the specially commissioned John Cobb marquetry commode with flanking torcheres in the cabinet room and the Florentine pietra-dura cabinets that give it its name; the Thomas Johnson mirrors in the state bedroom and others in the octagon room are a selection which alone would make Corsham a house of the highest distinction. The works of art include Michelangelo's 'The Sleeping Cupid' and porcelain is another arrow in an artistic quiver of seminal importance.

HAMPTWORTH LODGE, *Landford.*

Mr N. Anderson.
Tel: 0794 390215.

10 m south-east of Salisbury between Redlynch and Landford.
Open: end-March to end-April 2.15-5.
£3, children free.

Hamptworth Lodge is an ideal example of the derivative quality of Edwardian architecture. The handsome house set in the far corner of Wiltshire where the county runs into the New Forest looks convincingly Tudor from a distance and the external brick and timber construction is equally impressive. The original house was built in 1620and extensively altered during the 19th-century; but the seemingly authentic building is, externally, pure reproduction, rebuilt by Sir Guy Dawber between 1910-12.

Internally there are genuine Elizabethan and Jacobean overmantels removed from another house, but more important is the skilful arrangement of rooms around the spacious hall, which recalls the period of inspiration as well as being convenient - a high priority for Edwardians. Both Dawber and his client at Hamptworth, Harold Moffatt, were fervent enthusiasts for the Arts and Crafts and every detail of the work on the house exemplifies the movement .

The great hall contains an impressive hammer-beam roof, other rooms have finely worked plaster ceilings. Moffatt's Arts and Crafts enthusiasm is best shown in the fascinating selection of furniture that he carved himself in a rich variety of woods. The main rooms facing south and west look over the terraced gardens laid out to recreate the style of the 17th-century and completing an important period piece with the house and its contents.

LONGLEAT HOUSE, *Warminster.*

The Marquess of Bath.
Tel: 0985 844400.

6 m west of Warminster off A362.
Open: Daily all year except Christmas Day, Easter to Sept 10-6, rest of year 10-4, days and times of opening may vary.
Grounds entry £2, children 50p; House £4, children £2, concession.
Tea room.

A select band of England's greatest houses have been long at the forefront of opening to the public, houses that are unqustionably national treasures as well as private homes. Immediately one thinks of Longleat which opened its doors in 1949, perhaps the very first to do so on a commercial basis. The visitor's first view of Longleat, preferably from the wooded ridge known as Heaven's Gate, is impressive for even the most disinterested observer. For the enthusiast it is a magical revelation; the prototype great Elizabethan country house set in one of the most perfectly-planted 18th-century parks.

Sir John Thynne was only interested in money and architecture and combined the two to spectacular effect. Assisted by Robert Smythson, the architect at the helm of Elizabethan country house architecture and a Frenchman, Allen Maynard, Thynne produced a house of palatial size that combined the most memorable English mediaeval style, Perpendicular, with Renaissance classicism. Perpendicular produced the towering mullioned windows through which light floods and which combine with the silver-toned walls to extraordinary effect. The classical symmetry of the house's external shape, the details of pilasters and regularly arranged projecting bays was one of the first seen in an English house. The roofscape with a mixture of classical balustrade, finials and pepperpot turrets continues the sense of fusion to the house's upper limits.

The great hall shows that Thynne's arrangement of rooms was traditional (although they have been subsequently altered throughout); the classical composition of English interiors did not come until Inigo Jones. Maynard carved the amazing Mannerist stone fireplace - and was probably responsible for the exterior decoration as well. The hall's timbered roof was flattered by the later insertion of a library but the most extensive interior alterations were carried out by Jeffry Wyatville after 1806 and, more lavishly during the 1870s and 1880s in Italian style by John Diblee Crace for the 4th marquess - an Italophile and important collector.

The manner in which the exterior blends a fundamental Englishness with breathtaking continental influences continues inside. Huge Woottons hang in the hall, there are Tudor and Stuart portraits of canny-looking Thynnes and other important personages such as the Duchess of Richmond by Van Dyck, a good collection of portraits dating from the 16th to the 20th centuries, and gilded furniture from Wyatville's period. These are balanced - or perhaps overshadowed - by lavish Italianate ceilings, doorcases and chimney-pieces, Venetian mythological paintings, Venetian Baroque and French furniture, Kandler white Meissen birds and, the gem of the old masters, Titian's Rest on the Flight into Egypt.

Outside Russell Page, who first worked for the late Lord Bath during the 1930s, laid out the formal garden on the north side which extends to Wyatville's orangery and recalls the enormous parterres which were added around the house by London and Wise at the end of the 17th century, but removed by Brown when he began the park in 1757. Repton made a few subsequent alterations, joining the two lakes and removing some trees where they were too densely planted, but the setting remains Brown's and one of the outstanding landscape achievements of any period.

SHELDON MANOR, *Chippenham.*

Major Martin Gibbs.
Tel: 0249 653120.

1 m west of Chippenham, off A420.
Open: Easter Sun and Mon then Sun, Thur and Bank Hols to Oct 12.30-6.
Price available on request.
Home-made lunch/tea.

The west country is richly endowed with mediaeval or part-mediaeval manor houses, but most visitors seem to agree that there is something special about Sheldon. There are no famous names associated with its architectural evolution from the 13th century on, mediaeval builders were usually anonymous craftsmen, nonetheless the 13th-century porch which greets the visitor from behind two venerable yew trees is quite unique, a gem that only survives elsewhere in churches of the period. This was built by the crusader Sir Geoffrey Gascelyn who acquired Sheldon in 1256 and established his family there for 200 years.

In 1424 it was bought by the Hungerford family, at the time powerful and acquisitive Wiltshire landowers. They built the 15th-century wing to the right of the porch but their occupation was infrequent and it was 16th-century tenants who added the similarly gabled but taller wing to the left. By the late-17th century the Hungerfords had shot their bolt, Sheldon was sold and slumbered as a farmhouse for which the two barns were built during the 18th century, until 1917 when Henry Martin Gibbs bought it for his son.

Gibbs' taste was that of many late-Victorian romantics and ideally suited to Sheldon's atmosphere. No doubt he took great care to preserve the original water cistern in the buttressed porch whose vaulted ceiling supports an upper 'priest's' room. He would have approved of the linenfold panelling introduced by his predecessor, and studiously preserved the largely undisturbed layout of the rooms: dining room below a library (the original solar) in the 15th-century wing and the hall in the 16th-century wing, beyond the oak staircase. The contents he brought were well chosen, in particular the furniture which includes four Elizabethan oak refectory tables, Lancashire chairs, 'seaweed' marquetry and a pair of Dutch ebony cabinets. His enthusiasm for the aesthetic movement is demonstrated in the William de Morgan pottery, while surprising but no less suitable in its period romanticism, is the Tissot painting Marguerite a l'Eglise.

Major Gibbs and his wife have lived here since 1952 when, following a series of tenants, the house once again had gone into decline and required rejuvenation. This they have carried out to great effect, at the same time as providing their own major contribution in the garden with romantic planting on the terraces around the house, a maze which provides endless delight for children, and, at a distance, a formal water garden concealed by clipped hornbeams.

WILTON HOUSE, *Wilton.*

The Earl of Pembroke.
Tel: 0722 743115.

In Wilton on A30.
Open: end-March to mid-Oct daily except Sat, 11-6 (last entry 5).
£5.50, children £3.50, concessions £4.50
Restaurant.

Wilton represents the apogee of English aristocratic patronage and connoisseurship. Successive generations of Pembrokes commissioned, designed, purchased and entertained at all the right times in England's cultural development. In the 450 years since Henry VIII granted the abbey and estates of Wilton to William Pembroke in 1544 there appears to have been only one bad hat; the 7th earl who ran up debts, was accused of murder, convicted of manslaughter and sent to the Tower where he died in 1683. The present earl's career as a film producer may be unconventional but he is no less devoted to

Wilton than his scholarly father (who catalogued the collections), as confirmed by his imaginative additions to the gardens.

William Herbert's tenure of office through four Tudor reigns and earldom awarded by Edward VI propelled the family into political and social ascendancy which subsequent generations retained and built upon. His son married Mary sister of Sir Philip Sydney; they ushered in the first of Wilton's halcyon periods as a centre of Elizabethan and Stuart court life, continued by their sons the 3rd and 4th earls. Mary's brother, Spencer, Shakespeare, Isaac de Caus, Inigo Jones and John Webb were central characters. With the inheritance of the 8th earl in 1683 another golden era dawned, of scholarship, great collecting and the contributions by his son the 'architect earl'. His Palladian bridge across the Nadder beyond the lawns and cedars to the south of the house marked a watershed in the English landscape; it was copied at Stowe, Hagley Hall, Prior Park and by Catherine the Great at Tsarskoye Selo. The 10th earl commissioned work by Sir William Chambers, the 11th earl commissioned James Wyatt. Through the 19th and 20th centuries successive earls were soldiers, scholars and politicians, consolidating and caring for Wilton and its collections.

Chambers provides the introduction with his triumphal arch. No two fronts of the square house around a courtyard are the same, but the gentle Chilmark stone gives strong unity. The 1st earl's Elizabethan house is retained in the central portion of the east facade, and Wyatt built the vaulted Gothick cloisters that surround the courtyard on two levels. But is is the south front that is of seminal importance and provides Wilton's most enduring image. Its simple but majestic proportions and detail proved as influential as any other house on the development of English classicism. Its reputation heightens the question of its authorship. Philip the 4th earl certainly commissioned Isaac de Caux around 1636 and a drawing by de Caux survives. But the subsequent fire in 1647 gutted Wilton's interiors and the facade may have been partially rebuilt by John Webb, advised by his uncle Inigo Jones, albeit reproducing de Caux's original.

The partnership of the aging Jones and his nephew produced Wilton's interior tour de force, the Double Cube room, acknowledged to be both the most sumptuous and important 17th-century interior in England. The combination of the white and gold decoration, coved and painted trompe l'oeil ceiling, the marble chimneypiece, towering Corinthian doorcase at one end and the great Van Dyck portraits specially commissioned for their allotted spaces, is overpowering. The style continues in the adjacent single cube room.

In these rooms, the rest of the Jones-Webb state rooms and throughout the house, the visitor soon appreciates the endless quality of the picture collection which has few private rivals anywhere in Europe, the furniture with 18th-century highlights in the quantities of work by Kent and Chippendale, and works of art such as the 8th earl's collection of antique statues and busts.

YORKSHIRE
BRAMHAM PARK

BURTON AGNES HALL, *Driffield.*

Burton Agnes Hall Preservation Trust Ltd.
Tel: 0262 490324.

In Burton Agnes 6 m south-west of Bridlington on A166.
Open: April to end-Oct daily 11-5.
£3, children £2, concessions.
Tea room.

Burton Agnes is well suited to its exposed position and like other distinguished houses in the area defies the inhospitable nature of the surrounding wolds. The delightful gatehouse provides the ideal welcome to what lies beyond, rows of squat yews leading to the house. The family have had eight hundred years of continuity at Burton Agnes from Griffiths by marriage in 1654 to Boynton.

Built between 1601-10 it was one of the last major houses by Sir Robert Smythson. As with all his houses, there is plenty of originality: the combination of five-sided, semi-circular and square bays surmounted with battlements, balustrades and carved stone cartouches; the entrance concealed in the side of one of the square projections which also contain ascending statues in niches; over-sharp finialled gables; and the symmetry of windows, brick and stone quoining. The generous fenestration is exaggerated by the later sashes and white painting but greatly adds to the house's friendliness.

There is such a quantity of carved plaster panels and screens that Robin Feddon said there were so many 'figures of Virtues and Vices and other sententious motifs' that the house was 'like a perpetual sermon.' In the hall only the size of the elegant full-length portraits of Sir Griffith Boynton 6th Bt. and his wife by Francis Cotes allows them to compete with the Bunyan-like compositions. The smaller scale of the main bedrooms, the king's and queen's bedrooms make the combination of panelling and plaster ceilings more readily accessible.

Sir Griffith, his father and grandfather (four generations in a row bore the same name) were between them responsible for 18th-century alterations, including the coromandel screens in the Chinese room. An interesting 18th-century feature is the number of portaits and other paintings by Phillipe Mercier, a Frenchman born in Berlin who spent a number of years working in York.

A more recent and unusual addition to Burton Agnes is the array of late-19th and 20th century paintings collected by Mr Wickham-Boynton including works by Corot, Courbet, Boudin, Augustus John and a number of Impressionists. It was thanks to Mr Wickham-Boynton that the long gallery was restored after the ceiling had collapsed in 1870 and the room was divided into bedrooms. The work was carried out by Francis Johnson and included the reconstruction of the original barrel ceiling.

BURTON CONSTABLE HALL, *Humberside.*

Burton Constable Foundation.
Tel: 0964 5623400.

In Burton Constable, 7 m north-east of Hull, 1 m north of Sproatley off B1328.
Open: Easter to end-Sept, Sun to Thur inc, Sat in July and Aug, 1-4.15.
£3, children £1.50, concessions.
Tea room.

Burton Constable is an Elizabethan house that has the appearance of a great ship marooned on the desert flats of south-east Yorkshire. Always the home of the Constable family, it is the best combination of a mellow Elizabethan exterior, rich 18th-century interiors and eclectic collecting by the family from all periods. The presiding genius of the house is William Constable, collector, patron, antiquary and scientist (he was a patron of Priestley and friend of Banks). His Museum or Cabinet of curiosities with shells, minerals, scientific intruments, coins and medals etc has survived intact; one of the few of its kind to do so from the 18th century.

William Constable brought in a series of distinguished 18th-century architects; Timothy and Thomas Lightoller, James Wyatt and Thomas Atkinson among others, to modernise and improve the interiors with magnificent results. Chippendale made the set of gilded furniture for Wyatt's superb ballroom and an impressive array of other craftsmen supplied different work for the house. The picture collection has an extensive group of portraits of the families - mainly Catholic -with whom the Constables married.

SLEDMERE, *Driffield.*

Sir Tatton Sykes, Bt.
Tel: 0377 86028.

8 m north-west of Driffield, at junc of B1251 and B1253.
Open: Easter to end-Sept daily except Mon and Fri.
£2.75, children £1.50, concessions.
Restaurant.

House and estate at Sledmere have steadily matured since their inception in the mid-18th century. Then a small manor house and a tract of desolate land was transformed by the ingenuity of Richard Sykes, his brother Parsons Sykes (the agricultural improver), and his son Sir Christopher Sykes. The latter remodelled his father's modest house. The new neo-classical block, echoing both Carr of York and Samuel Wyatt, dominates the landscape and yet sits contentedly among the model stables, other outbuildings, cottages and farms.

Internally the house was redecorated with refined plasterwork by Joseph Rose. A series of gracious rooms on the ground floor act as a foil to the dramatically placed staircase leading to Sir Christopher's library, the outstanding interior which majestically spans the whole length of the first floor. Its windows look out to Capability Brown's park where great roundels seem to float like ships. The form and decoration of the library recreates Piranesi's evocations of the bath houses of ancient Rome. Here was housed Sir Christopher's superlative collection of books. Romney's marvellous double portrait of him with his wife, which hangs in the dining room, comfirm the charm and intelligence of this squire whose personality remains instilled in both house and estate.

The large number of rooms contain rich diversity of paintings, furniture and works of art. During the 19th century the famous Sledmere Stud was developed and the horse room affords a fascinating summary of British sporting pictures with works by Herring, Chalon and Ferneley. Elsewhere are portraits by Lely, Lawrence, Mengs and Grant, good Italian and Flemish paintings and furniture of comparable quality. The bedrooms contain a collection of lace work; other highlights include rare works of art ranging from Italian bronzes to a needlework of Columbus and Queen Isabella.

Sledmere was largely gutted by fire in 1911, mercifully most of the art collection was saved. The house was rebuilt with improvements and additions, such as a unique Turkish room based on the Sultans' apartments in Istanbul. The ability to improve and extend the house, its collections and surrounding estate continues unabated; the present owner Sir Tatton Sykes has conserved at the same time as adding both furniture and works of art, added lapis columns in the dining room, and new plasterwork in the main hall.

ALLERTON PARK, *Knaresborough.*

Gerald Arthur Rolph Foundation.
Tel: 0423 330927.

4 m west of Knaresborough, 1 m east of A1 on A59.
Open: Easter to end-Sept, Sun and Bank Hols, 1-5.
£3, children £2, concessions.

The clustered turrets and gables of Allerton are hardly visible from the A1 which passes a mile away, and only closer inspection reveals the true size of arguably the largest Gothick revival house to survive from the 19th century. Shortly before 1850 the 19th Lord Stourton commissioned George Martin to rebuild the existing Georgian house. Martin's work doubled the size and transformed it into an assembled union of gables, mullions, oriels and pointed turrets of constant variety. HIs most spectacular work came inside in the creation of the great hall, a heroic space often credited with being the largest room in England, rising some 80 feet to the top of a hammerbeam roof. A gallery runs around the first floor and at ground level the staircase leads up through a Tudor arch in a panelled oak screen. At right-angles to the hall a second axis extends through the saloon to the chapel.

Allerton had been empty for some years in 1983 when it was bought from the Stourton family by an American, Dr Gerald Rolph. He has carried out extensive restoration. Only a few of the original decorative fittings - such as massive wall brackets and Venetian chandeliers survive - but there is also some interesting Victorian furniture, some made by Holland and Son.

BRAMHAM PARK, *Wetherby.*

Mr and Mrs George Lane Fox.
Tel: 0937 844265.

5 m south of Wetherby on A1.
Open: mid-June to Sept, Sun, Tues, Wed, Thur and Bank Hol 1.15-5.
Price available on request.

'Bramham is a grand and unusual house, but its gardens are grander and even more unusual'. Pevsner's opinion is entirely accurate. The early-18th century house has many qualities but its gardens are the largest and best preserved French-inspired formal landscape in England. The whole ensemble was the creation of Robert Benson who inherited a fortune and the Bramham estate from his lawyer father and prospered as a politician and businessman becoming Lord Bingley and ending up as George II's treasurer. Contempories considered him socially inferior but aspersions cast on his origins could not be extended to his taste. The design of the house and garden were almost certainly his, based on what he had seen on a grand tour of France and Italy during the 1690s.

His work was consolidated by his daughter Harriet who married George Fox Lane. Thereafter Bramham's progress was less smooth. Disorder after their deaths in 1773 was followed by disaster during the Regency thanks to George Lane Fox 'the gambler' and his witty, pretty but hopelessly extravagant wife Georgina. As the debts mounted, in 1828 fire broke out and gutted the house. Their son 'the squire' eventually paid off his father's gambling debts of some £175,000 but could never contemplate rebuilding the house. The work did not start until 1906 when his grandson commissioned Detmar Blow and together they planned as accurate a reconstruction of Bingley's original as possible.

Bingley envisaged Bramham in the style of an Italian villa or casino and it retains that sense of quality in reduced scale on both the entrance side approached through splendid Baroque gate-piers and even more so on the garden front where Blow's new doorway and curving double staircase was a good replacement for a 19th-century bow window. The exact cube stone hall makes for an austere greeting but is enlivened by Reynolds full length portrait of 'Butcher' Cumberland and double doors lead into the gallery on the garden front, Blow's main alteration that replaced three smaller rooms. The impressive proportions are emphasised by full length family portraits reflected in equally tall pier glasses between the windows, and a flamboyant Lely of Popham Conway at one end.

The other main rooms are - while not small - warm and intimate. More good portraits, such as 'the gambler' looking dashing but slightly raddled by Hayter, mixing with notable sporting pictures (Bramham is home to the Bramham Moor Hounds), especially the Walker in the library and the Wootton in the sitting room, Dutch and Italian still lives and landscapes. Upstairs a charming set of water-colours by Ziegler depict Bramham before the fire.

The sunken parterre below the south front gives little idea of the true character of Bramham's gardens, but heading towards the fine temple by James Paine (who also built the splendid Tuscan stables flanking the forecourt) on one side the visitor is soon led into the series of grassy allees through woodland that cover two large areas. Here, the formal canals, temples and other architectural ornaments, and the constant revelation of spectacular vistas, allow for hours of absorbing exploration. The Gothick temple in particular has few peers among garden buildings and the damage wrought by a catastrophic gale has been made good by replanting.

CASTLE HOWARD, *York.*

The Hon Simon Howard.
Tel: 0653 648333.

15 m north-east of York off A64, 6 m west of Malton.
Open: daily mid-March to end-Oct.
£6, children £3.

Castle Howard never fails to excite the visitor. However you approach the extraordinary originality of Vanbrugh's buildings, and the powerful interplay of lakes, avenues, vistas and gardens have overpowering effect. This is not just a house but a massive estate which builds up to a crescendo around the Baroque palace at its centre. Here is a domestic building approached by columns, arches, pyramids and temples: a house surmounted by a dome, only previously seen in England on St Paul's cathedral.

The Howards of Castle Howard have always been great builders and collectors. The house and park were created for Charles Howard, 3rd Earl of Carlisle whose works of art form the bedrock of the collection, among which the paintings by Marco Ricci are a forte. His son acquired in Italy the famous collection of antiquities. These are still displayed as intended, in the passages and central hall and are complimentary to the Baroque exuberance of the architecture. The 5th earl completed the building. He also commissioned contemporary British paintings from Reynolds, Gainsborough and Zoffany, as well as purchasing a portion of the Orleans Collection of Old Masters. These include the Gentileschi and Guercino hanging in the Long Gallery. Further additions to the collection came during the life of the 9th earl, himself an artist. There is a room devoted to the achievements of the 9th earl and his friends, and a beautiful Italianate chapel with windows by Edward Burne-Jones.

The collections of English and European porcelain, works of art and furniture are equally strong. Much of the furniture of the 3rd earl's time has survived, added to by 18th-century French pieces and crisp neo-classical furniture by Linnell and Tatham. In one of the recently decorated bedrooms is Linnell's newly restored domed bed.

All of this might hve been lost when the Howard energy failed after the disastrous fire in 1940 when the south-east wing was gutted. George Howard, Lord Howard of Henderskelfe, and his successors made a brilliant job of restoring and opening the house. The treasures are well displayed and augmented by Vanbrugh's heroic grounds and the rose gardens. The visitor can enjoy Castle Howard in many ways; delightful walks in the grounds, rewarding study of works of art, a family day out, or an absorbing glimpse of one of the greatest 18th-century estates.

DUNCOMBE PARK, *Helmsley.*

Lord and Lady Feversham.
Tel: 0439 770213.

On edge of Helmsley town.
Open: Easter, Sun and Wed April and Oct, Sun to Thur May, June, Sept, Daily July and Aug, 11-5.
£4.50.
Restaurant.

The return of Lord Feversham to his family seat after it had been a girls' school for sixty years was considered admirably brave by some, foolhardy by others. A few years later, after restoration of uncompromising high standards, and with a clutch of awards, he would appear to have silenced the doubters.

At the end of the 17th century Charles Duncombe was possibly the richest man in the city of London. People were jealous when in 1689 he paid £90,000 for the profligate Duke of Buckingham's estates in Yorkshire, sold by the duke's trustees to pay debts after his death. Charles's portrait as an effete young man disguises his financial acumen. Helmsley was inherited by his nephew who assumed the Duncombe name and, in 1713 commissioned the gentleman Yorkshire architect William Wakefield to design a suitably impressive house. The result was authoritative Baroque. During the 1840s Barry replaced the original wings with the present ones and enclosed the giant forecourt; the result was even more impressive than the original, if slightly ponderous.

Disaster struck in 1879 when the main house was gutted by fire. Restoration was not begun until l895 and was carried out by William Young following the original 18th-century plan and style, but in classical Edwardian which produced an occasional flourish. The quality of the work could not be faulted: the window frames were all replaced with teak. They give the house a sombre look but have never needed to be replaced. The family's departure from Duncombe was caused by the death of the young 2nd earl at the Somme in 1916, following which the contents were sold and the house let.

Lord Feversham's restoration has aspired to the standards of craftsmanship of the 18th-century original and Edwardian replacements, and much of the joinery and other decorative work was done on the estate or by local firms. The 40ft-cube hall has giant Corinthian pilasters and stretches up to a circular roof panel; the ceiling has been repainted and the angels, putti and other details adorning doorway arches or walls have been restored. Central doors lead through to the saloon which stretches along the garden front for over 100 feet. The drawing room is decorated in rich yellow silk and, like the saloon, its plaster ceiling was originally done by George Jackson the Adam brothers' crafsman.

Family portraits include a lovely group of three daughters of the 1st earl as children, who became famous beauties (portraits of two as married ladies hang in the dining room), and a conversation piece by Soldi of Thomas Duncombe and his family; in the drawing room there are landscapes by Desiderio and in all rooms the furniture introduced by the Fevershams continues the theme of quality as well as being of adventurous variety.

Duncombe's most important feature lies outside the house, beyond the huge expanse of lawn that stretches away from the garden front between flanking blocks of woodland. Thomas Duncombe made a crucial contribution to the English landscape movement when he laid out the broad grass terrace that stretches betwen classical temples along the edge of the wooded Rye valley which drops away below. Later in the 18th century his grandson laid out a similar terrace - its deliberate picturesqueness showing the changes in taste - a short distance away on the estate, overlooking the ruined Rievaulx Abbey. The two together have been called the 'supreme masterpiece of the English landscape gardener' and should not be missed.

HAREWOOD HOUSE, *Leeds.*

The Earl of Harewood.
Tel: 0532 886331.

7 m south of Harrogate, 8 m north of Leeds on A61/A659.
Open: April to end-Oct daily, 11.
Price available on request.

18th-century Harewood extolled the composition of landscape, architecture and decoration which defined the acme of English country houses. It has long contained great treasures. Now, recent imaginative reorganization and rediscovery of long-hidden masterpieces have made it one of the country's great show houses. With certain changes, the arrangement and decoration of rooms - in particular the progression along the south front - remain one of Robert Adam's greatest achievements, on a par with Kedleston and Syon.

Edwin Lascelles, whose family fortune came from Barbadian sugar plantations, was a man of taste, but cautious and forthright. He only commissioned Carr of York to build his new house in 1759, when Carr had executed the stable block first and his plan was almost certainly preferred to one by William Chambers because of cost. Lascelles next consulted young Robert Adam, ambitious and in the ascendant. He was given control of the interiors, with the proviso from Lascelles, 'let us do everything properly and well, mais pas trop.'

The result gives little impression of any constraint. The sense of progression from room to room, the quality of design throughout are both masterful. Adam was also able, no doubt with advice and preferences from Lascelles, to commission the leading craftsmen; Joseph Rose and William Collins for decorative plasterwork, Angelica Kaufmann, Antonio Zucchi and Biagio Rebecca to paint decorative panels, and Thomas Chippendale to supply the furniture. In Robin Feddon's opinion, 'here is not only the best of Thomas Chippendale's work, but possibly the finest furniture ever to be made in England.' By the mid-1770s, when 'Capability' Brown had completed the park falling away from the house to the vast lake he created, Harewood was not so much a house as an expression of taste - this accounting for its regular illustraton by Turner, Girtin and other contempories whose superb watercolours provide brilliant evidence.

The 3rd Earl of Harewood - or more precisely his wife, Louisa a Thynne from Longleat - commissioned Charles Barry to enlarge the house. Carr's elegant roofline was replaced with an extra storey, his portico removed from the south front and the 18th-century lightness sunk in the impressively grand but lifeless classicism with which Barry encased the house. Along the south front he placed the broad Italianate terrace. Inside he remodelled the dining room, whence he removed Adam's chimneypiece from the gallery, and turned the saloon into the main library (there are three at Harewood.) The 20th century brought two distinguished new arrivals to Harewood, in 1922 the present Lord Harewood's father married the Princess Royal, daughter of George V and, having inherited the fortune of his great-uncle, the last Marquis of Clanricarde, collected the Old Masters, almost exclusively Italian but including El Greco' Allegory.

The rooms occupied by the 6th earl and the Princess Royal are among the first seen by visitors retain an evocatively period atmosphere. Beyond the full success of the present Lord and Lady Harewood's reorganization - greatly helped by Alec Cobbe's advice on redecoration and hanging of pictures - becomes apparent. The cabinets in the china room show off part of Harewood's incomparable Sevrès collected. The yellow drawing room has been redecorated to Adam's original colour, but the two climaxes are the cinnamon drawing room where Cobbe collected the Reynolds portraits including ravishing Lady Worsley, one of Edwin Lascelles' step-daughters, renowned for her affairs and looking the part in a red hunting habit. The gallery, long hung with family portraits, has had its chimneypiece returned, and contains the Old Masters. Two of the Chippendale mirrors were recently discovered dismantled in store.

What Edwin Lascelles would think of Epstein's great alabaster figure of Adam that stands alone in the centre of the hall, is hard to say but there is little doubt that both he and Adam would approve of the manner in which Lord and Lady Harewood have rejuvenated so much of their distinguished home.

KIPLIN HALL, *Scorton.*

Kiplin Hall Trust.
Tel: 0748 818178.

4 m east of Catterick off A1, on B6271 8 m north-west of Northallerton.
Open: Late-May to end-Aug, Sun, Wed and Bank Hol Mon, 2-5.
£2, £1 children.
Teas on Sun.

Kiplin Hall is a unique gem of Jacobean architecture, its quality enhanced by its delightfully small scale. At first sight its combination of steep gables and towers topped with octagonal ogival domes seems typical of the period and reminiscent of, for instance, Hatfield. But Kiplin's plan of a rectangle with a tower in the centre of each side - rather than an the corners as would be more usual - is unique. The similarity of certain features to Hatfield is not surprising; George Calvert who built Kiplin during the 1620s, was secretary to Robert Cecil, Earl of Salisbury before following his master as secretary to James I. Calvert was a pioneer of the new colonies in America. He founded the colony of Avalon in Newfoundland and later the state of Maryland whose capital took its name from his peerage, Lord Baltimore.

During the early 18th century the interiors of Kiplin were extensively remodelled by Christopher Crowe, who bought the house from his stepson Lord Baltimore. From 1705 to 1716 Crowe was British consul in Leghorn where he was a leading figure in the city's thriving mercantile and artistic community. Some of the fine Italian pictures that he collected still hang at Kiplin and when he returned to England he transformed most of the rooms with with early 18th century decoration. Around 1820 a Gothick wing was added for Lord Tyrconnel who married a Crowe heiress and from his family Kiplin passed to the Talbots.

Miss Bridget Talbot established a charitable trust in 1968. This important step was followed by urgently required restoration work; the Gothick wing was removed with the exception of the 19th-century library which was retained; otherwise the house returned to its original proportions. The balance of stone dressing and brickwork is particularly fine; one feels that Calvert absorbed the quality of his Cecil masters houses at Hatfield and Cranborne; many details such as the front door flanked by twin pillars are extremely similar. The safeguarding of an enchantinging house of such prime importance is a considerable achievement and it is to be hoped that the Trust is able to establish long-term security and continuing improvements at Kiplin.

NEWBY HALL, *Ripon.*

R.E.J. Compton Esq.
Tel: 0423 322583.

4 m south-east of Ripon on B6265.
Open: April to end-Sept daily except Mon (open Bank Hols) from 11.
Price available by telephone.

Newby Hall fits effortlessly into the gentle valley of the River Ure. The late-17th century connoisseur of country houses, Celia Fiennes, thought it 'the finest I saw in Yorkshire'. The gardens were largely designed by Major Edward Compton stretching from house to distant river. Now the house, gardens and surroundings have been totally renovated and restored by his son Robin Compton and his wife Jane, with substantial attractions for visitors.

Newby was built by the Blackett family and sold in 1748 to Richard Weddell who bought it for his son, William, a leading member of the Dilettanti Club. One hesitates to refer to Weddell's work at Newby as 'alterations'; it marked a highpoint of 18th-century taste. Batoni painted him twice, and the small oval and grand full-length both show an instantly appealing connoisseur. Weddell's grand tour produced two major trophies, his collection of classical sculpture and one of the six sets of Gobelins tapestries woven for English houses.

Inside the house remodelled by Carr of York, Adam designed the interiors. Joseph Rose executed the plasterwork, Angelica Kaufmann and Antonio Zucchi the painted panels. The Gobelins tapestry drawing room remains uniquely intact with Chippendale furniture covered in the same material. In Adam's sculpture gallery Weddell's collection remains as he arranged it, with the recent addition of his own bust by Nollekens surveying his trophies.

Weddell had no children and left Newby to the son of his cousin and close friend, Lord Grantham. His daughter Mary married Henry Vyner and inherited Newby which passed to their son Robert, then to his daughter, Mr Compton's grandmother. The Vyners added the Victorian wing where the billiards room contains a portrait of Frederick Vyner, murdered by Greek Brigands, whose death caused his mother to commission Burges's church.

Chippendale masterpieces and card tables by Vile are among furniture commissioned by Weddell. Portraits illustrate the different families connected with Newby: after Weddell come Granthams, de Greys, Vyners and Comptons. Other connexions constantly appear, trophies from the family's 19th-century racing successes and the delightful curiosity of the rare collection of chamber pots collected by Robert de Grey Vyner and arranged by Mrs Compton. The view from the house down Major Compton's 300-yard double herbacous borders is one of England's finest garden vistas.

NORTON CONYERS, *Ripon.*

Sir James Graham, Bt.
Tel: 0765 64333.

3 m north-west of Ripon near Wath, 3 m from A1.
Open: Bank Hols, Sun end-May to Sept and daily late-July 2-5.30.
£2.80, children £2.30, concessions.
Tea room (Sun and Bank Hols, otherwise by arrangement).

Charlotte Bronte visited Norton Conyers in 1839 and the house remains the most convincing model for Thornfield Hall in Jane Eyre. The direct link is the Graham family legend of a mad woman confined in the attics during the 18th century, but the whole mood of the roughcast house, its Dutch gabling a peculiarity in Yorkshire, is suitable. The Conyers were a powerful Norman family who owned the land by the time of Domesday. It was bought by the Nortons at the end of the 14th century, who remained until rashly taking part in the Catholic uprising of 1569; their estates were confiscated.

The earliest parts of the house date from the Conyers occupation. It was substantially rebuilt around 1500 in red brick with arrow-slits, one of which remains. The Grahams bought Norton Conyers in 1624, some time later they covered the brick in roughcast, added the gables and made internal changes such as the broad oak staircase - which is as Charlotte Bronte wrote, 'spacious and slippery.' The fine walled garden is early 18th-century and the slightly later park provides an expansive setting. The 5th baronet commissioned William Belwood (a York architect who worked under Adam at Harewood and Newby) to build the stables, add the south-facing bow windows and install chimneypieces and ceilings which remain today.

The Victorian Grahams were sporting squires and the hall, which survives from the 15th-century house, is dominated by the Ferneley painting of the Quorn hunt when Sir Bellingham Graham, 7th Bt., was master. He won the picture from the other sitters on the throw of a dice. His swaggering portrait by Beechey more than hints at the recklessness which proved ruinous and shortly before his death the house and contents were sold. His behavious is reputed to have driven his daughter into a nunnery, but fortunately his son was able to buy back the estate in 1882 and continuity was preserved. Much was not recovered from the sale but there is still an abundance of portraits; two Romneys, a group of the 5th baronet and his family by Zoffany's pupil Henry Walton and a Batoni of Sir Humphrey Morice who remains a mystery at Norton Conyers as he had no connexions with the Grahams.

RIPLEY CASTLE, *Harrogate.*

Sir Thomas Ingilby,Bt.
Tel: 0423 770152.

In Ripley, off A61 3 m north of Harrogate.
Open: April and Oct Sat and Sun; May Sat and Sun, Tues, Wed, Thur (11.30-3.30); June to Sept Sat, Sun, Tues, Wed, Thur, Bank Hols; 11.30-4.30.
£3.75, children £2, concessions.
Restaurant/Tea room.

Ingilbys, who came to England with William the Conqueror, have been at Ripley for nearly seven hundred years and this long establishment is confirmed in the satisfying unity of the castle with its neighbouring model village and expansive landscape park. The gatehouse is mediaeval and Sir William Ingilby built the tower in 1555. Otherwise the castle dates from substantial rebuilding during the 1780s by Sir John Ingilby. Unfortunately the work was due to be largely financed by the fortune of his wife's father, Sir Wharton Amcotts. When he refused to part with any money Sir John and his wife were forced to leave Ripley and live in exile in Europe for some years.

Despite such tribulations Ripley today presents a fine balance between its impressive battlemented stone exterior, and elegant well-proportioned interiors exemplified by the curving cantilevered staircase in part of the entrance hall. Carr of York was Sir John Ingilby's architect and the Gothic flavour of the exteriors is well balanced by the classical interiors, which well offset the few surviving older chambers such as the Knight's Chamber and the Tower Room. Ingilby portraits tell of the family's progress through unsettled Tudor times to the Civil War when the then Sir William Ingilby was among the king's defeated forces as the nearby battle of Marston Moor, and illustrate successive 18th and 19th-century generations. There are also a number of notable Old Masters and appealing 18th-century Ingilby dogs.

Fine chairs in the round drawing room tell of the connexion between Ripley and Thomas Chippendale, whose family had lived in the village for generations and whose father was an estate carpenter. The important collection of Maiolica is one feature of a rich variety of works of art which, with Ripley's flower gardens and park, make for a rewarding ensemble.

STOCKELD PARK, *Wetherby.*

Mr and Mrs P.G.F. Grant.
Tel: 0937 586101.

2 m north of Wetherby on A661.
Open: April to early-Oct, Thur only 2-5.
£1.50, children 75p.

Stockeld is a good example of the depth of quality displayed by Yorkshire country houses. Far smaller than its grand neighbours such as Harewood, it is nonetheless a house of considerable distinction and one of James Paine's foremost designs. The Roman Catholic Middleton family commissioned Paine in 1756 and Stockeld was complete in 1763. During the 19th century the house was bought by Robert John Foster whose family had founded the Black Dyke Mills, famous for its brass bands. In the 20th century Stockeld passed to the Grants by marriage to a Foster.

Paine's original house of three deep, pedimented blocks, was characteristically Palladian and yet full if ingenuity, designed to afford the maximum effect from a limited ground-plan. Inside his most spectacular achievement was the oval staircase hall which, as well as its cantilevered staircase with crinoline balusters by Paine's favourite ironworker called Wagge, has a bewildering array of architectural sleights of hand.

The Fosters made considerable changes at Stockeld, adding a large wing and raising the entrance so that the original ground floor was sunk into a basement. They remodelled interiors - but gave them suitably neo-classical appearances. The library with its screen of grand scagliola columns, was originally the gallery for the Middleton's chapel and the double doors to the drawing room, the broken pediments and plaster ceiling were all added by the Fosters. The drawing room chimneypiece is Paine's original; the one in the library was added and came from 145 Piccadilly, the London home of the Queen Mother's family. When the fireplace was inserted it was discovered that Paine's arrangement of flues was so complicated that rather than linking into it, a new one was built accounting for the curious single chimney stack on one side of the house.

The loss of the chapel in the house was rectified by the Fosters when they made another one adjacent to the stable block in what had been an old orangery. These alterations were designed by Detmar Blow and included a fine organ. These buildings and the fine park containing a cricket ground give Stockeld a setting to compliment its architectural distinction.

SUTTON PARK, *York.*

Mrs Nancie Sheffield.
Tel: 0347 810249.

8 m north of York on B1363.
Open: details available on application.
Price available on application.

The Sheffield family have been distinguished landowners in Lincolnshire and Yorkshire since the 16th century, but have only lived at Sutton Park since 1963. It was bought by Mrs Sheffield and her late husband as a replacement for Normanby Park in Lincolnshire, whose size, as well as wartime requisition and open-cast mining in the park, made it impractical to live in.

Sutton Park proved a delightful alternative; an elegant Palladian house attributed to Thomas Atkinson and built for the Harland family around 1740, the two wings being added roughly a decade later. Mrs Sheffield and her husband restored the interiors (notably the original plasterwork by Cortese and the pine panelling by Henry Flitcroft in the morning room), adding chimney-pieces from Normanby, a new dining room designed by Francis Johnson, a tortoiseshell-decorated tea room for displaying porcelain and decoprated the drawing room with fine Chinese wallpaper.

Although recently installed the contents reflect the family's long, dinstinguished history. John Sheffield was made Earl of Mulgrave by Charles II, later became Queen Anne's favourite and was elevated to Marquess of Normanby and Duke of Buckingham. His London home was Buckingham House, sold to George III in 1762 and replaced by Buckingham Palace. After his his death his natural son Charles was his heir, but the inheritance was contested by Buckingham's widow, duchess Catherine and the heirs of her previous marriage. They inherited the family estates in North Yorkshire and the Mulgrave barony. Charles Sheffield inherited the London property and the estates around Normanby.

A number of the fine books in the library came from the Duke of Buckingham's library at Buckingham House and Sutton Park contains other evidence of his period, not least the remarkable series of portraits of the duke, his three duchesses and their children, by Wissing, D'Agar, Kneller and Highmore. Jacopi's perspective drawing of the garden front of Buckingham House hangs over a fine Japanese chest and both came from Buckingham House. Elsewhere the portraits date back to Elizabethan generations of the family.

The collections of porcelain, Meissen, early-18th century Derby and Chelsea, Dutch and Oriental are a highlight; the furniture throughout is of fine quality. Outside Mrs Sheffield has created a delightful series of terraced gardens beyond which parkland stretches away with Brown-like roundels of trees.

SCOTLAND
Traquair House

ABBOTSFORD HOUSE, *Melrose.*

Mrs P. Maxwell-Scott.
Tel: 0896 2043.

3 m west of Melrose off A72.
Open: late-March to end-Oct daily 10-5, Sun 2-5.
£2.60, children £1.30.
Tea room.

Abbotsford is a shrine to the life and achievements of Sir Walter Scott. The affection that he poured into the place between 1811 when he purchased the original farm and his death in 1832 remains evident and accounts for the strong personal presence that survives.

It was the success of his writing - in particular the Waverley Novels begun in 1814 - which provided the necessary funds for Abbotsford. The very name, which Scott gave the place because it had been owned by the Abbot of Melrose whose monks had crossed the Tweed at a nearby ford, and the house itself, irregularly battlemented, turreted, towered and gabled, celebrated the romantic Scottish history that Scott extolled in his writing. Together the place and his books were the major impetus for the advent of Scottish baronial architecture and the explosion of Victorian enthusiasm for Scotland.

Scott had originally purchased a farm of 110 acres and extended the existing house. But in 1822 this was pulled down and replaced with the more substantial present one, to which the west wing was added during the 1850s. During the eight years from 1824 when he and his family first moved into the new house, Scott decorated and filled it with things that he had collected and with gifts from eminent friends and admirers: a lock of Bonnie Prince Charlie's hair; a glass that belonged to Burns; Rob Roy's purse; and a desk given to Scott by George IV (who made him a baronet in 1820); an urn from Byron.

The warm, rich character that Scott gave to Abbotsford radiates from his portrait by Raeburn in the Drawing Room and ensured that from the first year after his death, visitors would be irrestistably drawn - as they have been ever since. Queen Victoria went in 1867 (although she thought it was 'rather gloomy') and in 1883 a total of 1500 people. Assisted by the continuity of unbroken family ownership, the richly-carved wooden panelling, the important collection of armour, the library lined with leather-bound volumes and the quantity of artifacts together perpetuate the memory of one of Scotland's favourite sons.

AYTON CASTLE, *Eyemouth.*

D.I. Liddell-Grainger of Ayton.
Tel: 08907 81212.

7 m north of Berwick-on-Tweed on A1.
Open: May to Sept Sun 2-5.
£2, children free.

Visitors to Scotland arriving by the London to Edinburgh train receive an impressive welcome shortly after crossing the border at Berwick-on-Tweed; a few miles to the north the red sandstone baronial splendour of Ayton Castle suddenly appears, a roofscape of crow-stepped gables, pointed or battlemented turrets and chimneystacks which encapsulates the popular idea of a Victorian Scottish castle.

Originally built during the 1840s, it was the last major work by the leading Scottish baronial architect, James Gillespie Graham, who was commissioned by Ayton's owner, William Mitchell Innes. Graham was just completing work on Brodick Castle on the Isle of Arran and there are clear similarities with Ayton: although his tower at Brodick collapsed he was not deterred and built a similar, larger, one at Ayton - which still stands.

During the 1860s Graham's originally castle was extended with new work by David Bryce and subsequently James Maitland Wardrop, but during the 1880s the property was sold by the Mitchell Innes family. It was bought by Henry Liddell whose family became Liddell-Grainger in 1893. Recent restoration and redecoration have highlighted the important surviving features of Graham's interior work, notably the rich plaster and carved ceilings. Especially interesting is the later decorative work by Bonnar and Carfrae, pupils of David Ramsay Hay.

BALCASKIE, *Pittenweem.*

Balcaskie Estate Trust.
Tel: 0333 311202.

1 m north-west of Pittenweem.
Open: June to end-Aug Sat and Sun, 2-5.
£2.50, children £1.50, concessions.

Balcaskie represents the major watershed in Scottish architecture that was achieved in the career of the house's builder Sir William Bruce. Bruce puchased Balcaskie in 1665 and transformed it from a fortified tower-house to a classical mansion with terraced gardens and surrounding parkland, a style that he later perfected on a larger scale at Hopetoun and Kinross.

As one approaches the house's north-facing entrance the French-inspired classicism of the central block joined to flanking pavilions by low walls with niches is immediately evident. Bruce's leap forward into classicism continues inside the house, notably in the outstanding plaster ceilings by Dunsterville. (He was working for Bruce at Holyroodhouse at the time and it was easy for the architect to commission the work for his own house.) The library and dining room ceilings have frescoes of Fame and Daedalus and Icarus both attributed to Jacob de Wit.

Bruce sold Balcaskie in 1684 and in 1698 it as bought by Sir Robert Anstruther, whose family have lived here ever since. They carried out alterations during the 19th century and it is their portraits which decorate the various rooms, demonstrating a long tradition of military service. In the hall is the portrait of Major General Philip Anstruther, who was captured during the First China War of 1840-42 and kept in a cage by his captors for two weeks. The tastes of successive generations are reflected in the mixture of French and English furniture, but of all the contents, the most suitable is te longcase clock in the library by one of Soctland's most distinguished makers, John Smith of Pittenweem, Balcaskie's local village about a mile away.

Among the family's most inportant contributions at Balcaskie has been their steady development and replanting of Bruce's original terraced gardens. These lie on the south side of the house, providing the foreground for the magnificent view to the Bass Rock in the centre of the Firth of Forth, and were as innovative when built by Bruce as the house itself.

BLAIR CASTLE, *Blair Atholl.*

The Duke of Atholl.
Tel: 0796 481207.

Off A9 at Blair Atholl, 35 m north of Perth.
Open: April to end-Oct, daily, 10-6 (last admission 5).
£4.50, children £3.50, concessions.

Blair Castle presents a surprising contrast. From the outside the sprawling white-harled building composed of tall vertical blocks with propotionally small windows, crow-stepped gables and conical turrets is what one would expect of a ducal Scottish seat. The feeling is encouraged by the knowledge that the family has been established for over seven centuries on the site that holds a position of enormous strategic importance on the main route through Scotland.

But there is an air of spaciousness in Blair's setting that suggests something more elegant than a castle in the Highlands. Indeed there is, for the 2nd duke - possibly to atone for the anti-English activities of his brothers - created one of the most notable series of 18th-century interiors to be found in any Scottish house. The work was done in the English Georgian tradition, with a roll-call of distinguished craftsmen all making their contributions; among Scottish houses only the Duke of Argyll's Inverary Castle rivals Blair in this manner.

Many of the craftsmen were English. Thomas Clayton executed the superb plasterwork, at its most florid Baroque in the ceiling, wall panels and overmantel in the dining room and finely elegant in the frieze of the tea room. Thomas Carter carved the marble chimney-pieces and furniture was supplied by a series of leading makers John Hodson, George Cole and John Gordon. Throughout all the rooms open to the public the wide range of furniture is of unfailing quality.

A set of Brussels tapestries was made for Charles I and bought by the 1st Duke of Atholl when sold off by Cromwell. Among the pictures which chronicle successive generations of Atholls and Murrays the most enjoyable are conversation pieces of the 3rd and 4th dukes with their families by Johann Zoffany and David Allen. The most magnificent is the full length of the 1st marquess by Jacob de Witt on the picture staircase looking like, 'one of Louis XIV's marshals.'

To assist understanding of the castle's evolution it is suitable that the first and last major rooms among the thirty-plus seen, the entrance hall and the ballroom, both date from the Scottish baronial additions for the 7th duke during the 1870s, which incorporated the surviving mediaeval parts of the castle and some Georgian alterations and accounts for the present exterior appearance.

Today Blair's strategic position is more important in attracting visitors than for defensive reasons, and it is the most visited historic house in Scotland.

BLAIRQUHAN, *Maybole.*

James Hunter Blair.
Tel: 065 57 239.

14 m south of Ayr off A77.
Open: mid-July to mid-Aug afternoons except Mon.
£3, children £2, concessions.

The approach to Blairquhan, along a three-mile drive which capitalizes on the picturesque setting of the River Girvan, is the ideal preparation for the house that lies ahead, on first impressions a pure Gothick castellated mansion which J.P. Neale described in his Views of Seats as 'a correct specimen of the architecture of Henry VII's time.'

But the house's architect, William Burn, shared an enthusiasm for Greek revival architecture with Robert Smirke in whose offices he studied. Blairquhan, built in the 1820s during the height of the Greek revival movement, clearly reveals this inspiration in the clean crisp lines of the ashlar stone with which it is built and makes the house, both outside and in, an intriguing blend of styles.

The main rooms, all arranged round an impressive two-storey saloon with a double staircase beyond, form an easy progression enhanced by their elegant, unfussy proportions. Certainly Burns's work is an intriguing contrast to the fantasy-like appearance of some of his other projects, such as the extraordinary staircase at Harlaxton Hall in Lincolnshire. But perhaps the most enjoyable feature of Blairquhan's interiors is the survival of the furnishings and other works of art that Burns's patron, Sir David Hunter Blair originally commissioned for the house. Redecoration and modernisation by the present owner, James Hunter Blair, has done nothing to disturb this happy situation.

Without doubt the most important additions since Sir David's time is the collection of pictures by Scottish Colourist artists, put together by the present owner's father, Sir James. Notable among these are the works by F.C.B. Cadell which predominate in the picture gallery. And as one leaves, the house's setting confirms the great contribution made by Sir David's extensive tree planting which, with the natural landscape, does so much to display the house to its best effect.

BOWHILL, *Selkirk.*

The Duke of Buccleuch and Queensberry.
Tel: 0750 20732.

3 m west of Selkirk on A708.
Open: Daily in July 1-4.30.
£3.50, concessions.
Tea room.

The long, rambling house of Bowhill is well suited to the gentle contours of the Scottish Borders. Despite boasting a continuous length of 437 feet there is a softness about the building which inspired Sir Walter Scott - neighbour and frequent visitor during the period that the original 18th-century house was encased and expanded - to name it 'sweet Bowhill.'

Certainly it does not have the ducal grandeur of the other Buccleuch seats, Drumlanrig Castle or Boughton House and as a result the visitor may not be prepared for the inside which contains one of the most superlative art collections in any house in Britain. Here the family portraits are masterpieces and the collections of Old Master paintings, French furniture, continental porcelain alone are testament to the combination of munificent patronage and collecting which has characterised successive generations of the family.

In 1812 the 4th duke of Buccleuch commissioned William Atkinson to begin alterations to the house. The duke died five years later but the work was continued, later involving two more architects William Burn and David Bryce, by his son the 5th duke who was laird of Bowhill for the next sixty-five years. The arrangement of the house and much of its atmosphere originates from this halcyon period as home to the duke and duchess and their seven children.

Not suprisingly many of the contents were either commissioned or collected during the previous century, for it was the 3rd duke of Buccleuch who witnessed the union of the three families of Montagu, Douglas and Scott along with their estates, houses and possessions. In 1767 he married Elizabeth, daughter and heiress of George Duke of Montagu and just before the end of his life, in 1810, he succeeded to the dukedom of Queensbury with its accompanying titles and the Douglas estates.

As befitted one of England's greatest heiresses, Elizabeth Montagu was painted by Reynolds in a portrait at Bowhill that many experts consider his finest work. While she is almost regally elegant, Gainsborough's portrait of her husband in the dining room reveals a supremely cultivated gentleman. Their eldest son is the 'Pink Boy' by Reynolds but for most visitors it is the artist's portrait of his sister, Lady Caroline Scott, as 'Winter' which is the most enchanting discovery in the whole house.

Bowhill reminds visitors that the original Buccleuch earldom became a dukedom when the family heiress, Anne married James Duke of Monmouth, the son of Charles II and his most attractive mistress, Lucy Walter. The family (and their estates and titles) survived the upheaval of the duke's rebellion against his uncle James II and his execution in 1685. A number of the works of art at Bowhill were gifts to Monmouth from his father and the duke himself is remembered in the Monmouth room which appeals to varied taste: as well as grand full length portraits of himself (by Lely) and his duchess and two sons (by Kneller), there is his cradle, his wonderfully ornate saddle, and the shirt he wore at his execution.

Such upheavals seem far removed from Bowhill today and instead it is easier to envisage the assured connoiseurship which gathered together the Mortlake tapestries in the Gallery Hall and the full-length portraits below, the scenes by Canaletto, Guardi and Claude Lorrain and Jacob van Ruysdael, the 18th-century Sevres porcelain often either on or near contemporary French furniture and the numerous pieces that combine curiosity with quality, such as the longcase clock by the Scottish maker John Smith of Pittenweem, which plays 8 different Scottish airs every 24 hours but is silent from midnight Saturday until midnight Sunday. Equally important, the tradition established by the 5th duke during his long tenure, that Bowhill was the focus of a thriving estate, has been continued by succeeding generations and at no time more since the present duke succeeded in 1973.

BRAEMAR CASTLE, *Braemar.*

Captain A.A.C. Farquharson of Invercauld Trusts.
Tel: 03397 41224.

North-east of Braemar on A93.
Open: May to mid-Oct daily except Fri 10-6.
£1.70, children 90p, concessions.

It is ironic that Braemar is home to the Farquharsons, for it was built in the early 17th century by the Earls of Mar to fend off their threatening Farquharson neighbours. The vississitudes of the two families dominated the castle's development for nearly two centuries, during which time it was a ruined shell for 60 years after being burnt out in 1689 by the legendary 'Black Colonel' John Farquharson.

In 1732 the castle was purchased by the colonel's descendant, John Farquharson of Invercauld, but its ruined state rendered it uninhabitable and in 1748 he leased it to the Hanoverian government for £14 per annum, to house one of the garrisons established to control the Highlands after the Jacobite risings. At the time John Adam, brother of Robert, held the position of Master Mason to the Board of Ordnance, and as a result he designed the restoration of the castle necessary before it could house its garrison. It is his work, grafted onto the original 17th-century fortress, which is responsible for Braemar's appearance today.

No doubt because Adam was planning for defence, the castle was not expanded and it retains the appearance of a miniature fortress, its five-storey battlemented walls towering over the courtyard which he protected with the curtain wall. When the Farquharson family took up occupation in 1807 peace had been restored to Deeside and the small rooms of the garrison stronghold became a family home of surprising intimacy compared to the castle's imposing exterior. Nonetheless, despite the cosiness, there are plenty of reminders of Braemar's violent past, in particular the iron grill in a stone passage which covers the 'Laird's Pit' an uninviting stone cell into which unfortunate prisoners were dropped.

CAWDOR CASTLE, *Inverness.*

The Countess Cawdor.
Tel: 0667 404615.

South of Nairn on B9090.
Open: May to Oct daily 10-5.30 (last admission 5).
£4, children £2.20, concessions.
Restaurant.

The Cawdor motto is 'be mindful' and for centuries successive generations of the family were well advised to remember it. Their title of Thane (once held by many Scottish barons) derives from the Saxons who took the word from the Norse thegn 'trusted servant of the king.' Even without the shroud of legend that Shakespeare threw around the place in Macbeth there is plenty of evidence of violent goings-on which terminated in Culloden field only a few miles away.

Certainly they appear to have remembered the motto when building their castle. Even today with its surroundings of peaceful park and woods, and delightful gardens, Cawdor has an air of impregnability and gives the feeling that it was built with security firmly in mind, a feeling confirmed as one approaches across a small drawbridge.

The other buildings which now enclose small courtyards to the east and north of the tower date mainly from the 17th century, with additions during the 19th century which marked the beginning of unbroken - and peaceful - occupation by the family. A fire in 1819 burnt part of the tower and repairs by the 1st Earl Cawdor signalled the family's return after prolonged absence at homes in London and Wales .

Today Cawdor is very much the family base and paintings and other works of art have been brought to the castle from other houses. Many early pictures were destroyed in the fire but full length portraits of the the 1st Lord Cawdor by Reynolds, his wife Caroline (daughter of the Earl of Carlisle) by Beechey and their son, the 1st Earl of Cawdor, confirm their 18th-centurystatus.

Sets of tapestries, 17th-century Arras, Brussels and Franco-Flemish, depicting the story of Noah, the Arts and Sciences and the story of Don Quixote, are traditional decoration for castle walls. Less expected are the examples of modern and contemporary art that one discovers, including a bronze girl by the Japanese sculptor Churyo Sato; and a plate by James Campbell.

He is the brother of Hugh, 6th Earl Cawdor, who died in 1993 aged sixty-one and who did so much to make Cawdor enjoyable for visitors. With his blend of irreverence, wit and connoisseurship, well displayed in the guide that he wrote, he made Cawdor history that was fun and brought the place and its contents to life to a degree reflected by its enduring popularity.

DALMENY HOUSE, *South Queensferry.*

The Earl of Rosebery.
Tel: 031 331 1888.

3 m east of South Queensferry, 7 m west of Edinburgh, off A90.
Open: May to end-Sept, Sun 1-5.30, Mon and Tues 12-5.30.
£3.40, concessions.
Home-made teas.

Dalmeny is a house to return to; one visit gives a taste of the diverse art collection but will also leave the visitor wishing to see more. Fortunately it is the most accessible country house from Edinburgh. It is full of history and treasures. The family home of the Earls of Rosebery, it was built during the 1810s by the 4th earl's friend, Wilkins, designer of King's College Cambridge and the National Gallery. He created a fine Tudor-Gothic mansion with wondrous views up and down the Full of Firth.

The family's great art collection, including that of the present earl's grandmother, Hannah Rothschild, is clearly and carefully arranged. The hall boasts family portraits, original Wilkins furniture and the delightful Goya tapestries of 'Children at Play'. The adjacent library contains furniture owned by Warren Hastings. This room is now used as a family drawing room - not surprisingly when you enter the state drawing room. Here is a remarkable display of French 18th-century furniture of the highest quality, set on a Louis XIV Savonierie carpet and surrounded by Beauvais tapestries designed by Boucher. The paintings are by Greuze and his contemporaries and the small porcelain dog on a cushion from the Sevres factory is naturally modelled on Marie Antoinette's pet.

The Napoleon room comes as a wonderful contrast. The richness of the 18th century is replaced by masculine severity. Here are objects not normally seen outside France: the Appiani portraits of the Emperor; and the Lefevres and Gerard portraits of his family; the consular throne; his shaving stand with his own profile portrait life size in ormolu; furniture and personal possessions from St Helena. This rich diet is not assuaged in the dining room. Here hang not just the family portraits but the 18th-century political portraits by Gainsborough, Reynolds, Lawrence and Raeburn, collected by the 5th Earl who married Hannah Rothschild. He became Prime Minister during the 1890s, but once remarked that he would prefer to own the winner of the Derby - which he did in consecutive years.

In the family wing are rooms devoted to the passion for racing which generations of Roseberys have enjoyed under their famous Primrose yellow colours, as well as French porcelain, furniture and paintings, and a room devoted to the Rothschild family. They complete a house of intriguing historical and artistic interest.

DRUMLANRIG CASTLE, *Thornhill.*

The Duke of Buccleuch and Queensberry.
Tel: 0848 31682.

3 m north of Thornhill off A76.
Open: early-May to late-Aug daily except Thur 11-5 (Sun 1-5).
Price available on request.

The first view of Drumlanrig is an experience never forgotten and something that every country-house enthusiast should enjoy. Among the gentle wooded hills of Nithsdale the castle seems to float on an elevated plateau and from any time after mid-afternoon on a sunny day gives the impression of being spotlit as the sun picks up the pale pink hue of its sandstone. It presents an Arcadian harmony of architecture and landscape that few places can match.

The third castle on the site where Douglas's had lived for over three centuries, Drumlanrig was built between 1679 and 1691 by the 1st Duke of Queensberry, who became the most powerful man in Scotland after the restoration of Charles II. The existing site and old castle probably contributed to the plan of a rectangle around a central courtyard, but the new castle demonstrated the status of its builder and - to a startling degree on the entrance front - the Carolean Baroque style of the age. ne does not expect that the rich composition that Robin Feddon described; 'curving perron arcaded loggia, giant pilasters, ranks of peimented windows, balustrades, and a lavishly decorated porch...'

Drumlanrig and its gardens nearly bankrupted the duke, the fortunes were restored by his son before coming under seige again later in the 18th century. The wife of the 3rd duke was Kitty Hyde who one contemporary described as, 'Kitty, beautiful and young, and wild as colt untamed' and when her husband died without a son the titles and estates passed to his cousin William, a dissolute rake called 'Old Q' whose carryings-on in London took their toll on his Scottish estates. He had no sons, left his money to an illegitimate daughter who used it to launch the Wallace Collection. The Queensberry titles and estates passed to the Duke of Buccleuch.

From this moment serenity and a steady influx of artistic riches were the happy lot of the Douglas stronghold and Drumlanrig is a similar treasure-trove to the other Buccleuch homes, Bowhill and Boughton. Rembrant's 'Old Woman Reading', Leonardo da Vinci's 'Madonna with the Yardwinder' and Holbein's portrait of Sir Nicholas Carew - the three masterpieces among serried ranks of outstanding pictures, all came from the Montagu family. Much of the exquisite French furniture found in a number of rooms was similarly imported. Nonetheless Douglas and Queensberry family members are well represented; Kitty Queensberry is painted by Jean-Baptiste Van Loo and there is a conversation piece of her with her husband and two sons by George Knapton, while wood carving by Grinling Gibbons testifies to the quality of the 1st Duke of Queensberry's original decoration of the interiors.

The family's position and patronage at the time combine to make Drumlanrig an all-round illustration of 17th- and 18th-century art of the highest quality; the enlightened custodianship of subsequent generations has ensured that their connoisseurship is preserved for visitors to enjoy.

DUART CASTLE, *Isle of Mull.*

Sir Lachlan Maclean, Bt.
Tel: 06802 309.

2 m from Craignure off A849.
Open: May to mid-Oct, 10.30-6.
£3, children £1.50, concessions.
Tea room.

Even among Scottish castles Duart seems to encapsulate the strange combination of romance, violence and hardship integral to the history of the Highlands and their clans. Its remoteness is immediately evident as it is glimpsed, perched on a rocky promentary called Black Point that sticks out into the Sound of Mull facing Lismore Island and the mainland beyond.

Parts date from the 13th century, from which time until the end of the 17th century the Macleans appear to have been constantly fighting; amongst themselves, with the Macdonalds, but principally against the hated Argyll Campbells who, with support from the English governemnt, eventually defeated them in 1691. Duart was then razed in 1756 when the English garrison departed.

It remained a ruin for over two centuries until 1911 when the surviving building and peninsula on which it stood were purchased by Sir Fitzroy Maclean, 26th Chief of the Clan and a man in the mould of his ancestors, who fought as a Hussar in the Crimea and lived to be a hundred. He engaged the architect Sir John Burnet to rebuild the small castle and make it the habitable home visitors enjoy today. The castle contains regular reminders of stirring deeds by Macleans; dirks and uniforms and a portrait of Sir John Maclena who fought at Killiecrankie shortly before the clan's rout by the Campbells, as well as portraits of the castle's saviour, Sir Fitzroy and his son who was Chief Scout and Comptroller of Elizabeth II's Household. Duart's romantic history and position make it a place of irrestible pilgrimage for Macleans from the world over.

DUNROBIN CASTLE, *Golspie.*

The Countess of Sutherland.
Tel: 0408 633177/633268.

1 m north of Golspie on A9.
Open: Easter week-end (10.30-4.30, Sun 1-4.30), May to mid-Oct, Sat (10.30-5.30) Sun (1-5.30) closing 1 hour earlier May and Oct.
£3.20, children £1.60, concessions.
Tea room.

Perched dizzily above its terraced gardens, Dunrobin is the grandest and most impressive building in the northern Highlands. More modest predecessors were homes to the earls of Sutherland whose ancient title dates from the 13th century and whose vast estates stretched the length and breadth of the Highlands encompassing in excess of a million acres.

The earldom may be held by a female. In 1785 land and lineage became merged with huge wealth when Elizabeth Countess of Sutherland married George Marquess of Stafford. He inherited not only his own family's wealth and estates, but those of his uncle, the 3rd and last Duke of Bridgwater. Months before Lord Stafford's death in 1833 he was created 1st Duke of Sutherland and his wife therafter known as the Duchess-Countess.

Being a committed reformer and philanthropist the 1st duke's activities in the Highlands focused on the misguided Clearances that caused such unhappiness and ill-feeling, but his son had different ideas. He commissionioned the fashionable architect Charles Barry to remodel his three main country seats, Dunrobin, Trentham in Staffordshire and Cliveden on the Thames. Between 1835 and 1850 Barry transformed Dunrobin into the French-style chateau.

The 2nd duke, his son and grandson all entertained lavishly at Dunrobin. Queen Victoria made the long journey from Balmoral in 1872 and her son, Edward VII, to whom the comfort greatly appealed, was a more regular guest. In 1915 when the castle was being used as a hospital, fire gutted most of Barry's interiors and the 5th duke commissioned Sir Robert Lorimer to carry out extensive restoration.

Nonetheless the castle retains an atmosphere of grand Victorian Scottish living in its warmly panelled rooms. In recognition of her contribution to the family fortunes there are portraits of the Duchess-Countess by Hoppner, Reynolds and Lawrence. Dunrobin's zenith is evoked by two portraits of the 2nd duke's wife Harriet, one with her daughter Elizabeth by Lawrence, the other by Winterhalter and the later portrait of Eileen, 5th duchess, by de Lazlo. Foremost in the collection, however, are the pair of Canalettos of the Doge's Palace in the spacious drawing room that Lorimer made out of two smaller rooms.

DUNVEGAN CASTLE, *Isle of Skye.*

John MacLeod of Macleod.
Tel: 047 022206.

In Dunvegan 23 m west of Portree.
Open: end-March to end-Oct daily 10-5 (Sun 1-5).
£4.00, children £2.20, concessions.
Restaurant.

Inhabited by the Chiefs of the Clan Macleod for over 750 years, Dunvegan has a history stretching back to Norsemen and Celts. The family descend from Leod who, around 1270, first fortified the rocky site of Dunvegan. Until 1748 the only entrance to the castle was through the sea gate, reached via steps up from the sea and defended by barbican and portcullis. When Dr Johnson visited in 1773 the faithful Boswell recorded that the landward entrance dated from 1748. Evidence of various stages of the castle's development from Leod's time can be found, but, internally and externally Dunvegan dates from two substantial periods of work, during the 1790s when the 23rd Chief of the Macleod clan determined to make it a habitable home as much as a castle, and during the 1840s when the exterior gained its uniform castellated appearance.

No change could detract from Dunvegan's magical position and visitors find themselves steeped in distant history, admiring strange and romantic relics. The Fairy Flag is the most prized, followed by the Dunvegan Cup, a wooden vessel encased in silver filagree, which was given to Sir Rory Mor (the 16th Chief) by the O'Neills of Ulster, in thanks for his help in their fight against the English in 1596. The silver is inscribed and dated 1493 but the vessel is much older. Flora Macdonald, Bonnie Prince Charlie's saviour, lived here for a time as her daughter married the tutor to the young Chief. Many of her personal souvenirs of the Jacobite uprising are on view at the castle. The outstanding paintings are by Allan Ramsay, full-length portraits of the 22nd Chief and his second wife, he in full Macleod dress, every inch a Highlander.

EARLSHALL CASTLE, *Leuchars.*

The Baron and Baroness of Earlshall.
Tel: 0334 839205.

At Leuchars off A919.
Open: Easter, April to end-Oct, daily 1-5.15.
£3.20, children £1, concessions.
Tea room.

The coastal castle built by Sir William Bruce in 1546 gained belevolent restoration at the ideal time. In 1890 Earlshall was bought by Robert Mackenzie, a Perth bleach merchant who commissioned Robert Lorimer to restore the castle and design new gardens. Lorimer's career included a number of outstanding and sensitive restorations of Scottish castles and Earlshall is as good an example as any. In the gardens irregularly shaped yew topiary chessmen now seem to copy the conglomerate of battlements, steep crow-stepping and towering chimneys of the castle's roofscape.

As with a number of Scottish castles of the period, Earlshall's vertical strength gives the impression of being a collection of towers thrust together and one would not think there is room for the castle's chief glory, the long gallery with its fantastic 17th-century coved painted ceiling, decorated with the arms of leading Scottish families, and a host of other devices including a variety of mythological beasts such as the Ape of Arabia. The gallery was restored by Lorimer and the present owners have added their enormous collection of basket-hilted swords and rare 'twa-handed' Scottish swords, highlights of a more extensive collection of arms and armour. There is also a selection of Jacobite relics perpetuating the loyalty of Baxter (the baron's family name) ancestors who supported the cause and fought at Culloden.

When the Baxters bought Earlshall in 1983 it was once again in need of attention. Their restoration inside the castle and the resurrection of Lorimer's garden to which they have added quantites of new planting would certainly have met with his approval. As well as the military and historic contents (such as the set of bagpipes played at Waterloo) they have added the fine oak funiture is ideally suited to the warm panelled atmosphere of most rooms.

FASQUE HOUSE, *Fettercairn.*

The Gladstone family.
Tel: 05614 569/202.

1 m north of Fettercairn on B974.
Open: May to end-Sept daily except Fri 1.30-5.30.
£2, children £1, concessions.

Aberdeenshire is an area of Scotland richly endowed with substantial houses as opposed to castles, but few rival Fasque for scale and symmetry. Its broad stone front with castellated turrets in descending size from the centre and simple Georgian windows looking out over deer park is an impressive sight and one is not surprised to hear that the project ruined its builder, Sir Alexander Ramsay. His architect was Paterson of Edinburgh, who controlled the Scottish projects of the Adam brothers once they were based in London and Fasque has all the assertive confidence of this family partnership. The houses's interiors continue the tone of grand austerity, with the one architectural flourish of the double curving cantilevered staircase.

Ramsay's plight was exploited by John Gladstone who bought Fasque from him in 1830. A Leith boy who made a fortune in Liverpool, he returned home to Scotland to establish himself with a country seat. And it is the Gladstone connection which most people visit Fasque for, as John Gladstone's youngest son was W.E., the Liberal Prime Minister. Fasque was his home from 1830 until his father's death in 1851 and one can well imagine him immersing himself in the rows of leather-bound volumes in the library.

The Prime Minister's eldest brother Thomas succeeded to Fasque and the baronetcy their father had been given and he in turn was succeeded by his only son John who lived in the house until 1926. Thereafter the family based themselves at Hawarden Castle in Wales and only occupied Fasque on an occasional basis. The lack of change since the 1920s - fine Georgian and Regency furniture and paintings in the main rooms have not moved - means that visitors are able to enjoy a curiously unchanged period atmosphere.

FINLAYSTONE HOUSE, *Langbank.*

Mr and Mrs G. MacMillan.
Tel: 047554 285/505.

On A8 between Langbank and Port Glasgow.
Open: April to Aug Sun 2.30-4.30.
£1.50, children £1, concessions.
Tea room.

Overlooking the Clyde estuary a few miles west of Glasgow airport, Finlystone was for some four centuries a seat of the earls of Glencairn, whose number included an ardent supporter of John Knox, a Chancellor of Scotland and a leading patron of Burns. Their house dated from the 14th century but was rebuilt around 1760. The did not have long to enjoy their improvements; in 1796 the last earl died and that family's occupation of Finlaystone ended.

By the end of the 19th century the Clyde was among the most important shipping centres in the world and Finlaystone was bought by George Jardine Kidston, chairman of the Clyde Shipping Company. The house was in need of considerable repair and he commissioned Sir John James Burnett to carry out the work, completed around 1900. The house retained an 18th-century facade. The top storey (which Kidston added to accomodate his nine children) gave it an attractive hipped roof and dormers. On one side symmetry is interruputed by the square tower which rises above the roofline. In true plutocratic style Kidston lavished huge sums on the house. Marble pillars were inserted to support the old north wall, heavy marble chimneypieces added to the main rooms which were also given decorated plaster ceilings.

General Sir Gordon MacMillan married Kidston's granddaughter and their family have lived at Finlaystone since the Second World War. The Edwardian atmosphere survives in the house where new interests include an important collection of dolls in the billiard room. In recent years the MacMillans have made major new introductions in the garden, re-designing the walled garden and extending the traditional garden yew-hedges, herbaceous borders, and sweeping lawns by incorporating more informal areas in the surrouding woodland and unusual features such as the Celtic pattern of paving.

FLOORS CASTLE, *Kelso.*

The Duke of Roxburghe.
Tel: 0573 223333.

North of Kelso.
Open: Easter and end-April to end-Oct Sun-Thur, daily July and Aug 10.30-5.30, Oct Sun and Wed 10.30-4.30.
£3.40, children £1.70, concessions.
Restaurant.

As shown in the painting of 1809 by William Wilson which hangs in the castle, Floors as originally built by William Adam for the 1st Duke of Roxburghe between 1721-26 was one of the Borders' most impressive houses and enjoyed an enviable position overlooking the River Tweed. The position remains unchanged but alterations for the 6th duke, carried out by the Edinburgh architect William Playfair transformed impressive to palatial. Playfair joined the central block to its pavilions, and extended the whole so now the north - entrance - front seems endless in width while from the river to the south the roofscape is a dazzling melee of pepper-pot turrets, chimneys and castellations.

In 1903 the 8th duke followed the example of other leading aristocrats and married an American heiress, May Goelet of New York, and it is her contribution that makes the greatest impact in the rooms open to visitors. She inherited and expanded a superb art collection and also replaced Playfair's Scottish baronial style in some rooms with 18th-century recreations. She remodelled the drawing room to accomodate the set of 17th-century Brussels tapestries called the Triumph of the Gods that came from her family home in Long Island, and similarly transformed Playfair's ballroom to accomodate two equally fine Gobelins tapestries from the series Les Portieres des Dieux.

Many rooms contain Duchess May's oriental porcelain and French furniture, notably the Louis XV and XVI cabinets and commodes in the drawing room and the Louis XVI escritoire in the needle room. A more surprising discovery is her collection of paintings in the needle room including works by Matisse, Bonnard and the Englishman Sir Matthew Smith.

Duchess May's additions compliment the grand scale of Floors but there is a pleasing element of contrast in the smaller rooms such as the sitting room where the Wilson view of Floors hangs, the ante room with a rare early-16th century Gothic tapestry woven in Brussels and the hall where Hendrick Danckerts view of Charles II and his court walking in the Horse Guards is outstanding among a group of English topographical pictures. The series of likenesses of successive earls and dukes of Roxburghe was completed in 1988 with an arresting portrait of the present duke by Howard Morgan.

GLAMIS CASTLE, *Glamis.*

The Earl of Strathmore and Kinghorne.
Tel: 0307 840 242/393.

In Glamis.
Open: April to late-Oct daily 10.30-5.30 (last admission 4.45).
£4.20, children £2.30, concessions.
Restaurant.

The first view of Glamis, the unusually tall central block framed at the bottom of a long double avenue confirms expectations of romantic history, from the distant past as celebrated by Shakespeare in Macbeth, and more recently as the childhood home of Queen Elizabeth the Queen Mother who was born Lady Elizabeth Bowes Lyon. Like many Scottish castles Glamis is impressive rather than beautiful and one agrees with the poet Thomas Gray who visited in 1765 and wrote, 'Very singular and striking in appearance, like nothing I ever saw.'

A mediaeval royal hunting lodge, Glamis was the scene of the death of King Malcolm in 1034. In 1372 it was granted to Sir John Lyon by King Robert II and thus began the family's occupation which has continued unbroken ever since. Lyon became Lord Glamis in 1445 and during the 17th century Earls of Kinghorne and Strathmore, but most important for the family fortunes was the 18th-century marriage of the 9th earl to the heiress Mary Bowes of Durham, from which point the family name subsequently became Bowes Lyon.

From a 15th-century core parts of which are preserved in the central block Glamis expanded, mainly during the 17th century. At this time the west wing was added to balance the existing east wing of the old tower and this produced the unusual arrangement of the main entrance facing out from its tower on the angle of the two wings. The further eastern extension were made principally during the 19th century. It is this period which greets the visitor in the dining room where the combination of features, notably the ceiling, remain a vigorous Jacobean recreation. As was popular among Victorians, the family history is told in heraldry by the succession of shields arranged in chronological order.

The atmosphere of Glamis' distant, violent past is prevelent in the crypt and in Duncan's Hall (the legendary scene of Duncan's murder by Macbeth although the deed actually took place near Elgin); one can sympathise with Sir Walter Scott who wrote after staying in the castle, 'when I heard door after door shut, after my conductor had retired, I began to consider myself as too far from the living, and somewhat too near the dead.'

It is a relief to escape to warmer, more welcoming parts of the castle and the drawing room, billiard room and royal apartments in particular are full of delights. The 1621 plasterwork arched ceiling in the drawing room is the outstanding feature of the work by the 2nd earl and the overmantel with the royal arms is almost certainly contemporary. More plasterwork from the same period can be found in King Malcolm's bedroom which has a delicate ceiling pattern of the 2nd earl's cypher and coronet and his arms in the overmantel.

The billiard room is notable for the set of 17th-century English tapestries depicting the life of Nebuchadnezzar and The Fruit Market attributed to Frans Snyders. The drawing room contains the best selection of the castle's portraits, including a fine group of the 3rd earl and his sons and a more melancholy likeness of the 9th Lord Glamis aged eight; his great-grandmother was burnt as a witch by James V in 1540 for no better reason that hatred of her family.

Such disturbing memories disappear completely in the elegant but friendly royal apartments, arranged during the 1920s for the Duke and Duchess of York who became King George VI and Queen Elizabeth. One delightful touch by the young duchess's mother was to incorporate into the hangings that she worked for her daughter's bed the initials C and C (for herself and her husband) and the names and dates of birth of all their ten children. She also passed on to her daughter a love of gardening, evident in the enclosed Italian garden she created which makes a delightful contrast to the more expansive parkland surrounding the castle's approaches.

HOPETOUN HOUSE, *Scotland.*

The Hopetoun House Preservation Trust.
Tel: 031 331 2451.

2 m from Forth Road Bridge near South Queensferry off A904.
Open: daily April to end-Sept, 10-5.30 (last admission 4.45).
£3.80, children £1.90, concessions.
Restaurant/Tea room.

Hopetoun is Scotland's largest house, and could be considered architecturally the most important in that it was built by the country's two most distinguished classical architects - or architectural families - William Bruce and the Adams. Bruce's house built between 1699-1703 is preserved in the west-facing garden front and reveals distinct similarity to his own home Balcaskie in its French-influenced classicism. William Adam's entrance front begun in 1721 is altogether more monumental, the curving colonnades and pavilions with their cupola-topped towers balancing the massive proportions of the central block.

Inside the contrasting scales of classicism continue, with the important influence of the Hope family's elevation from the Earldom of Hopetoun dating from 1703, to the Marquessate of Linlithgow in 1902. the first marquess was the first Governor-General of Australia, his son was the longest serving Viceroy of India from 1936-43. Their full length portraits, both as Knights of the Thistle (Scotland's equivalent of the Garter), greet the visitor in the entrance hall which was completed by William Adam's son John.

The main staircase is Bruce's work, with rich wood carving by Alexander Eizat who worked for him at Holyroodhouse, as are the parlour and bedchamber in the centre of the west front, the last containing the splendid state bed made by Mathias Lock and supplied by James Cullen who was responsible for most of the furniture for the Adam apartments. Also in the bedroom is an unusual pattern chair which Cullen made for the 2nd earl to enable him to choose from a variety of carving styles. Here and continuing in rooms above are a series of allegorical paintings commissoned by the 1st earl from Philip Tideman.

The large library as it is now, was a conversion from a bedchamber and small drawing room in the early part of the 19th century by Sir James Gillespie Graham employed by the 4th Earl of Hopetoun. Three grand rooms make up the major Adam contribution inside Hopetoun, the yellow drawing room, red drawing room and dining room (which it became after considerable alteration during the early 19th century.) The two drawing rooms survive as remarkably complete examples of Adam decoration: rich coved plaster ceilings and suites of splendid furniture all as supplied for the original scheme by Cullen. The work at Hopetoun also reflects the classical education of Robert Adam; in 1754 he visited Italy with Charles Hope Vere (or Weir), the second son of the 1st earl, a journey that profoundly influenced his architectural style. The most impressive momento of is the marble chimneypiece in the red drawing room, for which Adam sent the design from Rome, to be carved by Michael Rysbrack. More poignant is the Nathaniel Dance portrait of the two Hope boys Charles and James with their tutor, the elder son, Charles, dying shortly afterwards aged twenty-six.

All three rooms contain fine paintings and among the portraits the most significant is the 2nd Earl Annandale by Andrea Procaccini. The earl was a noted connoisseur and collector, his sister married the first earl - no doubt the connection partially inspired his architectural commissions - and when Lord Annandale died his sister inherited his art collection. Most of it was dispersed during the 19th century when it was replaced with the present collection of Italian, Dutch and Flemish Old Masters.

George IV came to Hopetoun on his visit to Scotland in 1822 and knighted the artist Henry Raeburn and Captain Adam Ferguson, Keeper of the Scottish regalia, in the yellow drawing room. The king would certainly have appreciated the house's splendours, but he is unlikely to have made the journey to the roof as visitors can do today, to enjoy the spectacular views across Hopetoun's park to the Firth of Forth and its twin road and rail bridges.

INVERARAY CASTLE, *Inveraray.*

The Trustees of the 10th Duke of Argyll.
Tel: 0499 302203.

North of Inveraray on Loch Fyne.
Open: 1st Sat in April to 2nd Sun in Oct, daily except Fri, 2-5.30, July and Aug daily 10-5.30 (Sun 1-5.30).
£3.50, children £1.75, concessions.
Tea room.

The ancient seat of the Clan Campbell, of whom the Dukes of Argyll are head, was ruined Innis Chonnell Castle on Loch Awe when the 3rd duke inherited in 1743 and commissioned the Englishman Roger Morris to design the new castle outside its eponymous town. The family's pro-English connections, so hated by their enemies the Macleods and Macdonalds, dated from the 10th Earl of Argyll who was made a duke by William of Orange for his support in opposition to the Stuarts who had beheaded both his grandfather and father for treason.

Morris's castle, whose construction was supervised by William Adam and his two sons John and Robert, was a vigorous early example of the Gothic revival, its four-square proportions undiminished by any wings or extensions. The Gothic character was best displayed in Morris's central tower, 70 feet tall, although its impact was reduced by alterations by Anthony Salvin after the 1877 fire, when the original roof battlements were replaced by the present dormer windows. Salvin also added the conical turrets to the corner towers, making the castle's appearance more Scottish than the original, and redesigned the inside of the tower (which had been gutted) with the present armoury hall.

Internally Inveraray's main delight is the series of painted rooms designed by Robert Mylne for the 5th duke during the 1780s, which are without equal. The 5th duke and his beautiful Irish wife were Francophiles and most of the painters employed at Inveraray were French; the wonderful patterns have a lightness of touch compared, for instance, to painted rooms executed by Robert Adam. The decoration is complimented by an abundance of gilded chairs covered in French tapestry, by the set of Beauvais tapestries that hang in the drawing room with Hoppner's portrait of the 5th duke's daughter Lady Charlotte as Aurora.

The 5th duke's four sons were all painted in a notable series by Opie which hang in the saloon - originally the entrance hall - along with other distinguished family portraits. Elsewhere in the house are reminders of the marriage of the 9th duke to Queen Victoria's daughter, Princess Louise. This was six years before the first of Inverary's fires and the visitor should marvel that the family's determined efforts on two occasions have been so successful while sympathizing with the strain the restorations have placed on the estate.

KELBURN CASTLE, *Largs.*

The Earl of Glasgow.
Tel: 0475 568685.

On A78 between Largs and Fairlie.
Open: July and Aug pm.
£1.50 (castle only), concessions.

Kelburn, home of the Boyle family, Earls of Glasgow, is among the select group of Scottish castles vying for the unprovable distinction of being the country's oldest inhabited home. Their claim of the longest continuous occupation by a single family, the de Boyvilles (who came to Britain with William the Conqueror) since 1140, and evidence of the castle by the reign of Alexander III (1249-86), is impressive. Certainly they chose their position well, with the picturesque Kelburn glen tumbling down on one side and views across the Firth of Clyde to Arran and the closer island of Great Cumbrae - most of which they owned.

The earldom came to David Boyle in 1703 in thanks for his active support of the Act of Union. To demonstrate his new-found importance he trasformed Kelburn from a modest defensive tower house into a seat of substance by adding the wing which today forms the largest body of the castle. The family prospered for nearly two centuries, until the 6th earl threatened total ruin through - even by Victorian standards - one of the more unusual forms of profligacy, a mania for building churches. He funded their construction all over Scotland. Not his for long, however; by the 1880s he was bankrupt, the family's considerable estates and most of the contents of Kelburn were sold and the castle itself was only saved when his cousin - who eventually inherited the title - bought it in 1886.

The 7th earl was a sailor who served in the Crimea and China and became Governor-General of New Zealand. Kelburn today has many reminders of his career - some quite ordinary such as the quantity of marine pictures, other extraordinary such as the ghariol (a relative of the crocodile) which climbs the banisters of the 1st earl's impressive staircase.

Since opening Kelburn to the public the present earl and countess have emphasised the qualities of the castle's surroundings and made the old 18th-century home farm into the Kelburn Centre. It is along the path that follows the burn up its glen that one discovers the marvellous classical monument to the the 3rd earl, erected by his widow after his death in 1775, the design commissioned from no lesser figure than Robert Adam, by this time at the zenith of his career. The elegant monument's position here is entirely apt, for the 3rd earl's main contribution at Kelburn was landscaping the glen and improving the gardens which are integral to Kelburn's attraction. It is especially fortunate that the charming painting of his four children playing in the garden survives in the castle.

MANDERSTON, *Duns.*

Lord and Lady Palmer.
Tel: 0361 83450.

2 m east of Duns on A6105.
May to end-Sept Thur, Sun, Spring and Aug Bank Hol Mon 2-5.30.
Price on application.
Tea room.

Manderston can claim to be the most sumptous Edwardian house in Britain, and if anyone wants to savour the blend of opulence, indolence and quality that form the popular conception of upper-class life during that era, there is no better place to experience it. However derivative its architecture and every detail of its interior decoration the unfailing quality of the execution more than compensates.

It is the Edwardian story par excellence; a fortune made out of the most uninspiring of trades, hemp and herrings, is married to aristocratic grandeur, the daughter of Lord Scarsdale of Kedleston Hall, and Manderston and its policies are transformed like Cinderella. But for a cherry stone it might not have happened. The fortune was made by Sir William Miller, who himself first altered the original 18th-century house and gave it a French Renaissance look, but his eldest son William died a schoolboy at Eton after choking on a cherry stone and the inheritance pased to his younger brother, James. Little wonder he was always known as 'Lucky Jim'.

He inherited in 1887 and five years later married the Hon Eveline Curzon one of the eleven children of the rector Lord Scarsdale. She had been brought up at Robert Adam's masterpiece Kedleston and when her husband commissioned John Kinross - the best and most fashionable Scottish architect of the period - to begin work at Manderston, his wife's home was to be the model. Georgian elegance was to be blended with Edwardian comfort. The end result was impressive and expensive - fortunately Kinross had been told that there was no limit to the budget!

Externally .the house is faithful, immaculate neo-Georgian but even here there are the ingenious touches that all aided the easy flow of Edwardian life; at the base of the four Ionic pillars of the new entrance portico are metal lions' heads, two or which are bell-pulls in reach of a horseman's boot. It was, however, inside Manderston that Kinross worked to greatest effect and where the inspiration of Kedleston is constantly evident. From the oval entrance hall through vestibules and ante rooms to the main hall and a suite of reception rooms - a circular morning room, tea room, dining room, library, drawing room and ballroom (these two decorated as a pair in Sir James's racing colours of primrose and white) - the progression is a remarkable ensemble of Adam features; rich plaster ceilings and wall panels, urns on carved pedestals, inlaid marble floors, columns of varying order and arched doorcases containing perfectly hung mahogany doors.

The overall richness is enhanced by silk and velvet wall hangings and curtains - all original - gilded and painted covered in tapestry and French furniture, and the standard of work is almost unnervingly high. The climax - which some guests at Manderston's house parties may have secretly considered rather vulgar - is the cantilevered marble staircase with a swirling silver-plated balustrade and solid brass top rail.

Sir James ensured that not only his guests were afforded the utmost comfort. His passion for hunting and racing meant that his horses lived in what are widely acknowledged to be the grandest stables in Europe; one commentator wrote that their teak and tiled troughs were 'reminiscent of huxuriant hotel basins.' And it is the whole composition of Manderston: house, stables, gothic marble dairy, terraced gardens, the boathouse built for his wife in the style of a Swiss chalet, cottages, kennels and home farm - all designed by Kinross - and the huge gates gilded to catch the setting sun, which together submerge the visitor in a vision of luxurious torpor. The only note of melancholy is the knowledge that Sir James only enjoyed it for a few years. He died childless aged only forty-one from pneumonia brought on by a cold caught out hunting. Today Lord Palmer (the great-grandson of Sir James's sister) and his wife and children cope with maintaining Manderston to a standard his great-great-uncle would have approved of, without the army of staff that kept the wheels silently turning.

MELLERSTAIN, *Gordon.*

The Mellerstain Trust.
Tel: 0573 410225.

9 m north-east of Melrose, 7 m north-west of Kelso.
Open: Easter, May to end-Sept 12.30-4.30.
£3.50, chidren £1.50, concessions.
Tea room.

It is an indication of the grandeur of the earls of Haddington that until the present earl inherited the title, one of the finest Adam houses in Scotland was the family's secondary residence. They were among Scotland's foremost peers when, in 1717 the heir to the 6th earl married Rachel Baillie, heiress to Mellerstain. As their eldest son inherited the Haddington title and estates Mellerstain passed to their second son who built the house; two generations later his grandson inherited the earldom from his cousin.

George Baillie and his future wife, Lady Grisell, were a romantic couple who had suffered at the hands of the Stuart government and fled to Holland after his father had been executed. They subsequently saw their fortunes - and family estates - restored by the accession of William of Orange, after which they married in 1691. In 1725 George commissioned William Adam to build a new house at Mellerstain, but only two wings were completed. Forty years later, his grandson, also George (who had assumed the Baillie surname) commissioned William's son Robert Adam to complete the plan by building the required house between his father's two wings.

Mellerstain's north-facing entrance front, a harmonious balance of the father's wings and son's central block presents an elegantly welcoming scene. The south-facing front with its undecorated pattern of windows and castellated roof-line is austere to a point of bleakness and certainly not the younger Adam's most inspired design. In the succession of rooms along the south front: sitting room, library, music room, drawing room, small drawing room and small library (originally two rooms) Adam's skill at arranging a series of classical decorative compositions is triumphantly displayed. Each has a plaster ceiling, that in the library in pink and green with painted panels of Minerva flanked by Teaching and Learning by Zucci, perhaps the finest. The books were collected by Adam's patron and above their shelves are four classical reliefs and, in niches, portrait busts, two of Lady Grisell Baillie and her daughter Lady Murray by Roubillac. Adam's green and white marble fireplace sets the standard for those that follow in the other main rooms.

Adam's most coolly classical room is the apsed entrance hall and his hand continues in the double staircase and, indeed to the top of the house beyond the main bedrooms, where visitors discover the great gallery with a long curving ceiling, Ionic columns and a classical plaster freize. Throughout the house portraits illustrate members of the family through three hundred years, in many rooms hanging next to fine Dutch paintings and the furniture is of similar quality and varied interest.

In 1909 Sir Reginald Blomfield, the fashionable Edwardian architect and garden-designer, was commissioned to lay out the formal terraces below the south front which make an imposing foreground to the magnificent view that stretches over a long sweep of lawn to the lake and the Cheviot Hills in the background.

NEIDPATH CASTLE, *Peebles.*

Lady Elizabeth Benson.
Tel: 0721 720333.

1 m west of Peebles on A72.
Open: Easter to end-Sept Mon to Sat 11-5, Sun 1-5.
£1.50, children 75p, concessions.

Perched on a bluff overlooking the River Tweed, Neidpath's defensive origins are clear and the castle seems to have made few concessions to modernity since it was built during the late-14th century. Altered inside during the 16th and 17th centuries it was not extended and thus remains essentially a mediaeval tower house; a compact L-shape, with immensely thick walls, the height and limited ground-area giving maximum assistance to defenders warding off attack. This came regularly; in 1307 before the castle was built the local laird Sir Symon Fraser fought - and defeated - English armies three times in one day. Neidpath passed with his daughter to the Hay family who owned it for 380 years, becoming Earls and Marquesses of Tweeddale. In 1686 the 1st and last marquess sold Neidpath to the Duke of Queensberry; in 1810 it was inherited from the 3rd duke by the Earl of Wemyss.

Although partially ruined and unoccupied Neidpath gives an absorbing illustration of grim mediaeval life and how the castle was subsequently altered to provide a home with a modicum of comfort. Originally consisting of three main levels, all vaulted, these were divided during the 16th and 17th-century alterations, providing rooms with lower ceilings. Original mediaeval features such as arrow-slits, the corbels for defensive bretasches, and the guard room with a trap dropping into the grim pit-prison below, mix with later alterations including most of the windows and some panelling.

SCONE PALACE, *Perth.*

The Earl of Mansfield.
Tel: 0738 52300.

2 m north-east of Perth on A93.
Open: Good Fri to mid-Oct Mon to Sat 9.30-5 (Sun 1.30, July and Aug 10.)
£4.20, £2.30, concessions.
Restaurant/home-made teas.

Scone was steeped in Scottish history for centuries before Edward I removed its stone to Westminster to confirm the authority over Scotland of England's crowned kings, and continued to be thereafter until James VI conferred the property to Sir David Murray who initiated four centuries of family occupation.

After opposition to the Act of Union and active support for the Jacobite risings the family's fortunes might have been threatened but for William Murray, younger brother of the 6th Viscount Stormont, who became the outstanding lawyer of his generation. 'Silver-tongued Murray' ascended to twice become Lord Chief Justice and Chancellor. By judging in favour of a runaway slave and helped to launch the anti-slavery movement.

He lived mostly in London - in splendour at Kenwood House - and therefore Scone remained unchanged through his lifetime, as it did when his nephew inherited the earldom in 1793 but only lived for another three years. His son commissioned William Atkinson who had been introduced to the Gothic style by his tutor James Wyatt, to transform the old gabled house into Gothic; castle outside, palace within.

The Chancellor earl's portrait by Martin shows him with the Bernini bust of Homer of which he was so proud and today the portrait is flanked by the bust on one side and Rysbrack's bust of the earl on the other. They are in the library where the bookshelves are now mainly filled with Scone's magnificent porcelain: the 1st earl's oriental armorial set, 18th-century Meissen, Ludwigsberg and Sevres, early Chelsea, Worcester and Derby.

In the drawing room the set of Louis XV armchairs and the writing table made for Marie Antoinette by Riesener, are part of the extensive collection of French furniture brought to Scone by the 2nd earl, the family's most significant collector and ambassador in Paris from 1772-78. He also collected the seventy-plus Vernis Martin pieces which are unique. They are displayed in the gallery.

The dining room contains continental ivories and is hung with portraits, and old masters that are representative of the collection at Scone. The most delightful; Zoffany's portrait of his daughter Lady Elizabeth Murray with Dido the daughter of the 1st earl's housekeeper whom the great lawyer freed from slavery, was commissioned by the connoisseur 2nd earl.

THIRLESTANE CASTLE, *Lauder.*

Thirlestane Castle Trust.
Tel: 0578 722430.

28 m south of Edinburgh off A68.
Open: Easter, May, june and Sept Wed, Thur and Sun, July and Aug daily except Sat, 2-5 (last admission 4.30). £3.50, concessions. Tea room.

Thirlestane's massive T-shaped plan, with thrusting central towers and turrets extending into broad wings is the product of three phases of architectural activity; 1590 when the original keep was completed for John, 1st Lord Maitland who was Lord Chancellor of Scotland; 1672-78 when Sir William Bruce extended the castle for the chancellor's grandson the Duke of Lauderdale who had married the Countess of Dysart, heiress of Ham House; and 1840 when the Edinburgh partnership of David Bryce and William Burn added the matching wings and adapted many of the rooms for Victorian country-house life.

It was in 1972, however, that the most decisive point in the six centuries of Maitlands at Thirlestane was reached. Captain Maitland-Carew, the grandson of the 15th Earl of Lauderdale, inherited the castle from his grandmother with much of it in a dangerous state of disrepair; the resulting rescue operation was one of the most ambitious and successful carried out to date. Among the major problems, the central tower with which Bryce had topped the 16th-century keep in typically theatrical Victorian style, was in danger of collapsing and through the castle the fabric was in urgent need of attention. Grants from the Historic Buildings Council for Scotland enabled the repair work to be carried out. subsequently Captain Maitland-Carew passed most of Thirlestane and its contents into a charitable trust which could be endowed by the National Heritage Memorial Fund, thereby helping to assure its future.

Details of the 1590 castle are mostly obscured by the later work and it is Bruce's contribution that adds the greatest note of quality to Thirlestane. This is not surprising considering that his patron had been elevated to a dukedom by Charles II to whose five-membered Cabal his name supplied the last letter and who had, in 1672, married the Countess of Dysart, heiress of Ham House, whose formidable personality matched his own. Bruce's approach, a grand balustraded staircase leading to two new towers projecting from the old castle and a fine Baroque doorway demonstrated how Restoration architecture could be adapted to a Scottish castle. With access to the superlative craftsmen working either for himself at Holyroodhouse or for his patrons in their lavish remodelling of Ham, Bruce added some of the most vigorous interior features to be found in any Restoration house, notably the plaster ceilings which were mostly executed by the Englishman George Dunsterfield. The baroque doorcases in the ante room were almost certainly the work of Thomas Carter who was working at Ham.

Only portraits of Charles II himself evoke the Restoration period more forcefully than that of the red-haired duke over the dining-room fireplace, but as the rest of the room which is part of Bryce and Burn's work illustrates, Thirlestane moved on from his period and influence and successive generations enjoyed it as a country home rather than an illustration of political power. Paintings span the 17th, 18th and 19th centuries, but the furniture in most rooms dates from the 19th century. An important and unfailingly popular attraction - to both young and old - is the historic toy collection. The Maitland-Carew family live in the north wing and the south wing is given over to a museum of Border Country Life.

TOROSAY CASTLE, *Isle of Mull.*

Mr Christopher James.
Tel: 06802421.

South-east of Craignure on A849.
Open: Easter to mid-Oct 10.30-5.
£3.50, children £1, concessions.
Tea room.

For most visitors Torosay epitomises Victorian Scottish baronial and it is no surprise that its architect was a leading light of the movement, David Bryce. Compared to its more rugged and exposed neighbour Duart (a ruined shell when Torosay was being built during the 1850s), Torosay, set in neat protective parkland well illustrates the gentrification of Scotland by the Victorians. Its ambitions scale, however, proved too much for Bryce's patron, John Campbell. He was forced to sell in 1865, only seven years after completion and it was bought by Arbuthnot Charles Guthrie, ancestor of the present owner.

Inside and out Torosay provides an absorbing picture of Victorian and Edwardian life. Important additions were the three Italianate garden terraces below the south front and the statue walk lined with a series of 18th-century Venetian stone figures, all designed by Sir Robert Lorimer. They were commissioned by Walter Murray Guthrie whose first reaction on hearing he had inherited Torosay - which he had never seen - was to put it on the market - but fortunately his first visit changed his mind and he fell in love with the place. His wife was the daughter of Sir John Leslie, a polymath and accomplished artist. Some of his best pictures, including a full-length portrait of his wife and a more modest likeness of his four-year-old daughter hang in the castle.

TRAQUAIR HOUSE, *Innerleighten.*

C. Maxwell Scott of Traquair.
Tel: 0896 830323.

1 m from Innerleithen, at junction on B709 and B7062.
Open: Easter week, May to end-Sept daily 1.30-5 (July and Aug 10-5.)
Price available on request.
Tea Room.

The upper reaches of Tweeddale present some of the most beautiful Border country and the setting makes its own contribution to Traquair, perhaps the most eulogized of all Scottish houses. For more than three centuries from 1107, when Alexander I visited, Traquair was a royal demense, where Scottish kings stayed and hunted. In 1491, having earlier been given by James III to one of his favourites, it came to James Stuart, 1st laird of Traquair, who established five centuries of unbroken family occupation. Generations later, in 1745, the story goes that Prince Charles Edward stayed and as he left, his host the 5th Earl of Traquair, closed the gates and vowed they would never be opened until the Stuarts were restored to the English throne.

They have remained closed ever since and brought to Traquair a note of romance enhanced by the lack of change since that day. The family's period of greatest prosperity was during the 16th and 17th centuries, when the house was built in successive stages and they acquired an earldom (which died out in 1861). After 1745 their Jacobitism and catholicism meant safety in anonymity. They did not feel it safe to openly confirm their catholicism until emancipation came to Scotland during the 19th century, when the intimate chapel was built.

The view from the house which grew in stages from a 14th-century pele tower, across the forecourt with its elegant late-17th century screen and gates to the broad avenue beyond and the closed bear gates or 'Steekit Yetts' at the far end has not changed since 1745. Inside the period of the family's close involvement with the Scottish kings is widely represented. Mary Queen of Scots' rosary and crucifix and the cradle in which she rocked her son James VI and I, recall her visit with her husband Darnley and there is fine engraved Jacobite glass.

The library, which dates from the 18th century remains intact and is full of treasures; the Nuremberg Chronicle (1493), a Koberger Bible (1479) and a 14th-century iluminated psalter. The room has a cove painted unusually in grisaille which is one of a number of decorative curiosities in the house, in particular the trompe l'oeil overmante and overdoors. Most important, however, and the draw for visitors, is the atmosphere which pervades the whole place, enshrined in the stories and poetry that Traquair's history has inspired.

WALES

BODRHYDDAN HALL, *Rhuddlan, Clwyd.*

Col the Lord Langford.
Tel: 0745 590414.

2 m east of Rhuddlan, between A547 and B5332.
Open: June to Sept inclusive, Tues and Thur, 2-5.30.
£2, children £1.
Tea room.

Bodrhyddan displays one of the few surviving examples of the work of William Eden Nesfield, a Victorian architect who worked in the shadow of his better-known father, William Andrews Nesfield, the most fashionable garden designer of the High Victorian period. During the 1870s he made additions to the existing 17th-century house and gave it the distinctive 'Dutch' Queen Anne style entrance front that greets the visitor. His father, planned the formal garden which centres on the old front door on the south side, replacing the carriage circle at the end of the approach avenue.

Gates at the end of the avenue bear the Conwy crest of a Moor's head, given in recognition of their service in the Crusades and in the entrance hall the fine collection of armour came from Rhuddlan Castle of which Conwys were hereditary constable from 1399; their earlier establishment in the town is confirmed by the original charter from Edward I dated 1284 which is also displayed here. The great hall was the central room of the original house while the big dining room was added towards the end of the 18th century by William Shipley who married into the family and was dean of St Asaph while his father was bishop. The dean's portrait by Beechey hangs in the room, among other members of the family painted by Hudson, Vanderbank, Dahl, Ramsay and lesser artists. The bishop, painted by Reynolds, is also here, while his portrait by Devis is elsewhere.

Bodrhyddan must be the only house in Britain to boast the original body inside one of the two mummy cases brought back from Egypt by Richard and Charlotte Rowley in 1836 and another peculiarity is the Cantonese alter set looted by the French during the Peninsular War and subsequently captured from them after Waterloo.

BRYN BRAS CASTLE, *Llanrug, Gwynedd.*

Mr and Mrs N.E. Gray-Parry.
Tel: 0286 870210.

4 m east of Caernarfon, off A4086.
Open: Spring Bank Hol to end Sept daily 1-5 (mid-July & Aug 10.30-5).
£2.80, children £1.40, concessions.
Home-made teas.

Wales is rich with 18th and 19th century castles that revive the romance of the country's mediaeval examples, and Bryn Bras is one of the most typical. Positioned between Snowdon and the Menai Straits its turrets and battlements and the surrounding gardens nestle harmoniously into the foothills of the Llanberis valley which had long attracted enthusiasts for picturesque landscape before the castle was built during the 1830s. With its turrets and battlements it has the air of a toy fort, but the broad circular towers and the symmetrical central arches on the garden front add considerable substance.

Bryn Bras was possibly built by Thomas Hopper (who built the larger Penryn Castle a few miles away) for Thomas Williams, a prosperous Bangor lawyer, but following his death in 1874 it was sold in 1897 and changed hands a number of times until the present owners acquired it in 1964 and carried out welcome restoration. The library with richly carved panels and chimneypiece and the staircase hall are especially striking rooms, while the rejuvenation of the gardens has been an outstanding success. In front of the castle the two statues are impressive copies of Canova's pugilists Creugante and Damosseno in the Vatican Museum while the romantic woodland and water gardens, knot garden and borders - largely dating from when the castle was built - have all been carefully restored.

PENHOW CASTLE, *Newport, Gwent.*

Stephen Weeks.
Tel: 0633 400800.

On A48 midway between Chepstow and Newport.
Open: Easter to end Sept Wed-Sun, Aug daily 10-6, Wed through winter.
£2.95, children £1.65, concessions.

Penhow has been saved by the spirited restoration that Mr Weeks has carried out since buying the virtually ruined castle in 1973 and now visitors can enjoy its at times distinguished history that stretches back to the establishiment of the Norman foothold in Wales, at Chepstow, shortly after the Conquest.

One of a ring of castles that defended Chepstow from marauding Welshmen; early in the 12th century Penhow was granted to St Roger de St Maur, whose ancestor had travelled from the Touraine village of St Maur to accompany William the Conqueror to England, and whose descendents would adapt the name St Maur to Seymour, provide Henry VIII's favourite queen, Jane Seymour, and establish the titles Duke of Somerset and Marquess of Hertford. Sixteen years after the sadly premature death of Jane's son Edward VI the Seymour connexion with Penhow was severed with sale in 1569 and the castle embarked on four centuries of repeatedly changing ownership. The Lewis family made an important contribution during the late-17th century, but by the early-18th Penhow was tenanted as a farmhouse and its decline began.

The gradual extension of the castle from its Norman tower to include gatehouse, hall and later north wing, give Penhow an amorphous look, but its clustered appearance retains the air of defence that it was originally built for. Where possible the restoration has highlighted original features, notably the panels with inset paintings in the old parlour, the oak staircase and the surprisingly sophisticated dining room with Restoration plasterwork and broken pediments over the doorcases, all dating from the Lewis occupation. In the older parts of the castle the mediaeval and Tudor history is strongly evoked, the effect enhanced by the stereo audio-tours that Mr Weeks pioneered and which enables visitors to tour in imaginative seclusion.